体演中国系列主编　　[美] 简小滨
Perform China Series Editor: Xiaobin JIAN

体演苏州系列主编　　[美] 简小滨　逄成华
Perform Suzhou Series Editors: Xiaobin JIAN Chenghua FENG

Perform SUZHOU
a Course in Intermediate to Advanced Spoken Mandarin

———— 中高级中文听说教程 ————

体 演 苏 州

[美] 简小滨	[美] 王建芬	[美] 贾君卿	逄成华　著
Xiaobin JIAN	Jianfen WANG	Junqing JIA	Chenghua FENG

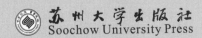

苏州大学出版社
Soochow University Press

Acknowledgement

The Performed Culture Approach developed by Galal Walker and Mari Noda, Department of East Asian Languages and Literatures at The Ohio State University, is basic to the conceptualization of this project. Specifically, their graduate seminars in Pedagogy in East Asian Languages and Culture in the years of 2013, 2014 and 2015 and the graduate students' works for those seminars had direct impacts on the shaping and completion of the materials as they are. The authors have also benefited greatly from the extensive discussions and collaborative work with colleagues and graduate students including Zhini ZENG, Xin ZHANG, Minru LI, Hanning CHEN, Cong LI, Donglin CHAI, Lulei SU, Kai LIANG, Bing MU, Haiyan FU, Chenxing JIN, Crista Cornelius, Alexandra Draggeim, Benjamin Reitz and Mario Degrantis. Especially, the concurrent development of the *Perform Suzhou* project and the *Perform Guangzhou* project by Xiaobin JIAN, Xin ZHANG and Zhini ZENG brought benefits to both projects' final formation and completion.

Many individuals contributed to this project at various stages and in various ways. Jining HAN, Huijun MA and Yan YANG provided crucial assistance in the drafting and audio-recording of the first two versions of *Perform Qingdao*, the prototype and predecessor of the current project. Xizhen QIN and Zhini ZENG utilized the earlier versions of the material when they were teaching at the OSU Intensive Chinese Language Qingdao Program and provided critical feedback. Xin ZHANG contributed significantly to the content of the last four units in the current version as well as provided illustrations to the drills. Crista Cornelius performed much needed initial proofreading of the earlier drafts. Juan CHEN created twenty-four illustrations for the dialogues that are very helpful to the learners in terms of visualization-contextualization. Feng PAN provided the initial design of the book cover and worked extensively on one of the most important components of this project— audio recording. Benjamin Reitz, Crista Cornelius, Cong LI, Xin ZHANG, Zhini ZENG, Adam Skov and Lydia Simon shared their valuable time and gracious voice in the audio program.

We thank the National East Asian Languages Resource Center at Ohio State University for its constant and generous support. Galal Walker is always the source for inspiration and guidance. Minru LI has been a strict and very knowledgeable editor who is critical in keeping the project in line and on time. Hanning CHEN designed the inviting book cover and provided important input to the functional layout of the book.

We would also like to express our gratitude to the students who participated in the OSU Intensive Chinese Language Qingdao Program, Suzhou Program and the Chinese Flagship Program in the past decade, and the Critical Language Scholarship Programs in the summers of 2013 and 2014. Their willingness to share their learning experiences with us is the greatest motivation for us to develop this project, and their feedback, including praises, criticisms and suggestions, helped to fine tune the project to its current state.

Finally, we thank our partners and colleagues at Soochow University. We thank the administrators at the School of Humanities for their foresight and their unwavering support for our programs and this project; the teachers in their Chinese as a Foreign Language Program for their devotion, flexibility and countless insightful suggestions; the student language partners for their time, participation and friendship; and the editors at Soochow University Press whose professionalism is both impressive and exemplar. Without the cooperation from our partners and colleagues at Soochow University, this project would have been impossible to complete.

目 录

Introduction /1

《体演苏州》教师使用建议 /6

《体演苏州》主要人物列表 /10

第一单元　抵达苏州 Settling Down

1.1　初次见面　三人行必有我师 /11
1.2　吃饭了　民以食为天 /26
1.3　买东西　货比三家 /37
学而时习之 /48

第二单元　校园生活 Campus Life

2.1　去哪儿　雪中送炭 /50
2.2　与老师交流　没有规矩，不成方圆 /61
2.3　组织活动　群策群力 /71
学而时习之 /83

第三单元　饮食交友 Food and Friendship

3.1　朋友小聚　客随主便 /86
3.2　家庭做客　礼轻情意重 /95
3.3　出席宴会　高朋满座 /108
学而时习之 /120

第四单元　游山玩水 Sightseeing

4.1　团队游　走马观花 /122

4.2　自助游　退而求其次 / 133
4.3　灵岩山　山不在高,有仙则名 / 145
学而时习之 / 155

第五单元　解决问题 Solving Problems

5.1　钱包丢了　吃一堑,长一智 / 157
5.2　咨询前台　宾至如归 / 166
5.3　空调病　寻医问药 / 176
学而时习之 / 187

第六单元　社会活动 Social Engagements

6.1　到社区去　一回生,两回熟 / 189
6.2　志愿服务　意在言外 / 200
6.3　参加会议　毛遂自荐 / 210
学而时习之 / 219

第七单元　调查研究 Research

7.1　确立话题　有的放矢 / 221
7.2　街头采访　循序渐进 / 231
7.3　口头报告　对答如流 / 242
学而时习之 / 256

第八单元　话说苏州 Talking about Suzhou

8.1　漫谈苏州　月是故乡明 / 258
8.2　苏州攻略　痛并快乐着 / 269
8.3　暂别苏州　依依不舍 / 281
学而时习之 / 294

附　录

附录1　Questions in "投石问路" / 297
附录2　Sample Narrations / 303

Introduction

Objectives and Expectations

Perform Suzhou has been developed to help you raise your level of sophistication in interacting with the local people while staying and studying in Suzhou. As the core material for the spoken development course at the intermediate and high levels, *Perform Suzhou* adopts the approach of the particular with community-specific and contextually-defined performances. *Performance* is the key concept in *Perform Suzhou*. A performance is a communicative event situated in a particular time and place with specified roles for the people directly engaged in the event and other people, either present or absent, who influence the event. By deliberately practicing the carefully selected performance scripts presented in this material and following the learning procedure we suggest, you are expected to:

1. **Become an expert in doing things in Suzhou.** As you are going to spend considerable time in Suzhou, you will be able to readily apply everything that is presented in this material outside the classroom. You will achieve your goal when you apply the vocabulary and expressions presented in this material to your actual living situations immediately and repeatedly and have gained acceptance from the people of the community because of your actions.

2. **Develop transferrable strategies that can be applied to new situations in the future.** *Perform Suzhou* provides you with concrete examples of scripts that can work in well-identified situations, but what you learn to do in Suzhou is generally applicable to other cities in China. Moreover, going through this learning process will equip you with the strategies and skills to effectively approach new communities and to make appropriate adjustments to new experiences in new situations. Dialogues presented in *Perform Suzhou* provide you with the basic scripts from which you can improvise in related but different contexts. Questions and notes are designed to focus on nuances associated with the context of the performance. Through closely working with the material, you will become a more perceptive learner whenever you engage in any new encounter.

3. Grow into an autonomous language and culture learner. *Perform Suzhou* supports a wide range of learners representing a wide range of Chinese proficiency levels and backgrounds. It is designed to give you flexibility and autonomy in determining the focus of your study. Following the learning procedure we suggest, you will become more skillful in dealing with performance scripts and exploiting the social environment around you. You are expected to learn the strategies that the two American characters use to convey and interpret intentions. But learners who have more background in Chinese, can also take the roles of the Chinese exemplars, using their strategies in different roles. All learners at this level will also work on narration strategies by telling stories about what is going on in the presented social interactions.

Components of *Perform Suzhou*

Perform Suzhou is composed of twenty-four stages, organized into eight units based on eight themes. These eight units cover topics that you need to handle immediately upon arrival, such as finding bus routes and meeting language partners, as well as activities that require more sophisticated knowledge of the people, places, and customs around you, such as planning a cultural activity and doing interviews in the local community.

Each stage approaches the theme from different perspectives, setting the stories around different groups of people, in different discourses. In every stage, there is a dialogue consisting of several performance scripts. The dialogue is designed to contextualize the performance scripts that involve the most important conversational strategies, which we expect you to make note of and practice actively. You may select or your teacher may assign a particular performance for you to perform and to create future improvised performances. Explanations, reflection questions, drills, exercises and culture notes are also provided in each stage to facilitate the overall oral practice with the performance scripts. Several field performance tasks and a list of useful expressions are provided at the end of each unit in a section titled 学而时习之. This section provides guidance for you to practice in real situations what you have learned from this unit.

An important component of *Perform Suzhou* is the audio program, which contains audio files for the warm-up questions, dialogues, drills, sample oral narrations and useful expression listed in the 学而时习之 section. A separate audio file is provided for each chunk of dialogue in the 知其所以然 section for you to focus on individual chunks and prepare for performance. The majority of your study time should be spent working with the audio materials to build automaticity in your performances.

All these components are presented in a sequence that we recommend you follow as an ideal learning procedure. But we also allow flexibility for approaching the material in different learning sequences based on different learning styles.

Below are suggestions on how to optimize your learning experience with this material.

Study Guide to *Perform Suzhou*

☞ Step 1: Warm-up 投石问路

This is the first section in every stage. It consists of five questions related to the dialogue you are about to listen to in the next section. After hearing each question in the audio program, you should pause the audio recording and orally respond to the question before moving on to the next one. There is space in this page for you to write down the key points of your answers. These notes may assist you in the upcoming class discussions. Through answering these questions, you may also be able to come up with some hypotheses about what might have happened in the dialogue.

☞ Step 2: Listening and Visualizing 边听边想

Each stage of *Perform Suzhou* contains a dialogue consisting of several performance scripts. When you complete all the five warm-up questions, you can proceed to listen to the audio of the dialogue. However, at this stage, don't refer to the text or rely on any written materials. When listening to the audio, try to visualize the dialogue in your mind, in terms of when and where the performance may take place, who are the people engaged, and what they aim to achieve through the interaction. The more vivid picture you are able to see in your mind, the more easily you will recall this performance later. You may need to listen several times before figuring out the whole story and being able to proceed to the notes section.

☞ Step 3: Listening with Scripts 耳闻目睹

After you have tried your best to visualize the story through listening, you may turn the page and listen to the audio again while following along in the printed text. As you listen, mark any places that you are unclear or have questions about. You may find answers to those questions in the section that follows.

☞ Step 4: Notes on Dialogues 知其所以然

知其所以然 consists of questions and explanations focusing on vocabulary, expressions, structures, conversational strategies and culture knowledge that we expect you to pay close attention to. Instead of directly telling you what the dialogue is about and why those representative characters act in certain ways, a few questions are designed in this section for you to assess your own understanding of the dialogue. You may already know the answers to many of those questions, so you can make good use of the questions to help you navigate through the notes in a more efficient way. But even if you are very uncertain about what you have come up with, you can always find answers in the notes following the questions.

☞ Step 5: Performance Scripts 体演文本

Among several performance scripts composing the dialogue, you are expected to perform only the designated performance scripts in class. Your teacher will designate the scripts to perform in class. To accelerate fluency in your performance, you should work closely with the Audio Program to practice line by line. You should practice each turn of the conversation, building from the end of the utterance, adding more and more parts to the front of it. This is an effective way for dealing with pronunciation; both in terms of memory and the accuracy of the syllables and words you produce. This backward buildup will preserve the tonal patterns of the original target sentence.

Do not start the practice until you have read through the notes.

☞ Step 6: Reflection and Elicitation 举一反三

举一反三 contains a list of questions that guides you to reflect on aspects of Chinese culture brought up in the dialogues. Some questions encourage you to read between the lines, to reflect on the hidden cultural aspects of the dialogue. Some other questions are used to elicit a new performance script that you will need to apply to a slightly changed situation. To complete this section, you should also write down your notes to get ready for the class discussion the next day. If you are asked to come up with a new performance script, try to check and practice the new script with your language partner before class.

☞ Step 7: Drills and Narrating Exercises 熟能生巧

熟能生巧 consists of strategy-based drills and narrating exercises. For each drill, you will either initiate the conversation or respond to an oral cue from another speaker. Listen to the instructions and examples carefully before doing each drill, as they point out what you are doing by means of your speech and the relative roles you and your conversation partner are playing with each other. Drills are designed to help you build automaticity in your speech, so please practice them with the audio by speaking aloud. (Get used to hearing yourself speaking accurately.) Take a break between each drill, especially at the beginning, as they are usually cognitively demanding.

The narration exercises are designed to help you practice relaying a story to another person who didn't experience what happened. Pay attention to the role you take either in enacting the performance or in observing the performance. Your perspective on what happened depends on the particular role you take. Therefore, the stories and emotions associated with the same event are likely to change as roles change. After you are done with your narration, refer to a sample narration in the appendix to see how you may improve your narration.

☞ Step 8: Notes on Expanded Culture-related Topics 言外有意

言外有意 delves into the depth of some culture-related topics including the Chinese idiom attached to each dialogue, cultural background information about the dialogue and some generated culture themes. The idiom is introduced as a tag to help you remember the dialogue in the future. Some notes such as the independent bookstore in China or the Chinese medical service system are culture facts that give you a general understanding about what is going on in the background. Some notes focus more on the behavioral aspects, such as how to behave as a guest at someone's house, and how to turn down a drink at a banquet. Occasionally, some links to other reading materials or online discussion are also included for students who have interests to explore further. After a close reading of each note item, try to discuss them with your language partner.

☞ Step 9: Field Performances 学而时习之

The "Performances" listed in this section provide opportunities to apply the strategies learned from the unit in real situations. They are sequenced according to the level of complexity. Depending on the specific contexts and turns of events, the "Acts" listed under each performance need not be performed in the exact order as listed; and they need not be performed all together in any actual encounter. Perform as appropriately and as effectively as you can. Be prepared to re-tell your experiences in class. Before you actually do the field performances, rehearse doing them with a Chinese friend. Also practice saying the useful expressions listed in this section after the accompanying audio. You may do each performance more than once. For example, you may do Performance 1 as you finish learning Stage 1 and do it again after you finish the whole unit.

Cited from *The Anecdotes of Confucius* (《论语》), "学而时习之" suggests that the pleasure of learning comes from timely application of what is learned. Therefore, these field performance tasks put you into situations where you may apply what you have learned.

Flexibility in the Learning Order

The sequence above is what we suggest as an effective learning procedure based on empirical studies and learning theories. However, we also recognize a need for some flexibility in approaching these sections in a slightly different order. For example, learners who want more background information before approaching the dialogue can do Step 6 or Step 8 or both before they do Step 2—listening to the audio and visualizing the performance. They may also do Step 6 and Step 8 before Step 5—practicing the performance scripts with the audio. However, we believe you will derive long-term benefit from doing the steps as they are ordered.

《体演苏州》教师使用建议

一、《体演苏州》之目标

《体演苏州》旨在引导学习者在苏州学习和生活期间更融洽地与中国人交流和沟通。作为一套中高级口语课的核心教材,《体演苏州》采用一系列与苏州当地文化紧密相连的"场景体演"为主要学习内容和方法,与当地社区与当地文化紧密相连这一点使本套教材与汉语学习领域中的大多数教材有所不同。"体演"是本套教材的核心理念。所谓"体演",指的是让学习者操练和表演一些精心设计的场景,这些场景必须是在某个特定的场合(时间)和地点展开,人物的角色和关系明确,并且是以沟通和交流的形式呈现的具有前因后果的事件。通过有效地学习这些反复斟酌而成的剧本并且表演场景,我们期望学生可以有这些收获:

1. 成为一位"苏州通"。所谓"苏州通",并不仅仅指学生对苏州了解多少,而是指他们能在当地文化中高效并得体地完成一系列任务。我们鼓励学生融入当地文化,与当地人有尽可能多的交流,所以学生在本套教材中学到的知识最终是为用于课外实践做准备的。我们要求学生及时并反复地使用教材中学到的词汇和表达与当地人进行得体的交流,从而建立起被接受并深入学习的渠道。

2. 具有实际应变的交际能力。《体演苏州》中选定的场景是学习者在中国其他城市都会遇到的,通过使用本套教材,学生不仅在苏州可以完成那些任务,而且可以把所学的知识运用到今后在中国的生活中。教材的设计对于培养学生的应变能力有所考量,对话的剧本以及呈现方式有助于学生分析掌握场景中的每个部分,并将所学到的知识应用到相似的场景中去。教材中"举一反三"和"知其所以然"部分引导学生关注与场景紧密相关的微言妙语,通过这样的训练来培养学生时时用心观察情景的学习习惯。

3. 成为自主自觉的语言和文化学习者。《体演苏州》针对的使用者有不同的学习背景和汉语水平,我们鼓励学习者在使用教材的过程中根据自己的汉语水平决定学习的重点。依循教材中建议的学习步骤,学生可以逐渐培养起读场景对话剧本的能力并善于利用与当地人交际的机会。对于大多数学生,我们引导他们关注作为外国人如何在中国文化中恰当地表达自己的看法和意图。而对于汉语水平比较高的学生,也可以让他们关注教材中中国人的角色,学习中国人的一些语言技巧。同时,通过讲述对话及场景的内容,学生的叙述能力将得到一定的锻炼和提高。

二、《体演苏州》之构成

《体演苏州》共有 8 单元,每个单元有 1 个主题,由 3 场"表演"组成,换言之,整套教材共有 24 场"表演"。这 8 个单元的主题涵盖了学生在苏州学习和生活的方方面面,包括抵达当地首先需要注意的事宜;如何使用当地的公共交通;如何与语伴们见面交流以及一些更有深意和难度的任务,比如如何策划一次文化活动、在当地社区进行采访;等等。

每单元的 3 场"表演"都从不同的角度来切入主题,并且涉及不同的角色、地点和交流方式。每一场表演的对话都由几幕组成,而这些对话中涵盖了最重要的交流和沟通的技巧。我们建议学生对于这些与技巧相关的表达做笔记,并反复地自觉练习。对话表演的剧本是为了让学生更好地掌握对话中的奥妙,并运用到更多的生活中类似的场景之中。每个场景都还包括了对于句型和对话内容的解释、口语操练、叙述练习和文化笔记,以便于学生进一步理解并口头操练学到的表达。每单元最后的"学而时习之"部分列出了一些供参考的田野任务,学生在学习一个单元的过程中,或者在学完一个单元之后,可以选做。

录音是整套教材中关键的一部分。教材中的"投石问路"部分、对话部分、"熟能生巧"部分以及每个单元最后的"知其所以然"部分都有相应的 MP3 录音。对话课文不仅有完整的录音,并有针对"知其所以然"部分的分段录音,便于学习者重点学习各个部分。学生在准备和复习的过程中应当需要大量地使用这些录音,而老师们也应当时时强调录音的重要性,并在设计课堂教学活动时考量到这一点。

每一场"表演"都具有这样 8 个部分:投石问路、边听边想、耳闻目睹、知其所以然、体演文本、举一反三、熟能生巧和言外有意。

三、《体演苏州》之使用

我们建议学生依以下步骤使用这 9 个组成部分,但已经形成有效学习习惯的学生也可以根据自己的习惯合理调整学习顺序。

☞ **第一步:投石问路**

投石问路是热身部分,包括 5 个问答式热身问题,这些问题与本场表演的对话和主题相关。在课本中并没有这 5 个问题的文本,因此学生需要使用录音来听这些问题,并作简短的回答。学生在回答问题的过程中可以在课本中预留的空间做一些笔记,并对接着要学习的对话内容做出一些猜测。这些热身问题并不是学习的重点,但为了鼓励学生在课前准备时坚持使用这一部分,老师需在每天的课堂中提到一至两个问题,或适时检查学生的笔记。

☞ 第二步：边听边想

在完成"投石问路"部分之后，读对话文本之前，学生需要反复听对话录音，并对对话中的场景、对话中的角色、人物的意图做出推断。授课老师需要时时强调录音先行于阅读文本的重要性，换言之，第二步始终应当先于之后几步。

☞ 第三步：耳闻目睹

学生在通过听录音来掌握对话大意之后，可以翻开文本。建议学生边听边看，并且标记之前没听出来或者有疑问的地方。这样在学习下一个部分的时候可以着重学习有疑问的部分。

☞ 第四步：知其所以然

"知其所以然"是向学生解释重要词汇、表达、句型、沟通策略以及文化知识的部分。这一部分以问题的形式引出，鼓励学生在读解释之前尝试回答这些问题。课堂教学活动需要适当地与"知其所以然"的内容有所联系。

☞ 第五步：体演文本

教师可根据课程需要提前指定体演文本中学生需要背诵及在课堂上表演的部分。学生应当在课前通过听录音，一句句反复操练那一部分的表演。一场表演的文本为了便于学习被分成了几个部分，我们建议学生在练习的过程中从句子的核心词入手记忆，并要求学生在阅读并理解了"知其所以然"之后才开始记忆对话文本。

☞ 第六步：举一反三

这一部分包括一系列对话课文中出现的与中国文化相关的思考题。有的问题鼓励学生在字里行间寻找对话中隐藏的文化点，也有一些问题引导学生思考如何将所学知识运用到类似的场景中去。学生应当在课前准备这些问题，并做一定的笔记，必要的时候也可以与语伴一起完成新对话的编写。授课老师在设计教学活动时需要包括对于这些问题的讨论。

☞ 第七步：熟能生巧

"熟能生巧"部分有两种练习：一种是说话技巧以及句型的操练，另一种是叙述能力的练习。每个操练都以对话的形式展开，学生有时需要引发话题，或者根据录音和图片提示来进行回答。这一步骤的目标是训练学生的听说能力，因此这里不提供这些练习的文本。教师应帮助学生抑制阅读与书写文本的冲动，引导他们通过反复聆听与对话来完成这一步骤的练习。

☞ 第八步：言外有意

《体演苏州》中的每一场"表演"都有一个成语或者俗语作为副标题来概括那一场的主题，那个成语的使用会在"言外有意"部分得到简要的解释。同时，"言外有意"还包括了一些中国文化中有趣、有意义也有学习价值的信息，比如中国的送礼文化、宴会礼仪、车牌号码的寓意等。这一部分也与所学对话的内容紧密相连，帮助学生更好地了解对话发生的大背景,并加深对对话内容的理解和记忆。学有余力的学生,也可以在这一部分找到一些具有一定难度的拓展阅读。我们鼓励学生在读完"言外有意"之后能发表自己的看法,与他们的语伴进行讨论。

☞ **第九步:学而时习之**

这一步是"体演"教学的目标,学生要运用所学技能在真实语境下完成交际任务。这部分所列出的田野任务按难度系数排列,越靠后的任务挑战性越大。每个任务下所列的场景不一定要全部进行,根据交流的实际情况,完成恰当的场景即可。然后在课堂上汇报完成任务的情况。在这一部分也列出了一些有用的表达,建议学生在做田野任务之前跟录音练习说这些表达。有条件的学生可以跟中国朋友提前演练田野任务。

《体演苏州》要求学生"知行合一",将课文中所学的知识用到他们在苏州的生活中去。在以"体演"为核心的汉语课堂中,老师们的任务并不是"讲授",而是"引导"。引导学生正确使用教材并在课堂中进行表演,以使学生能自信且得体地走出教室、使用中文架起一座真正的交流畅通的桥。

《体演苏州》主要人物列表

人物/ Roles	头像/ Image	配音/ Voice
周丹锐(Zhōu Dānruì),美国留学生,英文名字是Daniel		Benjamin Reitz
郑妮(Zhèng Nī),美国留学生,英文名字是Jenny		Crista Cornelius
孙浩(Sūn Hào),周丹锐的中文辅导老师,苏州大学的学生		李聪
赵奕歆(Zhào Yìxīn),郑妮的中文辅导老师,苏州大学的学生		张欣
秦晓岚(Qín Xiǎolán),项目主任,俄亥俄州立大学的老师		曾稚妮

第一单元　抵达苏州 Settling Down

1.1 初次见面

三人行必有我师

投石问路

Listen to the five questions in the audio and answer them based on your own experience. Be ready to discuss these questions in class. You may write down some notes in the space provided below.

1.
2.
3.
4.
5.

边听边想

Listen to the audio and try to visualize the dialogue in your mind. Think about who the speakers are, the kind of social relationship they have, and what their intentions might be.

🎧 耳闻目睹

Listen to the audio again while following along in the printed text. As you listen, mark any place that you are unclear or have questions about.

三人行必有我师
人物：周丹锐、孙浩

（开学第一天，周丹锐在学生活动中心跟辅导老师孙浩初次见面）

周丹锐：你好！我叫周丹锐，丹青的"丹"，精锐的"锐"。
孙　浩：很高兴认识你，我叫孙浩。
周丹锐：不好意思，你的名字怎么写？
孙　浩：孙浩，孙悟空的"孙"，"浩"是三点水右边一个告诉的"告"。
周丹锐：噢，浩浩荡荡的"浩"。(1/4)
孙　浩：对！你的中文说得不错啊，学了几年了？
周丹锐：没有没有，学了快两年了。你现在是几年级？读什么专业？
孙　浩：我是汉语言文学专业，读大三了。
周丹锐：那我可得多向你学习了。
孙　浩：你也是学中文专业的吗？
周丹锐：我主修国际关系，辅修中文。(2/4)
孙　浩：啊，快到午饭时间了，我下午还有点事儿，要不我们去吃饭吧，边吃边聊。
周丹锐：我和几个朋友约好一起去吃饭，咱们一起去吧，我正好给你们介绍一下。
孙　浩：好啊，那太好了。(3/4)

（午饭以后，孙浩和周丹锐在校园里走走）

孙　浩：周丹锐，下午有什么计划？
周丹锐：我要和郑妮去买手机卡。你知道在什么地方能买到吗？
孙　浩：校园里的一些超市就有卖的，外面路口的报亭也会有，我带你去吧。
周丹锐：不用，我们自己去就行了，别麻烦你了。
孙　浩：你最好和我们办同一家公司的手机卡，这样我们之间联系会便宜一些。我用的是移动。
周丹锐：等一等，这个我得记下来。
孙　浩：还是我跟你一起去看一下吧。
周丹锐：没事儿，我们应该可以解决，你不是说下午还有事儿吗？
孙　浩：有好多种套餐的，我怕你弄不清楚。
周丹锐：真的不用，你放心去忙你的吧。(4/4)

知其所以然

The dialogue is broken down into sections below for explanation and analysis. Study the notes and answer the questions for the underlined text.

1/4

(开学第一天,周丹锐在学生活动中心跟辅导老师孙浩初次见面)

周丹锐:你好！我叫周丹锐,<u>丹青的"丹",精锐的"锐"</u>。

孙浩:　很高兴认识你,我叫孙浩。

周丹锐:不好意思,你的名字怎么写？

孙浩:　<u>孙浩,孙悟空的"孙","浩"是三点水右边一个告诉的"告"</u>。

周丹锐:噢,浩浩荡荡的"浩"。

---

1. 周丹锐介绍自己的名字:"丹青的'丹',精锐的'锐'。"
   孙浩介绍自己的名字:"孙悟空的'孙','浩'是三点水右边一个告诉的'告'。"
   (1) 周丹锐还可以怎么介绍他自己的名字？＿＿＿＿的"丹",＿＿＿＿的"锐"。
   (2) 孙浩还可以怎么介绍他自己的名字？＿＿＿＿的"孙",＿＿＿＿的"浩"。
   (3) 如果周丹锐介绍自己的时候说"丹麦(Denmark)的'丹',锐角(acute angle)的'锐'",这和对话里的说法有什么不同？哪个好？

The fact that different Chinese characters can have the same pronunciation makes it difficult to know with certainty which characters a Chinese person uses to write their name. To turn a challenging situation into an advantageous one, Chinese speakers use various strategies to orally specify the characters in a name. Common strategies include describing the written form of a character and relating a character to a well-known expression with positive connotations. For example, Zhou Danrui identifies the characters in his given name by relating them to two words with positive connotations: 丹青(red-blue/green, painting, art, culture) and 精锐(sharp, elite). Sun Hao, on the other hand, modestly describes the written form of his given name "浩" by identifying its left and right components: i. e., "浩"是三点水右边一个告诉的"告". As a confirmation of understanding, Zhou Danrui demonstrates his knowledge of Chinese language and culture by relating the character 浩 to a highly recognizable and favorable idiom 浩浩荡荡(massive, mighty, grand).

Note that when describing the components of a character, a Chinese person usually follows the order of writing the character, that is, from left to right and from top to bottom. For example,"贾(jiǎ)"是西字头,下面一个宝贝的"贝";"张(zhāng)"是弓(gōng)长(cháng)"张" or "章(zhāng)"是立早"章"。

> **2/4**
>
> 孙浩： 对！你的中文说得不错啊,学了几年了？
> 周丹锐：没有没有,学了快两年了。你现在是几年级？读什么专业？
> 孙浩： 我是汉语言文学专业,读大三了。
> 周丹锐：那我可得多向你学习了。
> 孙浩： 你也是学中文专业的吗？
> 周丹锐：我主修国际关系,辅修中文。

2. 孙浩觉得周丹锐的中文不错,很好奇,所以问他："学了几年了？"

（1）孙浩为什么问"学了几年了",而不是"学了几年"？ _____

（2）在中国,如果你的中文老师说她以前在美国住过（现在搬回中国了）,你应该问她：

    A. 你在美国住了几年？

    B. 你在美国住了几年了？

（3）除了"几年""几个月""几个星期"之类的,你还可以怎么询问一个事件持续的时间？

The final 了 in 学了几年了 indicates that the action began in the past and continues to the present. Thus Sun Hao's question assumes Zhou Danrui is still in the process of learning Chinese. Without the final 了, the question would assume the action does not continue to the present. If you know your teacher lived for a period of time in the US but has now returned to China, you could ask：你在美国住了几年？

When you have no idea at all about the length of the duration, you may use 多久 (duōjiǔ) or 多长时间 instead of 几年/几个月/几个星期.

3. 周丹锐回应孙浩的称赞："没有没有。"

（1）周丹锐说"没有没有"是因为他觉得自己中文不太好吗？

（2）在这种情况下周丹锐还可以怎么说？（选两项）

    A. "谢谢,我已经学了两年了。"

    B. "哪里哪里,还得多练习！"

    C. "哪里哪里,你太客气了！"

（3）如果你的中国朋友去你家,跟你说："你家的院子真漂亮！"你怎么回答？

Nowadays, 没有没有 is a more common way to deflect a compliment than 哪里哪里 which sounds like an outdated cliché. It has also become increasingly common for people in China to accept compliments on appearance or personal possessions by saying 谢谢.

4. 周丹锐问孙浩的专业和年级,孙浩回答:"我是汉语言文学专业,读大三了。"孙浩问周丹锐的专业,周丹锐回答:"我主修国际关系,辅修中文。"

(1) 孙浩读大学三年级,所以他说"读大三了",如果他弟弟是高中一年级,他会怎么说?

(2) 如果你在大学是研究生二年级,你应该怎么简短地说明?

(3) 如果你有两个专业:经济学和中文,你怎么说明其中"经济学"是主要的专业?

大三 is short for 大学三年级. Similarly, second year in graduate school(研究生二年级) is shortened as 研二; first year in high school(高中一年级) is 高一; first year in middle school(初中一年级) is 初一. However, years in elementary school(e.g., 小学三年级) are less commonly shortened.

To refer to your major, you may use 我的专业是…… or 我主修……. You may also say 我主修……专业. 辅修 is used to indicate your minor field.

5. 周丹锐得知孙浩的专业以后,说:"那我可得多向你学习了。"

(1) 为什么周丹锐说他要向孙浩学习?学习什么? _____

(2) 如果孙浩不是辅导老师,只是普通大学生,周丹锐还可以怎么说?
_____

(3) 如果孙浩是数学专业的,他还会这么说吗? _____ 如果不会,应该怎么说呢? _____

(4) 如果周丹锐说"那我得多向你学了",没有"可",这句话表达的意思会有什么不同? _____

Indicating a desire to learn from others is a way of elevating their expertise or accomplishments relative to ones' own abilities. The form of complimenting others is often used when first meeting someone and learning about their academic or professional background. Even though the compliment seems to raise the status of the person being complimented, it actually lessens the social distance by establishing an area of common interest. In situations where the speakers are clearly equals, they may indicate an interest in developing a relationship without putting either person in a "lower/junior" position by saying 那我们可以多交流交流. A more socially neutral response 你的专业很有意思 serves simply to keep the conversation going.

In this structure, 可 is used to emphasize the statement 我得(děi)多向你学习了. In another context, if you really need the book which your friend has promised to bring you the next day, as you depart, you may say 你可别忘了带那本书 to emphasize your request.

> **3/4**
> 孙浩： 啊,快到午饭时间了,我下午还有点事儿,要不我们去吃饭吧,边吃边聊。
> 周丹锐：我和几个朋友约好一起去吃饭,咱们一起去吧,我正好给你们介绍一下。
> 孙浩： 好啊,那太好了。

6. 孙浩提议一起吃午饭:"快到午饭时间了。"

(1) 有什么字可以代替这里的"快"? _____

(2) 如果你一般12点睡觉,现在11点50了,你的朋友还在和你发短信聊天,你可以怎么说? _____

The structure 快到 + [action/event] + 时间了 indicates that it is about time to perform the action or it's about time for the event to take place. Some people may say 快要到 instead of the shortened 快到.

7. 孙浩提议吃饭的时候他们可以继续聊天:"边吃边聊。"

(1) 这里,孙浩说"边吃边谈"好不好?"聊"和"谈"有什么不同?

(2) 在去旅游的车上,你坐在老师旁边,你们可能:
   A. 聊了聊中国的交通问题。
   B. 谈了谈中国的交通问题。

(3) 你对中文课有一些看法,想跟老师说,你可以问老师:
   A. "老师,我能不能跟你聊聊我对中文课的看法?"
   B. "老师,我能不能跟你谈谈我对中文课的看法?"

聊 indicates a casual talk, whereas 谈 indicates an intentional discussion of a particular topic. For example, if a student needs to talk with a teacher about choosing a topic for an upcoming report, he or she might ask 老师,我能不能跟你谈谈我下周报告的话题? On the other hand, if the student happened to run into the teacher after class and the topic of their upcoming report came up while they were chatting casually, the student might describe the incident by saying 昨天,我跟老师聊了聊我下周报告的话题。

8. 周丹锐欢迎孙浩跟他和朋友们一起吃午饭:"我正好给你们介绍一下。"

(1) 这里"正好"表达周丹锐什么样的心情? _____

(2) 你正要拨打辅导老师的电话时,突然接到了辅导老师打来的电话,接通后你会说什么? _____

When 正好 is used before an action, it emphasizes that the situation happens to be right for that action. It usually conveys a sense of pleasant surprise at the coincidence. For example, if a Chinese person wants to ask his friend something and his friend happens to call him at that moment, the person may say 我正好有事想问你. In another context, if a Chinese person is thinking of getting help from a friend when that friend happens to turn up, the person may say to his friend 你来得正好,我正好想请你帮个忙.

4/4

(午饭以后,孙浩和周丹锐在校园里走走)

孙浩： 周丹锐,下午有什么计划?

周丹锐：我要和郑妮去买手机卡。你知道在什么地方能买到吗?

孙浩： 校园里的一些超市就有卖的,外面路口的报亭也会有,我带你去吧。

周丹锐：不用,我们自己去就行了,别麻烦你了。

孙浩： 你最好和我们办同一家公司的手机卡,这样我们之间联系会便宜一些。我用的是移动。

周丹锐：等一等,这个我得记下来。

孙浩： 还是我跟你一起去看一下吧。

周丹锐：没事儿,我们应该可以解决,你不是说下午还有事儿吗?

孙浩： 有好多种套餐的,我怕你弄不清楚。

周丹锐：真的不用,你放心去忙你的吧。

---

9. 孙浩建议周丹锐办和他同一家公司的手机卡:"这样我们之间联系会便宜一些。"

(1) 这里的"会"可以去掉吗? 可以换成"能"吗?

(2) 这里"会"的用法和下面哪三个句子一样?

　　A. 外面路口的报亭也会有。

　　B. 我刚学会开车了。

　　C. 你还是吃一点吧,不然下午会饿的。

　　D. 明天会不会下雨?

(3) 你的朋友一般用电脑看DVD,但有一天他来找你借DVD机,你问他为什么不用电脑播放,他的回答可能是下面哪一句?

　　A. "这张CD不能在电脑上播放。"

　　B. "这张CD不会在电脑上播放。"

In this dialogue, 会 is used to express a prediction with certainty. Only in northern dialects do people use 会 and 能 interchangeably in such contexts. Normally, 能 is not used to express prediction.

能 and 会 are both used to express ability. However, the use of 能 implies the speaker's belief that performing the skill is dependent on the agent's physical capability or permission from circumstance. On the other hand, the use of 会 implies the speaker's belief that performing the skill relies on the agent's willingness or natural development. For example, to ask a person recovering from a car accident if he is able to walk, a Chinese speaker will say 他能走路了吗? In contrast, to ask if a small child has the ability to walk, he will say 你儿子会走路了吗? Similarly, if a Chinese person finds that a newly bought CD does not play on his computer, he will say 这张CD不能在电脑上播放.

10. 周丹锐婉言谢绝孙浩陪自己去买手机卡:"你不是说下午还有事儿吗?"
(1) 周丹锐为什么要说"你不是说下午还有事儿吗"?
  A. 他觉得孙浩之前在说谎。
  B. 他想知道孙浩下午要做什么。
  C. 他提醒孙浩忙自己的事。
(2) 你的朋友说他星期五要去香港玩,但你星期六在学校里碰见他,你可以怎么说? _____

By asking a rhetorical question with the expectation of an affirmative answer, the structure 不是……吗 is used literally to indicate that the speaker is surprised, or confused, or even dismayed by a perceived discrepancy between the current situation and what was mentioned between 不是 and 吗. The structure 你不是说……吗 may indicate the speaker is a bit confused or annoyed by the current situation. For example, if you see your friend on campus who was supposed to be on a trip to Hong Kong, you may express your confusion by saying 你不是说要去香港玩的吗?

Note that in the dialogue, Zhou Danrui is not expecting an explanation from Sun Hao. Instead, by reminding Sun Hao of his other obligation, Zhou Danrui is politely refusing Sun Hao's offer by showing concern for his time.

11. 孙浩觉得应该陪周丹锐一起去:"我怕你弄不清楚。"
(1) 下面哪个字可以代替这里的"弄"?
  A. 做   B. 搞   C. 看   D. 懂
(2) 如果有一天你的朋友回来的时候手受伤了,你可以怎么问他受伤的过程?
_____
(3) 如果你一直想知道"手机卡"和"充值卡"有什么不同,查了几个网站之后你终于明白了,你可以怎么说? _____

Both 弄 and 搞 can be used in spoken contexts to denote actions in a general manner, e.g., 弄/搞好了,怎么弄/搞的,弄/搞不清楚,弄/搞明白了.

Note these differences: a) While in most cases 弄 and 搞 are interchangeable, people from northern China may tend to use 弄, whereas people in the south are more likely to use 搞; b) 搞 is more often associated with serious events or purposes, e.g., 搞活动,搞建

设，跟老师搞好关系，把经济搞上去.

12. 周丹锐再三谢绝孙浩的帮助："你放心去忙你的吧。"
（1）你觉得孙浩还会继续坚持陪周丹锐去买手机卡吗？＿＿＿＿＿＿
（2）这里的"放心"是让孙浩对什么放心？
　　A. 对孙浩自己下午要做的事放心。
　　B. 对周丹锐一个人办手机卡这件事放心。
（3）如果就说"你去忙你的吧"，不说"放心"可以吗？为什么？＿＿＿＿＿
（4）你在练习口头报告，你的室友一边看电视，一边不停地打断你，告诉你哪里错了，你想告诉他你不想被打断，可以怎么说？＿＿＿＿＿＿＿＿＿＿＿＿＿＿

你放心去 + [action] + 你的（+ object）is used to reassure the other person that he can go ahead and do what he needs to do, with an implication that the speaker wishes to be left alone. Depending on the context, the object needs not be specified. In Zhou Danrui's case, he could have said 你放心去忙你的事吧. In anther context, if a Chinese person knows his friend has a test to prepare, when the friend offers to help, the person may decline the offer by reassuring his friend 你放心去准备你的考试吧. 放心 may be replaced with 安心. Similarly, if your roommate keeps correcting you while you are rehearsing your oral presentation, you may say 你安心看你的电视吧, asking him to focus on what he is doing (i.e., watching TV) and stop interrupting you.

Note that without 放心 or 安心, the structure 你 + [action] + 你的…… can sound condescending.

体演文本

Review the sections of the dialogue assigned by your teacher by listening to the audio and role-playing with another Chinese speaker. Be ready to perform the assigned portion of the dialogue from memory in class.

举一反三

Answer the following questions and think about how the dialogue can be adapted for different situations.

1. 你怎么介绍你的中文名字？
2. 你能说出你老师的名字是怎么写的吗？语伴的名字呢？
3. 孙浩夸周丹锐的时候说"你的中文说得不错啊"。他为什么不说"你的中文说得真好"？如果你想夸你的中国朋友的汉字写得好，你会用"不错"还是"真好"？如果你要夸他英文说得好呢？
4. 如果周丹锐希望孙浩跟他一起去买电话卡，他可以怎么很客气地接受孙浩的帮助呢?

5. 周丹锐说:"你放心去忙你的吧。"你觉得这个说法会给孙浩什么样的感觉?

熟能生巧

Listen to the audio and perform the following drills until you feel confident with the items practiced.

☞ **Drill 1 Introducing a name**

When asked how to write someone's name, describe the characters using either or both strategies Sun Hao used to describe the characters in his name in the example below. The illustrations will provide you with Chinese names to be described.

例：

孙(sūn) = 孙悟空

浩(hào) = 氵 + 告诉

郑妮：不好意思，你的名字怎么写？

孙浩：孙浩，孙悟空的"孙"，"浩"是三点水右边一个告诉的"告"。

Now, you describe some of other Chinese friends' names to Sun Hao.

1. 赵(zhào)
   奕(yì) = 神采奕奕
   歆(xīn) = 音 + 欠

2. 马
   凌(líng)
   云(yún) = 壮志凌云 (zhuàng zhì líng yún)

3. 贾(jiǎ) = 西 + 贝
   哲(zhé) = 哲学

4. 秦(qín) = 秦始皇
   晓(xiǎo) = 拂(fú)晓
   岚(lán) = 山 + 风

☞ **Drill 2 Talking about the duration of an action that is still in process**

When you are told that someone is currently engaged in an experience, ask him or her how many years the person has been engaged in it. Try to say the question in its complete form although in natural conversation, a Chinese speaker may simply ask [verb] 了几年了.

例：

奕歆：我妈妈也在学英文。

周丹锐：她学英文学了几年了？

1.   2.   3.   4.

☞ **Drill 3 Talking about the duration of an action that is no longer in progress**

When you are told that someone used to be engaged in an experience, ask her how long that experience lasted. Try to say the question in its complete form although in natural conversation, a Chinese speaker may simply ask [verb] 了几年.

例:
奕歆: 我妈妈以前也学过英文。
丹锐: 她学英文学了几年?／她学了几年英文?
1.   2.   3.   4.

☞ **Drill 4 Inquiring one's year in school**

When told that someone is a student, ask what year the person is at school.

例:
奕歆: 我哥哥在北京上大学。
丹锐: 他现在是大学几年级?／他现在是大几?
1.   2.   3.   4.

☞ **Drill 5 Talking about academic majors**

例 1:（汉语言文学）
丹锐: 你读什么专业?
奕歆: 我是汉语言文学专业。

例 2:（国际关系/中文）
孙浩: 你的专业是什么?
郑妮: 我主修国际关系,辅修中文。

Practice with the following majors/minors as well as with your own.

English	中文名称	Pinyin
Anthropology	人类学	rénlèi xué
Chinese Language and Literature	汉语言文学	hàn yǔyán wénxué
Communications and Media	传媒	chuánméi
Education	教育	jiàoyù
Engineering	工程学	gōngchéng xué
Finance	金融	jīnróng
International Relations	国际关系	guójì guānxì
International Trade	国际贸易	guójì màoyì
Law	法律	fǎlǜ
Linguistics	语言学	yǔyán xué
Management	管理	guǎnlǐ

Drill 6 Accepting a proposal and adding to it

When something proposed by others coincides with your existing plan with other friends, accept the proposal and indicate that it would be good for the person to join you. Each of the illustrations provides you with your existing plan with other friends.

例：

孙浩：要不我们去食堂吃饭吧。

郑妮：好啊,我正好要和几个朋友去吃饭,一起去吧。

1.   2.   3.   4.

Drill 7 Seeking location to obtain something

When your friend asks you about your afternoon plan, tell him that you need to buy something and ask him where you can buy it. The illustrations provide you with the things you need to buy. In the following example, Zhou Danrui uses 在什么地方. You may also use 在哪儿.

例：

赵奕歆：下午你有什么计划?

周丹锐：我想去买手机卡,你知道在什么地方能买到吗?

1.    2.    3.   4.

Drill 8 Expressing certainty and strong probability

When asked, tell the person where he or she can acquire the item inquired by providing a definite option and a highly probable alternative. Each of the cues will provide two options that you can use.

例：校园里的超市/ 路口的报亭

赵奕歆：我要去买手机卡,你知道什么地方能买到吗?
周丹锐：校园里的超市就有卖的,路口的报亭也会有。
1. 校门口的小文具店/ 沃尔玛
2. 沃尔玛/ 京东网
3. 学校图书馆/ 大四的同学
4. 学校网站/ 秦老师

☞ Drill 9 Refusing an offer of help

When your friend offers to help, politely decline it by indicating that you can do it yourself.

例：

赵奕歆：我带你去买电话卡吧。
周丹锐：不用,我自己去就行了,别麻烦你了。
1.　　　　　2.　　　　　3.　　　　　4.

☞ Drill 10 Refusing an offer politely by showing concern for the other person's time

When your friend insists on helping, you refuse by remembering that your friend has another commitment to fulfill. Each of the illustrations provides information about your friend's other commitment.

孙浩：下午还是我跟你一起去电信营业厅去看一下吧。
郑妮：没事儿,我自己去看就行了,你不是说下午要去见女朋友吗?

1. 2.  3.  4.

☞ Drill 11 Refusing an offer politely by reassuring the other person that you can handle it

When your friend insists on an offer of help, you persist in refusing it by insisting that your friend proceed with his or her original plan. Each of the illustrations will provide information about what your friend could be doing instead of helping you.

例：

赵奕歆：有好多种手机卡的,我怕你弄不清楚,还是我跟你一起去看一下吧。
周丹锐：真的不用,你放心去写论文吧。

1. 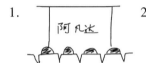 2.  3.  4.

Narration

Describe a new friend. One often gets an impression of a person from his or her words or behaviors. So, when you say what you think about the new friend, give concrete examples of what he or she has said or done. Listen to the example carefully to see how a Chinese student describes his new friend Zhou Danrui.

例：Liu Li describes her first impression of Zhou Danrui to her roommate Zhao Wenyuan.

赵文苑：你今天见了那个美国学生吧,快跟我说说?
刘丽：

嗯,今天我们一起吃的午饭。	1）Respond to the interlocutor;
孙浩的语伴中文名字叫周丹锐,"丹"是丹顶鹤的"丹",锐利的"锐"。才学了两年中文,不过说得很不错。	2）Provide basic information about your new friend (e.g. name, major, etc.);
他人挺友好的,就是可能刚认识还有点客气。	3）State your general impression of him or her;
听说他们几个要去买电话卡,我们怕他们搞不清楚有哪些手机套餐,本来想带他们去弄的,结果他再三坚持他自己可以解决,我们也就算了。	4）Give concrete examples of his words or behaviors to support your comment;
看来美国学生真是挺独立的。	5）End the narration by expressing your personal feeling or making a comment.

Now it's your turn!

Assume Zhou Danrui's role and describe Sun Hao to your classmate Zheng Ni, who is curious about your new tutor. After you are done, you may refer to a sample narration in the appendix and see how you can improve your narration.

郑妮：哎，丹锐，你的新辅导老师叫什么来着，看上去人挺好的啊？

言外有意

Read the cultural notes below and prepare questions for further discussion with Chinese people.

1. 三人行，必有我师（sānrén xíng bì yǒu wǒ shī）

Originally mentioned in Chapter Seven of *The Analects*（《论语·述而》），Confucius once said："三人行必有我师焉。" With the 焉（yān）dropped in most cases, this Confucian saying has become a conventional expression in today's everyday speech used to show one's humility and to compliment others. It encourages recognizing everyone's strengths and stresses the fact that we can always learn something from someone else.

2. 孙悟空、《西游记》、中国"四大名著"

Sūn Wùkōng（孙悟空），also known as the Monkey King in English, is the main character in the 16th century Chinese novel *Journey to the West*（《西游记》）. The fact that Sun Hao in the dialogue "naturally" specifies the "Sun" in his name as the same "Sun" in "Sun Wukong"（孙浩，孙悟空的"孙"），speaks to the popularity of the character and the novel.

Along with *Journey to the West*（《西游记》），two other 16th-century novels, *The Water Margin*（《水浒传》）and *Romance of the Three Kingdoms*（《三国演义》），and an 18th century novel *Dream of the Red Chamber*（《红楼梦》）are often referred to as the Four Great Classical Novels（"四大名著"）. Arguably, many would also add another 16th century novel, *The Plume in the Golden Vase*（《金瓶梅》）to the list. Becoming familiar with these famous literary works will help you better understand Chinese culture. Familiarize yourself with these famous literary works（e.g., their main characters and basic story lines）will help you better understand Chinese culture and better present yourself as an informed and serious Chinese learner.

1.2 吃饭了

民以食为天

🎧 **投石问路**

Listen to the five questions in the audio and answer them based on your own experience. Be ready to discuss these questions in class. You may write down some notes in the space provided below.

1.
2.
3.
4.
5.

🎧 **边听边想**

Listen to the audio and try to visualize the dialogue in your mind. Think about who the speakers are, the kind of social relationship they have, and what their intentions might be.

🎧 耳闻目睹

Listen to the audio again while following along in the printed text. As you listen, mark any place that you are unclear or have questions about.

民以食为天
人物：周丹锐、孙浩、郑妮、赵奕歆

（中午刚下课，周丹锐、孙浩、赵奕歆和郑妮在去食堂的路上）

周丹锐：终于下课了，我都要饿死了……哇，好香啊！

赵奕歆：前面就是食堂了。

郑　妮：在食堂吃饭可以用现金吗？

孙　浩：在学校食堂吃饭一般都用校园卡，不过你们没有校园卡也没关系，今天可以刷我的卡。

周丹锐：校园卡？是这个吧。

赵奕歆：对，就是这个，你们卡里充值了吗？

郑　妮：充值？

赵奕歆：就是往卡里存钱。

郑　妮：不知道啊，这是我第一次来食堂。（1/4）

赵奕歆：没关系，旁边就有圈存机，可以往卡上存钱。等一下吃完饭一起去看看，这顿就先刷我的卡吧。

周丹锐：还是先去充值吧。我带了信用卡。

孙　浩：美国信用卡可能不行，这次就先用我的饭卡吧。

周丹锐：那我取了钱马上还你。

孙　浩：不用了，不用了，这次算我的吧。

周丹锐：那好吧，谢谢你，下次我来请。（2/4）

（在食堂，周丹锐他们四个人排队打饭）

周丹锐：好多东西啊，看上去都很好吃。

郑　妮：那个是什么啊，好吃吗？

赵奕歆：那个是糖醋排骨，应该还可以吧，不过这儿的菜没有我妈做的好吃，有机会你们要来我家尝尝我妈的手艺。

郑　妮：好啊好啊。（3/4）

孙　浩：你们看着喜欢什么就告诉服务员，最后我来刷卡。

周丹锐：这菜叫什么？

赵奕歆：这个是古老肉。不过有些菜我也说不上名字，你就指着说要这个要那个就行了。哎，郑妮，你怎么光吃青菜呀？

郑　妮：好吃的太多了，这样吃一个夏天，还不发胖?!（4/4）

知其所以然

The dialogue is broken down into sections below for explanation and analysis. Study the notes and answer the questions for the underlined text.

1/4

（中午刚下课,周丹锐、孙浩、赵奕歆和郑妮在去食堂的路上）

周丹锐：终于下课了,<u>我都要饿死了</u>……哇,好香啊!

赵奕歆：前面就是食堂了。

郑妮：　在食堂吃饭可以用现金吗?

孙浩：　在学校食堂吃饭一般都用校园卡,不过你们没有校园卡也没关系,今天可以刷我的卡。

周丹锐：校园卡? 是这个吧。

赵奕歆：对,就是这个,你们卡里充值了吗?

郑妮：　充值?

赵奕歆：就是往卡里存钱。

郑妮：　不知道啊,这是我第一次来食堂。

---

1. 下课了,周丹锐感觉特别饿,他说:"我都要饿死了。"

（1）周丹锐说他要"饿死了",是因为如果再不吃东西他真的会死吗?
_____

（2）"我要饿死了"和"我要饿晕了"哪一个比较严重? _____

（3）如果你为了做作业半夜一点还没睡,感觉很困,可以怎么说?
_____

（4）如果你的好朋友问你她的新衣服怎么样,你可以说"美死了"吗? "美晕了"了呢? _____

The structure ［adjective］+ 死/晕了 is used to express feelings with exaggeration. It is generally used between people who have a close relationship. The feelings expressed with 死了 can be either negative (e.g., 饿死了,困死了,难受死了) or positive (e.g., 美死了,高兴死了). However, 晕了 mostly expresses negative feelings (e.g., 饿晕了,忙晕了,气晕了).

2/4

赵奕歆：没关系,旁边就有圈存机,可以往卡上存钱。等一下吃完饭一起去看看,这顿就先刷我的卡吧。

周丹锐：还是先去充值吧。我带了信用卡。

孙浩：　美国信用卡可能不行,这次就先用我的饭卡吧。

> 周丹锐：那我取了钱马上还你。
> 孙浩：　不用了，不用了，这次算我的吧。
> 周丹锐：那好吧，谢谢你，下次我来请。

2. 赵奕歆告诉丹锐圈存机的作用，她说："旁边就有圈存机，可以往卡上存钱。"
（1）这里的"上"还可以用什么词代替？_____
（2）别往菜_____加那么多盐，不健康。
　　A. 上　　　　　　B. 内　　　　　　C. 里
（3）电视_____正在放奥运会的相关新闻。
　　A. 上　　　　　　B. 里　　　　　　C. 上/里

上 and 里 are usually used to denote physical or conceptual location/direction. When denoting conceptual location/direction, 上 and 里 can be used interchangeably. For example, both 往卡上存钱 and 往卡里存钱 refer to the action of putting money onto the card. Similarly, to refer to information obtained from the TV, a Chinese person may use either 在电视上看到的 or 在电视里看到的. To report something read from a book, a Chinese person may use either "书上说……" or "书里说……". However, 上 and 里 are not interchangeable when used to denote physical location/direction. For example, to say that a card is inside a book, it is only appropriate to say 卡在书里. In contrast, 卡在书上 would indicate that the card is on top of a book. In another context, to request more salt to be added into a dish, a Chinese person would say 往菜里加点盐. If the request is to add some decoration on the dish, he would say 在菜上放一朵花.

3. 孙浩不让周丹锐还他午饭钱，他说："这次算我的吧。"
（1）孙浩说"这次算我的吧"，意思是他要做什么？_____
（2）这里孙浩能不能说"这次我请客吧"？为什么？_____
（3）还有什么情况下可以用"算我的"吗？_____

算我的 is often used by a Chinese speaker to claim responsibility. In this dialogue, Sun Hao is offering to take the responsibility for paying. 算我的 is slightly different from 我请客 in that 算我的 is often used as an on-the-spot decision, whereas you often have a reason or plan to 请客. This is why Zhou Danrui's response 下次我来请 sounds appropriate in the context. Similarly, when discussing if a course of action should be taken, a person who is worried about possible negative outcomes may ask："出了问题怎么办？" If you respond with "出了问题算我的", you are bravely claiming responsibility for whatever may happen.

> **3/4**
>
> (在食堂,周丹锐他们四个人排队打饭)
>
> 周丹锐:好多东西啊,看上去都很好吃。
>
> 郑妮： 那个是什么啊,好吃吗?
>
> 赵奕歆:那个是糖醋排骨,<u>应该还可以吧</u>,不过这儿的菜没有我妈做的好吃,<u>有机会你们要来我家尝尝我妈的手艺</u>。
>
> 郑妮： 好啊好啊。

4. 赵奕歆邀请周丹锐和郑妮去她家,她说:"有机会你们要来我家……"

(1) 这里的"有机会"还可以用什么词代替? _____

(2) 你觉得这里郑妮应该说"好啊好啊"吗? 为什么? _____

(3) 如果你的朋友跟你打电话时说他搬了新家,并邀请你有机会去他家玩,你可以怎么回答? _____

有机会 is used to propose doing something if there is a chance. Some similar phrases include 有时间, 有空 and 下次. Such a proposal can simply be an intention of being nice, or it may be a pretext for an actual invitation. The other person typically expresses acceptance by saying 好啊好啊 or 谢谢, without asking for details. In the case of an actual invitation, the person inviting will suggest details, such as a specific time and place. A polite response like 太麻烦你了吧 shows appreciation, but not necessarily acceptance of the invitation.

5. 郑妮去赵奕歆家的时候,赵奕歆说可以"尝尝我妈妈的手艺"。

(1) 这里"手艺"是什么意思? 为什么可以"尝尝"? _____

(2) 你的朋友需要理发,你觉得你去过的一家理发店理发不错,你给朋友推荐这家店的时候可以怎么说? _____

The basic meaning of 手艺 is "skills or craftsmanship" and it extends to include the products of such skills or craftsmanship. Here, 手艺 refers to Yixin's mother's cooking, which one would enjoy tasting. Similarly, to recommend a barber to a friend, a Chinese speaker may say 那家店的手艺不错 or 那家店的理发师手艺不错.

> **4/4**
>
> 孙浩： 你们看着喜欢什么就告诉服务员,最后我来刷卡。
>
> 周丹锐:这菜叫什么?
>
> 赵奕歆:这个是古老肉。不过<u>有些</u>菜我也<u>说不上名字</u>,你就指着说要这个要那个就行了。哎,郑妮,你怎么<u>光</u>吃青菜呀?
>
> 郑妮： 好吃的太多了,这样吃一个夏天,还不发胖?!

6. 赵奕歆也不知道所有菜的名字,"不过有些菜我也说不上名字"。
   (1) 她"说不上名字"是因为记不得还是不知道? _____
   (2) 可以把这里的"说不上"换成"说不出"吗? _____
   (3) 在你的生活中有什么你"说不出"的事情吗? _____

说不上 is used to denote that you are unable to name or categorize something even though you have some idea about it. In this dialogue, Zhao Yixin could also have used 说不出 to express that she could not name some of the dishes in the cafeteria.

Note that 说不出 can also be used in contexts in which someone is unwilling or unable to verbalize his/her feeling or thoughts about something. For example, 我说不出现在的感觉 and 我心里有种说不出的感觉.

7. 赵奕歆看见郑妮买的都是青菜,问她:"哎,郑妮,你怎么光吃青菜呀?"
   (1) 这里"光"的用法和下面哪两句的用法类似?
       A. 别光说我,这件事你也有责任。
       B. 秋天的阳光最美。
       C. 我能不能光买练习册,不买课本?
       D. 这张光盘是买课本时送的。
   (2) 如果你给弟弟 20 块钱去买牛奶和水。他回来的时候拿了很多水,但是没有牛奶,你不明白为什么,可以怎么问他? _____

光 is used to indicate a lack of variety. In the dialogue, Zhao Yixin may be surprised because Zheng Ni is not eating other varieties of food like meat or beans. In another context, if you ask your brother to buy milk and water and your brother comes back with only water, you may ask him: 你怎么光买了水啊? As another example, if a Chinese person keeps blaming his partner for failing to meet the deadline for their group project, his partner may contest by saying: 别光说我,这件事你也有责任. Similarly, if a textbook and workbook seem to be a set and you only need the workbook, you may ask: 我能不能光买练习册,不买课本?

体演文本

Review the sections of the dialogue assigned by your teacher by listening to the audio and role-playing with another Chinese speaker. Be ready to perform the assigned portion of the dialogue from memory in class.

举一反三

Answer the following questions and think about how the dialogue can be adapted for different situations.

1. 如果你的好朋友想请你吃饭，你会说什么？
2. 如果想请你吃饭的人不是好朋友，而是你当天刚认识的人，你会说什么呢？
3. 赵奕歆对郑妮说"有机会你们要来我家尝尝我妈的手艺"是真的邀请吗？如果不是真的邀请，她说这句话的目的是什么？
4. 你一般怎么判断哪些情况是真的邀请，哪些情况不是？

熟能生巧

Listen to the audio and perform the following drills until you feel confident with the items practiced.

☞ Drill 1 Expressing relief

When you are informed of a situation, comment that it finally comes and explain why you have been looking forward to it. Each of the illustrations indicates where you are and how you are feeling.

例：

赵奕歆：前面就是食堂了。

周丹锐：终于要到食堂了，我都要饿死了。

1. 2. 3. 4.

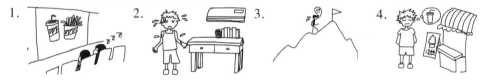

☞ Drill 2 Explaining a customary procedure and offering to help

When your friend asks if something can be done in a certain way, explain the customary way of doing it in your community and offer to help out in case she is not prepared. Each of the illustrations indicates the customary way of doing things.

例：

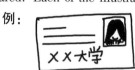

同学：在食堂吃饭可以用现金吗？

周丹锐：我们一般都用校园卡，不过你没有也没关系，可以先刷我的。

☞ Drill 3 Showing consideration by limiting inconvenience to others

When someone offers to help you out of trouble, accept it politely by showing consideration for the inconvenience that the person might experience. Listen to the model and then accept the following offers of help by expressing what you will do to limit the inconvenience they cause.

例：
赵奕歆：如果你还没取钱的话，先用我的吧。
周丹锐：那我取了钱马上还给你。
1.   2.   3.   4.

☞ Drill 4 Displaying hospitality

When your friend assumes something about you that's admirable, confirm it and then casually invite the person to experience it in person. The cues indicate the experiences for which you may invite your friend.

例：尝
孙浩：你妈妈做的菜一定很好吃吧？
郑妮：对啊，有机会你一定要来尝尝我妈做的菜。
1. 听
2. 看
3. 参观
4. 坐

☞ Drill 5 Making a casual proposal

In this drill, when you realize you share the same interest as your friend, give a positive response and propose to do that activity together in the future.

例：
奕歆：我特喜欢喝咖啡。你呢？
丹锐：我也喜欢，有机会我们一起去喝咖啡吧。
1.   2.   3.   4.

Narration

Narrate a new experience. In this drill, you will practice telling the story of having learned something from a new experience.

例：Zhou Danrui shares what he learned from the new dining experience at the campus cafeteria with his classmate Mary who invites him to try the food at the cafeteria.

梅瑞：周丹锐，听说苏大食堂的饭菜挺不错。我们今天去那儿吃吧。

周丹锐：

好啊。其实昨天中午我和我的中文语伴去过了。	1) Respond to the interlocutor;
你知道吗，在食堂吃饭必须用校园卡。我以前从来没在中国大学食堂吃过饭，还以为跟餐馆一样可以用现金。	2) State your ignorance of certain knowledge or wrong assumption due to lack of prior experience;
昨天去的时候才发现他们不收现金。	3) State the new information learned from the experience;
我虽然有卡，但是里面没钱。幸好是跟语伴一起去的，他用他的卡帮我付了钱。	4) Elaborate on your experience if necessary;
你的校园卡充值了吗？	5) End the narration by inviting the other person to comment.

Now it's your turn!

1. You are Zheng Ni. When Miss Zhang, a local teacher, asks you if you have tried the campus cafeteria, tell her what you learned from your experience at the Chinese campus cafeteria yesterday. After you are done, you may refer to a sample narration in the appendix and see how you can improve your narration.

张老师：郑妮，苏大食堂的饭菜挺不错的。你们去那儿吃过了吗？

2. When asked by a local teacher if you've gotten used to life in Suzhou, tell her something you've recently discovered through a new experience.

老师：怎么样？习惯不习惯这里的生活？

言外有意

Read the cultural notes below and prepare questions for further discussion with Chinese people.

1. 民以食为天（mín yǐ shí wéi tiān）Food is the first consideration of people.

The set expression 民以食为天 first appeared in《汉书·郦食其传》(Lì Shíqí Zhuàn, Hànshū) over two thousand years ago. It is still frequently used in contemporary Chinese, especially in relatively formal contexts, as a pretext for an enthusiastic discussion about food, such as in commercials of food on restaurants. To begin an introduction to Suzhou cuisine, a TV host may say：俗话说"民以食为天"，有谁能挡得住美食的诱惑？今天我们就来谈谈苏州的美食. With this ancient expression quoted, it sounds as if all the emotions and resources spent on food are forgivable, understandable, or even admirable. Similarly, a restaurant may be decorated with a huge calligraphy saying 民以食为天.

2. 礼尚往来：下次我来请

Gift giving is an important part of Chinese culture. When socializing with colleagues or friends, one golden rule about gifting is to sustain the reciprocity. This rule also applies to whoever pays the bill at a restaurant. In our dialogue, Zhou Danrui eventually accepted Sun Hao's offer to pay for his lunch by saying 那好吧，谢谢你，下次我来请. This is culturally appropriate and establishes the expectation that Zhou Danrui will pay the next time they eat together. Inviting each other to meals is a very common way of maintaining network of relationship in China. Urban young people sometimes follow the Western custom of going Dutch（AA 制）, but if your Chinese friend insists on paying for your meal, don't forget to say 下次我来请 and then do it!

3. 懂中国人说话的意图

Understanding the literal meaning of an expression does not always result in understanding the intention（意图）behind the words. Yet accurately assessing others' intentions is essential to effective communication.

For example, in the dialogue, Zhao Yixin's saying of 有机会你们要来我家尝尝我妈的手艺 had better be understood as a polite expression（客气话）intended to communicate goodwill instead of an actual invitation. An appropriate response will be a casual acknowledgement of the person's good intentions, such as "好啊好啊" or "谢谢啦".

Similarly, Zhao Yixin is not being critical when she asks Zheng Ni "你怎么光吃青菜啊" since Chinese people often show their care and concern by expressing reproach. Such comments should not be interpreted as interference in one's personal life but as concern for one's overall well-being. Don't stop at the literal meanings of the words. There is more to explore!

4. 吃了吗？

This can be a casual greeting between friends when they meet around meal time, and generally you are expected to reply with 吃过了 or 这就去吃, followed by 你呢? to greet back. A similarly tricky question is 上哪儿. When these questions are asked on the street, it is usually not necessary to give an elaborate explanation.

  Living in a Chinese community, you may often hear people ask you obvious questions like 看书呢？跑步啊？or 等车啊？when they can clearly see what you are doing. Those are just greetings or "ice-breakers"—greeting or initiating an interaction by mentioning the obvious, to which the other person can only give affirmative responses.

1.3 买东西

货比三家

🎧 投石问路

Listen to the five questions in the audio and answer them based on your own experience. Be ready to discuss these questions in class. You may write down some notes in the space provided below.

1.
2.
3.
4.
5.

🎧 边听边想

Listen to the audio and try to visualize the dialogue in your mind. Think about who the speakers are, the kind of social relationship they have, and what their intentions might be.

耳闻目睹

Listen to the audio again while following along in the printed text. As you listen, mark any place that you are unclear or have questions about.

货比三家

人物：周丹锐、孙浩、店员

（孙浩和周丹锐在欧尚超市买东西）

孙　浩：你不是说有好多东西要买吗？怎么就买了几个衣架啊？

周丹锐：我没找到我在美国经常吃的那种麦片。

孙　浩：哦。这里的进口食品已经算很多了，如果这儿还没有，就要去沃尔玛了。(1/4)

周丹锐：离这儿远吗？

孙　浩：不算远，在印象城有一家，坐车20来分钟就可以了。那儿是个大型购物中心。

周丹锐：太好了，我应该也可以在那里买到篮球鞋吧。

孙　浩：对，那儿有好几家运动品牌专卖店。

周丹锐：那我下午就去那边看看，你知道坐几路公交能到吗？

孙　浩：坐2路或者261路都能到。要不我陪你一起去？

周丹锐：没事儿，我自己去就行了。(2/4)

（周丹锐在印象城的某个运动品牌专卖店里）

店　员：看运动鞋吗？这里都是我们今年最新款的，价格都是在五六百到七八百元之间。

周丹锐：我想买双篮球鞋。现在有什么优惠活动吗？

店　员：那边一些去年的旧款式，现在打七折。

周丹锐：这双不错，打七折是多少钱？

店　员：386。你穿多大号的，我拿一双给你试试吧。

周丹锐：44号。(3/4)

（丹锐试完鞋）

周丹锐：还能再打点儿折吗？

店　员：不行了，这已经是最低折扣了。我最多再送你一双袜子，只能这样了。

周丹锐：噢，这样啊。那我先去别家看看，等会儿再回来。

店　员：好吧，那我给你留着啊。其实你眼光很好的，这双鞋真的很实惠，前天还卖五百多呢。……那一会儿再回来啊！(4/4)

知其所以然

The dialogue is broken down into sections below for explanation and analysis. Study the notes and answer the questions for the underlined text.

1/4

（孙浩和周丹锐在欧尚超市买东西）

孙浩： 你不是说有好多东西要买吗？怎么就买了几个衣架啊？

周丹锐：我没找到我在美国经常吃的那种麦片。

孙浩： 哦。<u>这里的进口食品已经算很多了</u>，如果这儿还没有，就要去沃尔玛了。

---

1. 孙浩没想到周丹锐买的东西那么少，他说："怎么就买了几个衣架啊？"

   （1）这里"就"的用法跟下面哪两句的用法类似？

   A. 我昨天下午很累，一回家就睡了。

   B. 好的，我现在就去买。

   C. 昨天去 KTV 的人太多了，我就唱了两首歌。

   D. 我钱包里就 20 块钱，不够打车。

   （2）你今天的作业是写一篇作文，你花半小时写完了。如果同学问你："今天的作业怎么样？"

   A. 为了强调作业很少，你可以怎么用"就"回答他？ _____

   B. 为了强调很快能写完，你怎么用"就"回答他？ _____

Here, Sun Hao uses 就 to indicate that Zhou Danrui is buying less than what he has expected. Similarly, to tell his friend that he did not get to sing as many songs as he had expected to, he may say 我就唱了两首歌. To emphasize that he does not have enough cash for a taxi, he may say 我钱包里就 20 块钱，不够打车.

In other contexts, 就 may also be used to indicate that things are done in an immediate manner. For example, if your friend recommends you a very good book, you may respond 好的，我现在就去买 to indicate that you will go and buy it right away. To emphasize that your homework is very small in amount, you may say 就一篇作文. To emphasize that homework takes little time to finish, you may say 我花半小时就写完了 or 半小时就能写完.

2. 周丹锐在欧尚超市没买到麦片，孙浩觉得有点意外，说："这里的进口食品已经算很多了。"

   （1）如果孙浩不用"算"，只说"已经很多了"，语气会有什么不同？

（2）在小店买东西的时候，你跟老板讲价。如果老板说"已经算很便宜了"，你还能讲价吗？_____

By adding 算 to the statement 很多, Sun Hao avoids sounding assertive. With 已经算很多了, Sun Hao leaves room for the possibility that other stores may have bigger collections of imported foods. Similarly, a vendor's response 已经算很便宜了 gives away the fact that there is still room for further negotiation of the price.

算 may also be used to soften the tone of negation, e.g., 不算远, which you will encounter in the next section. Similarly, to correct the assumption 你们是同学吧, a Chinese person may say 不算同学, 只是一起参加过一次夏令营(summer camp).

2/4

周丹锐：离这儿远吗？
孙浩：　不算远，在印象城有一家，坐车20来分钟就可以了。那儿是个大型购物中心。
周丹锐：太好了，我应该也可以在那里买到篮球鞋吧。
孙浩：　对，那儿有好几家运动品牌专卖店。
周丹锐：那我下午就去那边看看，你知道坐几路公交能到吗？
孙浩：　坐2路或者261路都能到。要不我陪你一起去？
周丹锐：没事儿，我自己去就行了。

3. 孙浩告诉周丹锐沃尔玛离学校不太远，他说"坐车20来分钟就可以了"。
（1）孙浩说"坐车20来分钟就可以了"，这句话还可以怎么说？_____
（2）如果你的室友问你背对话要花多长时间，你怎么回答？_____
（3）假设一个中国朋友问你："每天跑步跑多长时间？"你可以怎么回答？
_____

The table below shows different patterns that can be used to express approximate amounts. These patterns can be used for time, distance and quantity.

Pattern	Example	Meaning
number + 来 + classifier	40 来分钟	more than 40 minutes
number + 多 + classifier	40 多分钟	
number + classifier + 左右	40 分钟左右	40 minutes more or less
差不多 + number + classifier	差不多 40 分钟	
大概 + number + classifier	大概 40 分钟	approximately 40 minutes
大约 + number + classifier	大约 40 分钟	

第一单元 抵达苏州 Settling Down | 41

Note that 大约 is less colloquial than the other patterns listed here.

4. 周丹锐想坐公交车去印象城,他问孙浩:"你知道坐几路公交能到吗?"
(1) 下面哪些说法跟"坐公交"表示一样的交通方式?
  A. 坐公共汽车 B. 坐公车 C. 坐公交车 D. 坐车
(2) 在苏州,除了坐公交,还有什么其他交通方式?_____
  你在苏州怎么去印象城?_____

坐公共汽车,坐公车,坐公交车 and 坐车 may all be used by Chinese speakers to refer to taking a bus. Different buses are usually specified as〔number〕+ 路, indicating the route of a bus, as in 你可以坐公交车 21 路或者 261 路. Note that if the number reaches three digits you would read each digit singularly, e.g., for 261, a Chinese speaker would say "èr liù yī" or "èr liù yāo". Three-or-more-digit bus numbers are also rarely followed with the word 路.

While 坐车 in general is a casual way of saying "taking a bus", 打车 is a casual way of saying "taking a taxi". For example, if you and your friend plan to go to Walmart and you wonder if the two of you should take a bus or a taxi, you may ask:"我们坐车去还是打车去?"

3/4

(周丹锐在印象城的某个运动品牌专卖店里)
店员: 看运动鞋吗? 这里都是我们今年最新款的,价格都是在五六百到七八百元之间。
周丹锐:我想买双篮球鞋。现在有什么优惠活动吗?
店员: 那边一些去年的旧款式,现在打七折。
周丹锐:这双不错,打七折是多少钱?
店员: 386。你穿多大号的,我拿一双给你试试吧。
周丹锐:44 号。

---

5. 店员首先推荐店里的新款鞋,她说"这里都是我们今年最新款的"。
(1) 买衣服或者鞋子的时候,你一般先看"新款的"还是"旧款的"? 为什么?
_____
(2) 在 SWATCH 手表店,店员大概会先给客人看哪些手表?_____
(3) 假设你在衣服店看中了一件衣服,但是不知道是给男生穿还是女生穿的。你可以怎么问? _____

Here 款 is short for 款式, referring to the style or design of a product. The items in fashion stores are often categorized according to their styles or design, and are referred to as 新款(new styles), 旧款/老款 (old styles), 男款(men's style), 女款 (women's style) and 儿童款(children's style). If a woman likes a certain type of men's jacket, she may ask the shop assistant 这种外套有女款的吗? to find out if there are similar coats designed for women.

4/4

(丹锐试完鞋)
周丹锐：还能再打点儿折吗？
店员：   不行了，这已经是最低折扣了。我最多再送你一双袜子，只能这样了。
周丹锐：噢，这样啊。那我先去别家看看，等会儿再回来。
店员：   好吧，那我给你留着啊。其实你眼光很好的，这双鞋真的很实惠，前天还卖五百多呢。……那一会儿再回来啊！

---

6. 周丹锐决定要先货比三家，店员希望他回来买鞋，她说"那我给你留着啊"。
（1）在对话里，店员给周丹锐留着什么？为什么？_____
（2）假如你给你女朋友做了晚饭，但是她晚上有课，你可以告诉她什么？
_____
（3）假如你在买电影票，付钱时发现现金不够，需要取钱。你可以怎么对售票员说？_____

给……留着 is used to show that something will be reserved or saved for someone. When using this structure to make requests you can substitute 给 with 帮 to sound more polite. For example, if a person finds that he does not have enough cash for a movie ticket and would like the cashier to save the ticket for him, he might say 我去取点钱，能帮我留着这张票吗?

7. 店员很巧妙地推销那双鞋，她说"你眼光很好的"，既夸奖周丹锐，又夸了那双鞋。
（1）在对话里，店员说周丹锐的眼光好，为什么？_____
（2）假如你在一家衣服店工作。你可以对客人说什么样的话？_____
（3）假如一个女人总是找不到令她满意的男朋友，但其实她以前的那些男朋友都是很优秀的人。你可以怎么总结她没有男友的原因？_____

眼光 means vision or judgement. Hence, "你的眼光真好！" praises someone for having good taste or judgement. Phrases like these are often used by salespeople to compliment potential customers. Sometimes this can sound a bit like flattery or 拍马屁 (lit. patting the horse's rear). The phrase "眼光很高", on the other hand, is often used with sarcastic tone to talk about unrealistically high aspirations.

Note that to say someone has bad taste or no taste, "没有眼光" can be used.

8. 店员继续夸那双鞋,她说"这双鞋真的很实惠"。
(1) 假如你是专卖店的店员,你可以怎么介绍旧款式的运动鞋? _____
(2) 在对话中,店员为什么说"这双鞋很实惠",而没有说"这双鞋很便宜"? _____
(3) 如果你和朋友逛服装店,你看到一件衣服又便宜又好,你可以对你朋友说什么? _____

实惠 is used to describe something of good quality that is also inexpensive. It differs from 便宜 in that 便宜 only indicates a low price, but does not necessarily entail good quality. For example, a company might want to emphasize that their good products are priced economically by saying 我们的产品经济实惠. It's also possible to get a good deal on an expensive item. Even though the cost is relatively high, the price is considered 划算(huá suàn) or 值(zhí) in view of the high quality of the product.

体演文本

Review the sections of the dialogue assigned by your teacher by listening to the audio and role-playing with another Chinese speaker. Be ready to perform the assigned portion of the dialogue from memory in class.

举一反三

Answer the following questions and think about how the dialogue can be adapted for different situations.

1. 对话里孙浩说"要不我陪你一起去",你觉得他是真的很想陪周丹锐一起去呢,还是只是客气一下?如果他说"我陪你一起去吧",意思会有什么不同?
2. 如果周丹锐希望孙浩陪他去,孙浩说"要不我陪你一起去"的时候,他可以怎么回答?
3. 进了商场遇到工作人员向你热情推荐商品但你不想要的情况,你怎么做?
4. 周丹锐用哪些技巧讨价还价?你在中国用过这些技巧吗?你觉得哪一个最有效?
5. 假设你买了双运动鞋,穿几天以后觉得不太喜欢。到商店退鞋的时候你怎么跟店员说?

熟能生巧

Listen to the audio and perform the following drills until you feel confident with the items practiced.

☞ Drill 1 Expressing an approximation

When asked to confirm information, such as a distance, length, price, age or size, use 不算 to give a negative response without sounding categorical. Then on the basis of the visual prompts below, provide an approximate estimate using the structure [number] + 来 + classifier.

例：

赵奕歆：那家书店离这儿远吗？

周丹锐：不算远，20来分钟吧。

1.  2.   3.  4.

☞ Drill 2 Providing a range

When asked about something, tell her about the range of it. Each of the illustrations will provide you with the range you can use.

例：

赵奕歆：那些运动鞋的价格怎么样？

丹锐：都是在500到700之间。

1.  2.  3. 4.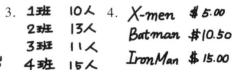

☞ Drill 3 Calculating the discounted price

When your friend asks how much you paid for something, describe the original price and how much of a discount you got. Each of the illustrations shows the original price and the promotion.

例：

周丹锐：你这双篮球鞋挺不错，多少钱买的？

郑妮：这双原价400块，我买的时候打七折，才花了280。

第一单元 抵达苏州 Settling Down | 45

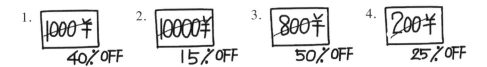

☞ Drill 4 Negotiating price at a department store

In this drill, assume that you really want to buy an item. When the shop assistant encourages you to buy a certain item, make one final attempt to bring down the price.

例：

店员：这双是我们店卖得最好的鞋。

周丹锐：还有什么其他优惠活动吗？这双鞋再优惠一点我就买了。

☞ Drill 5 Negotiating price at an open market

When the vendor encourages you to buy a certain item, request a lower price by promising her that you will bring more friends next time.

例：

老板：你眼光真好,这款手套就剩最后两副了。

郑妮：再给我便宜一点吧,这副手套再便宜一点我就买了,下次还带朋友过来。

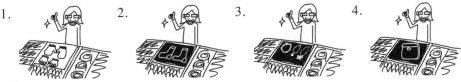

☞ Drill 6 Requesting a better offer

When the shop assistant gives you a good offer, ask her if you can get an even better one.

例：

店员：我给你便宜一点，150块钱怎么样？

周丹锐：还能再便宜一点儿吗？

1.　　　　　2.　　　　　3.　　　　　4.

☞ **Drill 7 Indicating no further room for negotiation**

When asked if you can do something, indicate that there is nothing can be done because the situation has already been changed to the greatest extent possible.

例：

周丹锐：还能再便宜一点儿吗？

店员：不行了，这已经是最便宜了。

1.　　　　　2.　　　　　3.　　　　　4.

Narration

Practice sharing shopping experiences.

例：The next day, upon hearing about the good deal Zhou Danrui got on his basketball shoes, Zheng Ni wonders how one could negotiate price at brand stores. Assume Zhou Danrui's role and explain how you got the good deal.

郑妮：专卖店不是不可以砍价吗？

周丹锐：

是不可以砍价。	1) Confirm;
不过他们会有一些优惠活动，比如一些旧款鞋会打折卖。	2) Explain that they have promotions;
而且买东西的时候一定要货比三家。有时候别的店会有更好、更便宜的。	3) Mention another strategy of getting better deals;
比如我今天看的第一双鞋，他们现在打七折，原价500多，打了折还要差不多400块。我问店员能不能再优惠点，她说最多能送我一双袜子。我觉得还是太贵，就去了别的店转了转，找到了一双一样的。原价也是500多，但是打五折，我只花了不到300块就拿下了。	4) Demonstrate the strategy with your own experience.

Now it's your turn!

Share one shopping experience that you had in China. Describe the deal you got and share any strategies you used for getting a better deal.

言外有意

Read the cultural notes below and prepare questions for further discussion with Chinese people.

1. 货比三家(huò bǐ sān jiā)

Many people in China tend to believe that smart shoppers compare similar items from different stores. To encourage someone to "shop around" more before making a purchase, you can say 买东西要货比三家,再去别的地方看看. Zhou Danrui could be described as a smart shopper by saying 他买东西总是货比三家.

2. 在中国生活之必备技能之一:讨价还价

Living in China, you will probably want to learn how to bargain. You may have noticed that most big chains and public facilities in China set fixed price for their products and services, leaving no room for bargaining. However, in a lot of shopping contexts, bargaining is the norm rather than exception. For example, in a specialty store or upscale boutique, even though they have posted prices, you can still ask if any discounts are available by asking 有没有优惠活动(Is there any promotion going on?). You might get a pair of free sock as a bonus for buying a pair of shoes. In short, just because a store appears to be a non-bargaining establishment, it never hurts to ask about discounts, especially if you are making a large purchase.

学而时习之

By carrying out the field performances in this section, you will be practicing in real situations what you have learned from this unit. The "Performances" listed here are sequenced according to levels of complexity. Depending on the specific contexts and turns of events, the "Acts" listed under each performance need not be performed in the exact order as listed; and they need not be performed all together in any actual encounter. Perform as appropriately and as effectively as you can. Be prepared to re-tell your experiences in class.

Before you actually do the field performances, rehearse doing them with a Chinese friend. The "Useful Expressions" box below provides you with some expressions you may use for these performances. For now, try saying them after the audio.

Useful Expressions

1. 等车呢！/你是苏大的学生吧？
2. 你篮球打得真好。
3. 不好意思，请问……怎么写？
4. 你读什么专业？你现在是几年级？
5. 你在这里工作了多久了？
6. 有机会我们一起……吧！
7. 这附近有没有……
8. 你知不知道在哪儿可以……
9. 你是哪儿的人？你老家在哪儿？
10. 你喜欢苏州吗？
11. 你觉得苏州跟你的老家比怎么样？
12. 你的家人都在苏州吗？
13. 你有兄弟姐妹吗？
14. 你们现在有什么优惠活动吗？
15. 还能再打点儿折吗？
16. 你再优惠一点我就买了。
17. 这些是新款的吗？
18. 我能试试吗？
19. 还是有点贵。我再去别家看看。

Make it a habit to carry a notebook with you and take notes on your interactions with Chinese people.

☞ **Performance 1 Making new friends**

Approach someone you do not previously know on campus and start a conversation with the person in Chinese.

_____ Act 1: Mention an action that the person is obviously doing.

_____ Act 2: Compliment the person on a skill.

_____ Act 3: Introduce yourself and describe the characters in your Chinese name.

_____ Act 4: Learn the person's name and request a description of the characters.

____ Act 5: Exchange majors (or occupations) and year at college (or year in that occupation).

____ Act 6: Ask about life in the neighborhood.

____ Act 7: Propose to do something together in the near future.

____ Act 8: Express your excitement about meeting the person.

____ Act 9: Exchange contact information.

____ Act 10: Exchange hometown information.

____ Act 11: Exchange impressions of the places you have been to.

☞ **Performance 2 Being a friendly customer**

Chitchat with any of these persons: 1) a person at the front desk of your hotel; 2) a taxi driver; 3) the owner of a small store or restaurant that you frequently go to; 4) an assistant at the store or restaurant.

____ Act 1: Compliment certain aspects of the person's business or service.

____ Act 2: Introduce yourself to the person.

____ Act 3: Learn about the person's name and request a description of the characters.

____ Act 4: Ask about the duration of being in the current job.

____ Act 5: Exchange hometown information.

____ Act 6: Ask if the person's family is in Suzhou.

____ Act 7: Learn about the excitement and/or challenges in their life.

____ Act 8: Describe your needs or preferences and request a recommendation.

☞ **Performance 3 Being a smart shopper**

Visit a shopping center or a market and find a good deal for something you would like to buy.

____ Act 1: Explain what you are looking for.

____ Act 2: Ask about their current promotion.

____ Act 3: Request to have a close look at an item or try it on.

____ Act 4: Ask for further discounts.

____ Act 5: Explain that you would like to visit other stores before you take the deal.

____ Act 6: Promise you will recommend the store to your friends.

第二单元

校园生活 Campus Life

2.1 去哪儿

雪中送炭

投石问路

Listen to the five questions in the audio and answer them based on your own experience. Be ready to discuss these questions in class. You may write down some notes in the space provided below.

1.
2.
3.
4.
5.

边听边想

Listen to the audio and try to visualize the dialogue in your mind. Think about who the speakers are, the kind of social relationship they have, and what their intentions might be.

🎧 耳闻目睹

Listen to the audio again while following along in the printed text. As you listen, mark any place that you are unclear or have questions about.

雪中送炭

人物：周丹锐、秦老师、公交司机、乘客

（上午秦老师刚下课，周丹锐有问题要问秦老师）
周丹锐：秦老师，请问苏州有没有适合搞文化活动的书店？
秦老师：有啊，猫的天空之城听说过吗？他们经常搞一些文化沙龙活动。
周丹锐：那家书店离学校远吗？
秦老师：苏州有好几家猫的天空之城，离这里最近的应该是平江路那家。
周丹锐：要是坐出租车大概要多少钱？
秦老师：起步价就够了，不过有时候很难打到车。坐公交车很方便的，很多车都可以直接到。
周丹锐：好的，那我在百度上查查公交路线吧。谢谢老师。（1/4）
（下午，在苏大附近的公交车站，2路公交车进站，周丹锐和另一位乘客上车）
周丹锐：师傅，我到平江路下，多少钱？
司机：　两块，在这儿投币。
周丹锐：哎呀，我没有零钱。十块的能找吗？
司机：　找不了，我们这是无人售票车。
乘客：　刷我的卡吧。
周丹锐：那怎么好意思……（2/4）
（丹锐和那位乘客两人坐下）
周丹锐：刚才真是太谢谢你了，我给你钱吧。
乘客：　不用了。你是留学生吧？
周丹锐：嗯，我在苏州大学学中文。对了，你刚才用的那个卡是苏州的公交卡吗？
乘客：　对，就是苏州的交通卡，叫市民卡。坐公交车、出租车、地铁都能用，还可以在很多便利店刷卡结账。
周丹锐：刷卡比用现金便宜吗？
乘客：　嗯，便宜一点，公交车打六折。坐地铁九五折。主要是图个方便，要不然老得随身带着零钱。（3/4）
周丹锐：这个卡有没有申请费之类的？
乘客：　办新卡要收20块押金。
周丹锐：外国人也可以办市民卡吗？
乘客：　应该可以吧。你可以随便找个充值点问问。……我这站就下了。再见啊。

周丹锐：谢谢你，再见。(4/4)

知其所以然

The dialogue is broken down into sections below for explanation and analysis. Study the notes and answer the questions for the underlined text.

1/4

（上午秦老师刚下课，周丹锐有问题要问秦老师）

周丹锐：秦老师，请问苏州有没有适合<u>搞</u>文化活动的书店？

秦老师：有啊，猫的天空之城听说过吗？他们经常搞<u>一些文化沙龙活动</u>。

周丹锐：那家书店离学校远吗？

秦老师：苏州有好几家猫的天空之城，离这里最近的应该是<u>平江路那家</u>。

周丹锐：要是坐出租车大概要多少钱？

秦老师：起步价就够了，不过有时候很难打到车。坐公交车很方便的，很多车都可以直接到。

周丹锐：好的，那我在百度上<u>查查</u>公交路线吧。谢谢老师。

---

1. 周丹锐想找一个书店搞活动，他问秦老师："请问苏州有没有适合搞文化活动的书店？"

   (1) 如果不用"搞"，你会怎么问这个问题？ _____

   (2) 你觉得"搞"和你用的词有什么区别？ _____

   (3) "2008年北京搞了奥运会"，这句话你觉得对吗？ _____

   "奥运会期间北京搞了很多活动"，这句话你觉得对吗？ _____

As noted in Lesson 1.1 知其所以然, the verb 搞 has the basic meaning of "to have something done" or "to have something arranged". In this dialogue, 搞 can be understood as "to hold" or "to organize". Depending on the specific activity involved and, more importantly, who is talking about it to whom and for what purpose, 搞 and 举办 may or may not be interchangeable when expressing the idea "to hold" or "to organize". Generally speaking, 举办 sounds more formal, official and serious than 搞. For example, when chatting among peers, a Chinese speaker may say 我们每周搞一次文化活动; whereas a written invitation to participate in a school anniversary may say 下个月我们学校要举办校庆活动. For activities reported in news, 举办 is almost always preferred over 搞 (e.g., 2008年中国举办了奥运会; or 广东省政府举办改革开放三十周年纪念活动). The focus in 奥运会期间北京搞了很多活动, is on 活动 and not 奥运会, so either 搞 or 举办 can be used depending on who is talking to whom and for what purpose.

2. 文化沙龙

The term 文化沙龙（Culture Salon）covers a wide range of activities such as book clubs, poetry readings, film screenings, "underground" music or drama performances, art shows, lectures series and discussions. These activities are especially popular among Chinese college students and young urban professionals. These cultural events are often initiated on or organized through the social networking service website douban.com. Cultural salons are often held in privately-owned bookstores, like the one Miss Qin suggests in the dialogue.

2/4

（下午，在苏大附近的公交车站，2路公交车进站，周丹锐和另一位乘客上车）

周丹锐：师傅，我到平江路下，多少钱？

司机：　两块，在这儿投币。

周丹锐：哎呀，我没有零钱。十块的能找吗？

司机：　找不了，我们这是无人售票车。

乘客：　刷我的卡吧。

周丹锐：那怎么好意思……

---

3. 周丹锐上了无人售票公交车，可是没有零钱，他问司机："十块的能找吗？"

(1) 这里"找"跟下面哪三个句子中的"找"用法相同？

　　A. 我没找到你的零钱。

　　B. 老板，您还没找我钱。

　　C. 100块的我找不开。

　　D. 此券复印无效，不能转售，不设找零，不能兑换现金。

(2) 你的朋友帮你在网上买一本书，花了49元，你还钱的时候给他一张50元的，你的朋友身上没有零钱，你可以怎么说？＿＿＿＿＿＿＿＿＿＿

Here 找 is short for 找钱, which refers to the action of giving change to a bigger bill. It may also be short for 找开, in which the complement 开 indicates the result of the action (i.e., giving change). Therefore, when the result can be attained, you say 找得开/能找开; otherwise, you say 找不开。If you see 不设找零 on a vending machine or a coupon, you should not expect change. Here, 零 is 零钱（small change）. To request another person to keep the change, you may say 你不用找我钱了 or 不用找了。

4. 司机没办法帮丹锐，他说"找不了"。

(1) 如果司机说"找不开"，意思会有什么不同？＿＿＿＿＿＿＿＿＿＿

(2) 你和朋友两个人在餐馆吃饭，朋友提议点一整只烤鸭，你觉得可能太多了，你怎么说？＿＿＿＿＿＿＿＿＿＿

（3）你和朋友约好周末去旅游，可是学校突然有安排。你怎么给朋友解释你不去的原因？_____

In 找不了，了 is pronounced "liǎo". [verb] + 得了/不了 is used to express possibility or capability. Here, the driver is explaining that it is not possible to provide change for Zhou Danrui's 10-*yuan* bill. In the dialogue, if the driver had used 找不开, he would be indicating that he did not have enough small change for the ￥10 bill. This would leave open the possibility that the driver is willing to make change, but he happens not to be able to do so at the moment. 找不了 conveys the sense that change is not normally provided on this bus.

In another context, when your friend wants to order a whole roast duck, you may ask her "一只烤鸭，我们（两个人）吃得了吗？", indicating your doubt that the two of you can eat all of it. Your friend might respond affirmatively 吃得了 or negatively 吃不了. In still another example, when explaining why you have to cancel your trip, you could say 学校突然有事，所以去不了了.

5. 那位乘客提出帮周丹锐刷卡的时候，周丹锐说："那怎么好意思……"

（1）周丹锐说"那怎么好意思"是表示接受还是拒绝那位乘客的帮助？
_____

（2）你觉得"……"中周丹锐可能说什么？_____

（3）在这种情况下，为了表达同样的意图，周丹锐还可以怎么说？
_____

（4）你在中国朋友家做客，朋友发现你很喜欢吃他家的一种糖果，所以你离开的时候，他让你把剩下的糖果带走去吃，你礼貌地接受糖果的时候可以怎么说？
_____

那怎么好意思 is used when you are offered something that you would like to accept. It is a tricky expression because it appears to be a refusal but your readiness to accept the offer is implied. If your intention is to accept, you may offer something in return as Zhou Danrui does when he says 我给你钱吧. If you want to make sure the offer is genuine, you may continue to decline by explaining how impolite it would be for you to accept it. For example, if your friend offers to let you use her only bike, you may say 那怎么好意思，你自己就没得骑了. If your friend's offer is sincere, she will insist and then you may politely accept.

Alternatively, you may say 那我就不客气了. While both expressions imply your appreciation of the offer, 那怎么好意思 entails your apology for causing the other person to make the offer; whereas 那我就不客气了 indicates that you feel obliged to accept the offer in the light of the other person's sincerity. Therefore, 那我就不客气了 is typically used after multiple attempts to decline the offer. Chinese people usually do not accept an offer directly by saying 谢谢 or even 那真是太感谢了. Instead, these expressions of gratitude are used after accepting an offer. Using them in the place of 那怎么好意思 or 那我就不客气了 will cause you to sound too eager to accept the offer and not polite enough.

3/4

（周丹锐和那位乘车两人坐下）
周丹锐：刚才真是太谢谢你了,我给你钱吧。
乘　客：不用了。你是留学生吧?
周丹锐：嗯,我在苏州大学学中文。对了,你刚才用的那个卡是苏州的公交卡吗?
乘　客：对,就是苏州的交通卡,叫市民卡。坐公交车、出租车、地铁都能用,还可以在很多便利店刷卡结账。
周丹锐：刷卡比用现金便宜吗?
乘　客：嗯,便宜一点,公交车打六折。坐地铁九五折。主要是图个方便,要不然老得随身带着零钱。

---

6. 周丹锐问那位乘客用公交卡是不是比用现金便宜,乘客告诉他"主要是图个方便"。
（1）乘客说他用公交卡的主要原因是什么? ＿＿＿＿＿＿＿＿＿＿＿＿＿＿＿＿
（2）你觉得这位乘客对于苏州现在的公交卡是不是特别满意? ＿＿＿＿＿＿＿
（3）你的朋友知道你不喜欢住小公寓,当他知道你决定租学校附近的一个很小的公寓的时候,他很不理解,你怎么给他解释? ＿＿＿＿＿＿＿＿＿＿＿＿＿＿＿

图（个）+ [something] is used in spoken language to indicate the desired benefit of doing something despite all the undesired aspects. In the dialogue, the passenger uses 图个方便 because the bus pass is not really that cheap, indicating convenience is its only real benefit. In another context, if a Chinese person is asked why he ended up staying at a hotel even if he thinks it is dirty and inconvenient, he may reply 我就是图个便宜, indicating that the cheap price was his sole motivation. In yet another context, if your close friend has been going all out to help another person who is not grateful at all, you may strongly discourage him by saying "你这么帮他图个什么啊?" indicating that you do not see any reason why your friend should continue helping the person. In the following example, 我租这个房间主要是图个方便,要不然每天上学太远, the conjunction 要不然 makes explicit the situation you are trying to avoid.

7. 苏州的公交车都是无人售票的,如果没有公交卡乘客就"老得随身带着零钱"。

（1）乘客喜欢"随身带着零钱"吗？你怎么知道？_____

（2）下面哪个句子里的"老"或"老是"不可以换成"总是"？

  A. 最近怎么<u>老</u>下雨啊？我都没有衣服换了。

  B. 中文的声调真难，我<u>老是</u>说不好第三声。

  C. 你<u>老</u>家还有什么人？

  D. 我们班有个同学<u>老</u>迟到。

老 or 老是 is used in spoken language to indicate the speaker's impatience with a persisting situation. Here, the passenger is indicating her aversion towards having to carry small change for bus rides all the time. Similarly, you may say 怎么老下雨 to complain about persistent rain, or say 我老是说不好第三声 to complain about your ongoing failure to pronounce the third tone correctly. 我们班有个同学老迟到 indicates your impatience with the classmate who always comes late for class.

总是 is also used to indicate a persisting situation; however, it does not imply impatience or complaint. In written contexts, 总是 is more common.

4/4

周丹锐：这个卡有没有申请费<u>之类的</u>？

乘客： 办新卡要收20块押金。

周丹锐：外国人也可以办市民卡吗？

乘客： 应该可以吧。你可以<u>随便</u>找个充值点问问。……我这站就下了。再见啊。

周丹锐：谢谢你，再见。

---

8. 周丹锐想知道办公交卡有些什么费用，他问那位乘客："这个卡有没有申请费之类的？"

（1）你觉得周丹锐有没有在其他城市办公交卡的经验？为什么？_____

（2）如果你问你的语伴办公交卡需要带什么，他说需要带护照之类的证件，这是不是说明他对办卡很熟悉？_____

（3）如果别人问你喜欢什么电影，你会怎么回答？_____

[item(s)] + 之类的 is used to sum up what has been mentioned before 之类的 as example(s) of a certain category. The representative items mentioned here can range from one to a few, but usually no more than three. For example, you can ask if your friend likes certain types of Sci-Fi movies by saying 你喜欢《超人》之类的科幻片吗？or 你喜欢《蝙蝠侠》《蜘蛛侠》和《变形金刚》之类的科幻片吗？

9. 乘客不确定外国人是不是也可以办市民卡，她建议周丹锐"随便找个充值点问问"。

（1）周丹锐应该去哪一个充值点问办卡的事？＿＿＿＿＿＿＿＿＿＿＿＿＿

（2）如果你的朋友问你明天要去逛街还是去看电影，而你想让你朋友来做决定，你怎么回答？＿＿＿＿＿＿＿＿＿＿＿＿＿＿＿＿

（3）如果你的中国朋友说一位大学老师穿衣服穿得太随便了。你觉得那个老师大概穿什么样的衣服？＿＿＿＿＿＿＿＿＿＿＿＿＿＿＿＿

随便 often used to indicate that something is done without much planning or that any outcome will be acceptable. For example, 因为担心迟到,他随便穿了件外衣就出门了 (Because he was concerned about being late, he threw on his coat and left). When 随便 is expressed as a response to a question about a choice, the speaker may or may not really mean it is OK either way, but it certainly puts the burden on the interlocutor to come up with a suitable suggestion.

体演文本

Review the sections of the dialogue assigned by your teacher by listening to the audio and role-playing with another Chinese speaker. Be ready to perform the assigned portion of the dialogue from memory in class.

举一反三

Answer the following questions and think about how the dialogue can be adapted for different situations.

1. 你觉得猫的天空之城是什么样的书店？请用几个形容词描述你的猜想。你的国家有类似的书店吗？
2. 周丹锐说的"文化活动"可能是什么样的活动？
3. 乘客为什么对周丹锐那么热情友好？是苏州人特别热情吗？
4. 在你看来外国人在中国受欢迎吗？
5. 假设上公交车的时候发现你没带零钱,也没有交通卡。你觉得你可以怎么做？

熟能生巧

Listen to the audio and perform the following drills until you feel confident with the items practiced.

☞ Drill 1 Specifying the purpose of something

When asked what kind of object or place you are looking for, identify the purpose you have in mind for it. The cues provide you with the activities you would like to do.

例：搞文化活动

赵奕歆：你要找什么样的书店？

周丹锐：我想找适合搞文化活动的书店。

1. 骑自行车
2. 朋友聚会
3. 长期住
4. 自学中文

☞ Drill 2 Expressing minor reservation

When you are asked whether something has a certain advantage, first confirm the advantage and then mention a minor disadvantage it has. The illustrations below provide you with the minor disadvantages.

例：

周丹锐：去书店坐出租车起步价就够了吗？
赵奕歆：对，起步价就够了，就是有时候不容易打车。

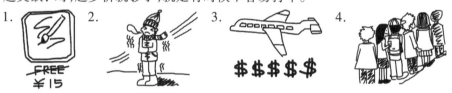

☞ Drill 3 Finding out if an offer is genuine

When your friend generously offers you something in light of your apparent interest in or need for it, respond with 那怎么好意思 and add to this ambiguous refusal in a way that would help you find out whether or not the offer is sincere.

例：
赵奕歆：刷我的卡吧。
周丹锐：那怎么好意思（我给你钱吧）。
1.　　　　　　　2.　　　　　　　3.　　　　　　　4.

☞ Drill 4 Highlighting an advantage

When your friend asks how two things compare, negate his or her assumption in a way that clarifies what you view as the sole advantage of one thing over another. Each of the cues below indicates the primary advantage you see in the situation.

例：方便
朋友：坐公交车刷卡比投币便宜吗？

周丹锐：不便宜。主要是图个方便。
1. 轻松
2. 安静
3. 便宜
4. 新鲜

☞ Drill 5 Finding out the general requirement for doing something

When your friend provides a suggestion, ask him or her about the kind of fees that may be involved. Each of the illustrations indicates one of the possible fees that may apply.

例：

赵奕歆：你可以办一张学生卡。
周丹锐：办学生卡有没有申请费之类的？

1.  2.   3.   4.

Narration

Practice narrating Zhou Danrui's incident on the bus to different audiences—a peer and a teacher.

例：Zhou Danrui responds to his friend Zhao Yixin, who asks him about his visit to the bookstore last weekend. He tells her what happened on the bus.

赵奕歆：周末去书店考察得怎么样？
周丹锐：

别提了，我算是体会到雪中送炭的温暖了。	1) Begin with a general comment on the story;
我上了2路车才发现那是无人售票车，可我身上没带零钱，十块的司机又说找不了。	2) State the difficulty you encountered, and elaborate on it if necessary;
正不知道怎么办的时候，另一个乘客帮我刷了卡。真是多亏了她，要不然就太尴尬了。	3) State the solution to your problem;
我打算也去办一张公交卡，有机会也给别人"送送炭"。	4) End the narration with your personal feeling and comments.

Now it's your turn!

Imagine that you are Zhou Danrui and your teacher Wang Dan is making a small talk with you and asks you about your weekend. Tell her about your incident on the bus.

王老师：周丹锐，这个周末过得怎么样？

言外有意

Read the cultural notes below and prepare questions for further discussion with Chinese people.

1. 雪中送炭（xuě zhōng sòng tàn）

The passenger on the bus who kindly paid Zhou Danrui's bus fare with his own bus pass can be described as "sending charcoal to someone on a snowy day" because of saving Zhou Danrui from the embarrassment of having no change to ride the bus. Later when Zhou Danrui relates his story to someone else, he could say 那个乘客给我的帮助真是雪中送炭，我特别感谢他！Upon hearing Zhou Danrui's story, his friend who was once in the same situation but no one helped him may comment 你怎么那么幸运?! 我上次在"雪中"的时候怎么就没有人给我"送炭"呢？Note how this person uses this idiom creatively.

2. 中国的独立书店 Independent bookstores in China.

Independent bookstores like 猫的天空之城 are important places for informal gatherings, especially to discuss non-mainstream topics such as independent movies, new translations of foreign books to Chinese, etc. Such bookstores are often not just a place to buy things, but, more importantly, a place where one goes to spend several hours, while sipping a cup of coffee. Sometimes there are even books you can borrow for the day for in-store use.

These bookstores often hold cultural salons, where young people gather to read, talk and socialize. However, due to the precarious condition of the Chinese book market, independent bookstores are facing a number of dilemmas. For more related information, you may search online for the article 独立书店的困境 written by Wang Xueliang（王学良）.

2.2 与老师交流

没有规矩，不成方圆

🎧 投石问路

Listen to the five questions in the audio and answer them based on your own experience. Be ready to discuss these questions in class. You may write down some notes in the space provided below.

1.
2.
3.
4.
5.

🎧 边听边想

Listen to the audio and try to visualize the dialogue in your mind. Think about who the speakers are, the kind of social relationship they have, and what their intentions might be.

🎧 耳闻目睹

Listen to the audio again while following along in the printed text. As you listen, mark any place that you are unclear or have questions about.

没有规矩，不成方圆

人物：周丹锐、郑妮、张老师

（上课前，同学们都陆续来到了教室，周丹锐拿着面包走进来）

郑　妮：早！

周丹锐：哎呀，早上复习对话，饭都没来得及吃。你每天背对话花多长时间啊？

郑　妮：加上和奕歆一起练习的时间，大概30分钟吧。(1/4)

周丹锐：我不明白，为什么非得让我们一个字一个字地背下来，还要在全班面前表演，你觉不觉得有点浪费时间？

郑　妮：我倒是挺喜欢上课表演对话的方式。比方说前两天学的在食堂打饭，在课上练过一次以后，我再去食堂打饭的时候就觉得熟练多了。

周丹锐：背过的句子，在说的时候倒是真的特别顺口。(2/4)

（张老师开始上课，周丹锐还在吃面包）

张老师：同学们好，现在上课了。今天秦老师生病了，我来给她代课……（看见周丹锐在吃面包）周丹锐，你还没吃早饭吗？

周丹锐：不好意思，刚才没来得及吃完。

张老师：上课的时候最好不要吃东西，不要影响其他同学上课。

周丹锐：对不起。(3/4)

（下课以后，周丹锐走上讲台跟张老师道歉）

周丹锐：张老师，刚才真的很对不起。其实秦老师也告诉过我们不要在课堂上吃东西。

张老师：没事，你们刚来，以后多注意就好了。

周丹锐：以后我一定注意。另外，张老师，我还有一件事想请您帮忙。

张老师：什么事儿？

周丹锐：我们活动部每周五下午都会组织文化沙龙活动，就一些大家感兴趣的话题进行讨论。我们想邀请您做我们这周的特邀嘉宾，不知道您有没有空？

张老师：没问题，到时候把你们要讨论的话题事先告诉我一下。(4/4)

📖 知其所以然

The dialogue is broken down into sections below for explanation and analysis. Study the notes and answer the questions for the underlined text.

> **1/4**
> （上课前，同学们都陆续来到了教室，周丹锐拿着面包走进来）
> 郑　妮：早！
> 周丹锐：哎呀，早上复习对话，饭都没来得及吃。你每天背对话花多长时间啊？
> 郑　妮：加上和奕歆一起练习的时间，大概30分钟吧。

1. 周丹锐觉得背对话太费时间，有点不高兴，他说："饭都没来得及吃"。
   （1）周丹锐吃早饭了吗？为什么？_____
   （2）周丹锐说"饭都没来得及吃"的意思是什么？
       A. 三顿饭都没有时间吃。
       B. 连吃早饭都没有时间。
       C. 同学们都没有时间吃饭。
   （3）如果你和室友要一起去参加活动，你担心迟到，所以跟室友说"快点，快点"，但你的室友说"来得及，来得及"，你觉得他的意思是什么？
       A. 别急，还有时间，不会迟到。
       B. 好的，我马上就好，马上就可以出发了。

来得及 + [verb] is used to state that there is enough time for someone to complete something. The opposite can either be 来不及 + [verb], stating that there will not be enough time for someone to complete something (e.g., 车来晚了，我上班要来不及了), or 没来得及 + [verb], stating that someone was not able to complete something within a given time frame (e.g., 早上复习对话，没来得及吃).

饭都没来得及吃 or 连饭都没来得及吃 is an emphatic structure for 没来得及吃饭. The emphatic structure highlights Zhou Danrui's complaint that memorizing dialogs is so time-consuming that he does not even have time for breakfast, which is important and does not take much time.

> **2/4**
> 周丹锐：我不明白，为什么非得让我们一个字一个字地背下来，还要在全班面前表演，你觉不觉得有点浪费时间？
> 郑　妮：我倒是挺喜欢上课表演对话的方式。比方说前两天学的在食堂打饭，在课上练过一次以后，我再去食堂打饭的时候就觉得熟练多了。
> 周丹锐：背过的句子，在说的时候倒是真的特别顺口。

2. 周丹锐不喜欢背对话，所以抱怨说："为什么非得让我们一个字一个字地背下来？"

（1）这里的"非得(děi)"可以换成什么词？
    A. 不得不　　　　　　B. 一定要　　　　　C. 不要
（2）如果你听到同学小王说"我今天非得把这个对话背下来"，这说明：
    A. 小王不喜欢背对话。　　B. 这个对话很难。　　C. 小王很懒。
（3）你听到你的中国朋友在抱怨她的丈夫，说"只要是他决定的事，他就非得那样做，谁的意见都改变不了他"。你觉得她的丈夫是个什么样的人？_____
（4）这里周丹锐说"一个字一个字地"，说明他觉得背对话的活动怎么样？
    A. 很费时间，而且没有必要。　　　　B. 要求很高，很难。

非得 is a colloquial way to say 一定要. When 非得 is often used with the interrogatives 干嘛 or 为什么, it conveys a strong complaint about the action stated. In the dialogue, Zhou Danrui is expressing a strong aversion to memorizing the dialogs. The expression 一个字一个字地 (word by word, indicating a sense of tediousness) in the same sentence adds strength to this complaint.

When not paired with interrogative words, 非得 + [action] can be used to express one's determination to get something done no matter what. The expression 不可 can be optionally attached at the end to add strength to the determination. For example, a student who is struggling to perform a dialogue from memory but is determined not to give up may say 我今天非得把这个对话背下来不可！ Note that 非得 is more often used in spoken language whereas 一定要 is preferred in written contexts.

While 一个字一个字地 can be literally understood as "word for word", the phrase used here is to exaggerate the tediousness of the action in question. In a more formal context, or in written Chinese, the idiom 逐字逐句 is a good alternative for this phrase.

3. 郑妮不同意周丹锐的看法，她说："我倒是挺喜欢上课表演对话的方式。"
（1）为什么郑妮用了"倒是"，而不直接说"我挺喜欢上课表演对话的方式"？
_____
（2）为什么周丹锐用了"倒是"，而不直接说"背过的句子，在说的时候真的特别顺口"？_____
（3）你跟中国朋友一起看完电影，他说电影很没意思，但是你不同意，你可以怎么表达你的不同看法？_____

Adding 倒是 or just 倒 in front of a statement is a way to make a point contrary to what has been expressed earlier while reducing the abruptness of such a turn of events. Thus, after hearing Zhou Danrui air his complaint about performing in front of the whole class, Zheng Ni states her opposing opinion by saying 我倒是很喜欢上课表演的方式. Even though Zhou Danrui questions the value of dialogue memorization, he still admits that the memorized script did help to make his speech sound smoother, saying 背过的句子，在说的

时候倒是真的特别顺口。

4. 周丹锐觉得郑妮说的有道理，背过的句子，因为说过很多次，所以说的时候特别顺口。

（1）你的同学说"我手机上的新软件，用起来很顺手"，你觉得他的意思是这个软件怎么样？_____

（2）对你来说什么样的事情做起来比较顺手？_____

（3）老师对同学们说"多听点不顺耳的话有好处"，在这里什么是"不顺耳的话"？为什么有好处？_____

（4）这些日子有没有让你觉得不太顺心的事情？_____

顺 means "to move in the same direction" and by extension "to flow smoothly". Thus 顺口 indicates "smooth or natural sounding speech". 顺 can also pair with other body parts to form terms to indicate that things are working smoothly according to the respective senses, such as 顺耳，顺眼，顺手 and 顺心.

3/4

（张老师开始上课，周丹锐还在吃面包）

张老师：同学们好，现在上课了。今天秦老师生病了，我来给她代课……（看见周丹锐在吃面包）周丹锐，你还没吃早饭吗？

周丹锐：不好意思，刚才没来得及吃完。

张老师：上课的时候最好不要吃东西，不要影响其他同学上课。

周丹锐：对不起。

---

5. 张老师再次提示周丹锐不要在上课的时候吃东西："不要影响其他同学上课。"

（1）张老师用了很多方法委婉地建议周丹锐不要在课堂上吃东西，请在上面画出这些表达。

（2）张老师让周丹锐"不要影响其他同学上课"，你觉得她真正要表达的意思是什么？_____

When Miss Zhang tells Zhou Danrui 不要影响同学们上课, her focus is not on the extent to which Zhou Danrui's eating in class was distracting or disruptive to others. Instead this is another reason she uses to strengthen her demand that Zhou Danrui stop eating in class.

4/4

（下课以后，周丹锐走上讲台跟张老师道歉。）

周丹锐：张老师，刚才真的很对不起。其实秦老师也告诉过我们不要在课堂上吃东西。

张老师：没事，你们刚来，以后多注意就好了。

> 周丹锐：以后我一定注意。另外，张老师，我还有一件事想请您帮忙。
> 张老师：什么事儿？
> 周丹锐：我们活动部每周五下午都会组织文化沙龙活动，就一些大家感兴趣的话题进行讨论。我们想邀请您做我们这周的特邀嘉宾，不知道您有没有空？
> 张老师：没问题，到时候把你们要讨论的话题事先告诉我一下。

6. 周丹锐跟张老师道歉，张老师说："没事，你们刚来，以后多注意就好了。"
（1）你觉得张老师说这句话表示她很友好，觉得这事儿没什么关系吗？
_____
（2）你的中文老师不小心写错了你的名字，向你道歉。你可以回答"没关系，以后多注意就好了"吗？为什么？_____
（3）如果不行，你应该怎么说比较好？_____

以后多注意 is usually used by superiors to mildly warn their subordinates not to commit the same mistake again. When you are told 以后多注意 by a senior, you need to take it very seriously. On the other hand, be aware that if you say this to someone, you are positioning yourself as the superior and it may upset the relationship if your interlocutor is not in fact your subordinate.

体演文本

Review the sections of the dialogue assigned by your teacher by listening to the audio and role-playing with another Chinese speaker. Be ready to perform the assigned portion of the dialogue from memory in class.

举一反三

Answer the following questions and think about how the dialogue can be adapted for different situations.

1. 周丹锐上课时给张老师什么印象？下课后呢？

2. 对话里周丹锐三次跟张老师表达歉意，每次所用的表达都不一样：第一次他说"不好意思"，第二次说"对不起"，最后一次说"刚才真的很对不起"。这表明周丹锐态度发生了怎样的变化？你知道中国人怎么使用这些不同的表达歉意的方式吗？

3. 张老师在周丹锐最后一次道歉后，说"以后多注意就好了"，你觉得她说这话时的语气怎么样？你在中国的时候听到过"以后多注意"这句话吗？是谁说的？是在什么情况下说的？

4. 周丹锐一开始没有听出张老师话里的意思，让老师不太高兴了。如果想要避免这种情况，他应该怎么做？

5. 如果由于身体的原因,根据医生的建议,周丹锐有必要在上课时吃些东西,他可以怎么跟老师解释?

🎧 熟能生巧

Listen to the audio and perform the following drills until you feel confident with the items practiced.

☞ **Drill 1　Explaining why you haven't done something**

When asked about a task you are expected to have done, explain that you have been occupied with something else and did not have enough time to get the task done. The cues will provide you with the excuses you can use.

例:

郑妮:丹锐,你还没吃早饭吗?
周丹锐:早上背对话,没来得及吃。

1. 　2. 　3. 　4.

☞ **Drill 2　Mildly expressing disagreement**

When presented with some stereotypical impressions about what Americans like, respond by expressing that your preferences are different.

例:
朋友:你们美国人都不喜欢上课表演对话,对不对?
郑妮:不一定,我倒是挺喜欢上课表演对话。

1.　　　　　　2.　　　　　　3.　　　　　　4.

☞ **Drill 3　Complaining about a requirement**

When a peer tells you about a requirement that you think is unreasonable, use 为什么非得……才……to complain about it.

例:
赵奕歆:你没有把对话背下来,所以说的时候不顺口。
周丹锐:为什么非得把对话背下来说的时候才能顺口呢?

1.　　　　　　2.　　　　　　3.　　　　　　4.

☞ Drill 4 Expressing determination

When a friend suggests that you give up on something, explain that you are determined to do it.

例：

赵奕歆：那个对话你实在背不下来就算了吧。

周丹锐：不行，我今天非得把它背下来不可。

1.　　　　　　2.　　　　　　3.　　　　　　4.

☞ Drill 5 Requesting advance notification

When invited to attend an event, accept the invitation and request to be informed of the details ahead of time. The cues provide you with the details you would like to know ahead of time.

例：主题

赵奕歆：我们每个星期有个学生会活动，你有没有空来参加？

周丹锐：没问题，到时候把你们活动的主题事先告诉我一下。

1. 地点

2. 具体时间

3. 人数

4. 流程

Narration

Narrate the incident of Zhou Danrui eating breakfast in class from the perspective of different participants in it.

例：Miss Zhang responds to Miss Qin, who is concerned about Miss Zhang's feeling about the incident in class. Pay attention to how Miss Zhang downplays the effect of Zhou Danrui's misconduct. Why does she do it?

秦老师：张老师，谢谢你帮我代课。听说今天周丹锐在课上让你生气了吧？

张老师：

噢，没什么，也不是什么大事。他们刚来，可能还不太习惯这边的规矩。	1) Respond by downplaying the effect;
一边听课一边吃面包。我一开始没直接说他，只问他："你还没吃早饭吗？"他没明白我的意思，说了句"噢，刚才没来得及吃完"，然后接着吃。后来我就直接告诉他上课的时候最好不要吃东西。	2) Describe the incident;

续表

不过他态度挺好的。我那样一说,他马上就没吃了,下课以后还主动跟我道歉了。	3) End the narration by indicating that problems are solved.

Now it's your turn!

Assume the role of Zhou Danrui. When Miss Qin asks you about the incident in class today, apologize and explain what happened. Try to emphasize that you did not intend to offend the teacher.

秦老师：周丹锐,今天上课的时候怎么回事啊?

言外有意

Read the cultural notes below and prepare questions for further discussion with Chinese people.

1. 没有规矩,不成方圆 (méiyǒu guīju, bù chéng fāngyuán)

This is an idiomatic phrase that is used to emphasize the importance of having norms and standards. 规 refers to the tool used for making circles (i.e., 圆形), and 矩 refers to the tool used for making squares (i.e., 方形). Therefore, literally, the phrase means "without these tools, one cannot make round and square shapes". 规矩 refers to regulations and rules. For example, you are teaching a group of kids English and in the first class you want to announce some classroom regulations, you may begin with 俗话说,没有规矩,不成方圆。下面我就说一下我的课堂的一些规矩。Or, if your students complain about certain rules and ask why they have to observe the regulations, you may say 因为没有规矩,不成方圆.

2. 师生礼仪 Teacher-student relationship.

China has a long tradition of 尊师重教(zūn shī zhòng jiào, respecting teachers and their teaching). One famous Chinese saying which reflects this tradition is 一日为师,终身为父. According to this tradition, students are supposed to show respect and honor to their teachers. Contradicting or disobeying a teacher is considered disrespectful.

As a result, classroom etiquette in China differs in some important ways from Western cultural contexts. Here are some expectations Chinese teachers have of their students:

(1) 用"老师好"向老师问好。老师好 is preferred to the more generic 你好.

(2) 在教室里要脱帽。Do not wear a hat in class.

(3) 别打断老师说话。Do not interrupt when the teacher is talking.

(4) 课堂上坐姿端正,不跷二郎腿。In class, sit up straight with both feet on the

floor.

（5）课堂上不经老师允许不可以随便走出教室。Do not leave the classroom without permission from the teacher.

It is always appropriate to express appreciation to your teacher when you have learned a lot from his/her class; however, you should be careful to avoid giving the impression that you are evaluating the teacher's performance. For example, a teacher would be happy to hear you say 谢谢老师,我很喜欢我们今天的讨论,我学到了很多东西, but would feel offended if you said 这堂课上得很好!

3. 背诵与智慧 Reciting and intelligence.

Chinese discourse traditionally values the ability to 引经据典(yǐn jīng jù diǎn, cite from classic or ancient works). Therefore, children in China are taught to memorize famous quotes from classics and poems. Their ability to recite these quotes is considered a demonstration of intelligence and good education. For learners of Chinese as a foreign language, memorizing and reciting chunks of spoken discourse helps develop fluency. Your ability to appropriately use Chinese idioms or quote from Chinese classics will give Chinese people a positive impression of both your Chinese level and your status as an educated adult.

2.3 组织活动

群策群力

投石问路

Listen to the five questions in the audio and answer them based on your own experience. Be ready to discuss these questions in class. You may write down some notes in the space provided below.

1.
2.
3.
4.
5.

边听边想

Listen to the audio and try to visualize the dialogue in your mind. Think about who the speakers are, the kind of social relationship they have, and what their intentions might be.

耳闻目睹

Listen to the audio again while following along in the printed text. As you listen, mark any place that you are unclear or have questions about.

群策群力

人物：周丹锐、孙浩、郑妮、赵奕歆

（下课了，孙浩、周丹锐、赵奕歆、郑妮都还留在教室里讨论有关文化活动的事）

孙浩： 我们商量一下这个星期的文化讨论活动怎么搞吧？

周丹锐：上个星期是我们同学们自己讨论的，这次能不能和外面的人讨论？

赵奕歆：外面的人？你是说不是学生的人吗？这可能会很有意思。

孙浩： 有意思是有意思，可是学校是不会让那么多校外的人来校内参加活动的。(1/4)

周丹锐：那我们去秦老师上次跟我说过的那个书店行不行？

郑妮： 那个很有名的书店吗？好像听你说起过。

孙浩： 那个书店我去过，叫猫的天空之城，他们经常搞一些文化沙龙。

赵奕歆：不如我们和他们商量一下，一起把这次文化讨论活动办成一个文化沙龙。

孙浩： 那我们吃完午饭就一起去那边看看，跟他们的老板谈谈吧。(2/4)

赵奕歆：丹锐跟郑妮也一起去吧。书店的人看到老外会好说话一些，特别是会说中文的老外。

郑妮： 可是我午饭后要和几个同学去欧尚超市买东西。

周丹锐：我下午也约了人。我们晚一点去行不行？顺便一起吃个晚饭。

郑妮： 是啊，其实我也很想去那个书店看看的。

赵奕歆：行啊。那就五点半在学校门口集合，怎么样？

周丹锐：好，到时候见！(3/4)

（孙浩他们四人在校门口集合，准备上路去书店）

郑妮： 独立日快到了，我们组织同学们一起去金鸡湖边放烟花庆祝一下吧。

赵奕歆：独立日就相当于美国的国庆节吗？

周丹锐：可以这么说。独立日嘛，就是庆祝美国独立的节日。不过既然是在中国过节，我们是不是该组织一些不一样的活动来庆祝，比如志愿服务之类的？

孙浩： 我去请示一下苏大的老师和领导吧，说不定可以和校志愿队合作。

郑妮： 我们也去问问秦老师，看她有什么建议。(4/4)

知其所以然

The dialogue is broken down into sections below for explanation and analysis. Study the notes and answer the questions for the underlined text.

1/4

（下课了，孙浩、周丹锐、赵奕歆、郑妮都还留在教室里讨论有关文化活动的事）

孙浩：　我们商量一下这个星期的文化讨论活动怎么搞吧？

周丹锐：上个星期是我们同学们自己讨论的，这次能不能和外面的人讨论？

赵奕歆：外面的人？你是说不是学生的人吗？这可能会很有意思。

孙浩：　<u>有意思是有意思，可是</u>学校是不会让那么多校外的人来校内参加活动的。

---

1. 赵奕歆觉得周丹锐的提议很有意思，但是孙浩说："有意思是有意思，可是……"

（1）孙浩同意赵奕歆的看法吗？＿＿＿＿＿＿＿＿＿＿＿＿＿＿＿＿

（2）孙浩为什么觉得周丹锐的提议不可行？＿＿＿＿＿＿＿＿＿＿＿＿＿＿

（3）你听说校门口一家饭馆的菜很好吃，你问你的中国朋友是不是真的，她说："好吃是好吃，可是……"你觉得她接下来会说什么？＿＿＿＿＿＿＿＿＿＿＿

A 是 A，可是 + [problem] is a colloquial way of introducing a contradictory comment while agreeing with the other person's comment. In this structure, the "A 是 A" part confirms the other person's statement while creating the expectation of a turning point introduced by 可是. Here, Sun Hao is expressing his concern that the university may not allow so many non-students to come to campus, even if, like Zhao Yixin says, it will be interesting to involve non-students in the activity. For example, when your friend suggests that you go to the activity center by taxi, but you are concerned about the cost, you can say 打车去方便是方便，可是太贵了。

In written discourse, you would use the structure 虽然 A，但是 + [problem]. For example, 打车去虽然方便，但是太贵了。

2/4

周丹锐：那我们去秦老师上次跟我说过的那个书店行不行？

郑妮：　那个很有名的书店吗？好像听你说起过。

孙浩：　那个书店我去过，叫猫的天空之城，他们经常搞一些文化沙龙。

> 赵奕歆：不如我们和他们商量一下，一起把这次文化讨论活动办成一个文化沙龙。
> 孙浩：　那我们吃完午饭就一起去那边看看，跟他们的老板谈谈吧。

2. 赵奕歆对于文化讨论活动的形式有个提议，她说："不如我们和他们商量一下，一起把这次文化讨论活动办成一个文化沙龙。"

　　(1) 这里"不如"可以换成"要不"吗？＿＿＿＿＿＿＿＿＿＿＿＿＿
　　(2) 这里"文化讨论活动"和"文化沙龙"是什么关系？＿＿＿＿＿＿＿＿＿＿
　　(3) 这里的"办"可以换成什么词？＿＿＿＿＿＿＿＿＿＿＿＿＿

Here, 不如 is used to initiate a casual proposal. In this context, it can be used interchangeably with 要不. A slight difference would be that 不如 sounds a little less colloquial. 不如 is also commonly used in written contexts to make a comparison. For example, to compare 苏州 and 上海, a Chinese person may write 苏州不如上海热闹. In spoken language, the person will probably say 苏州没有上海热闹.

The structure 把［Event A］办成［Event B］can be used to suggest holding Event A in the form of Event B. In informal contexts, you may say 把……搞成 instead of 把……办成.

3/4

> 赵奕歆：丹锐跟郑妮也一起去吧。书店的人看到老外会好说话一些，特别是会说中文的老外。
> 郑妮：　可是我午饭后要和几个同学去欧尚超市买东西。
> 周丹锐：我下午也约了人。我们晚一点去行不行？顺便一起吃个晚饭。
> 郑妮：　是啊，其实我也很想去那个书店看看的。
> 赵奕歆：行啊。那就五点半在学校门口集合，怎么样？
> 周丹锐：好，到时候见！

3. 奕歆建议周丹锐和郑妮跟他们一起去跟书店老板商量，她说："书店的人看到老外会好说话一些。"

　　(1) 如果书店的人"好说话"，对于赵奕歆他们有什么好处？＿＿＿＿＿＿＿＿
　　(2) 这里"好说话"的具体意思是什么？
　　　　A. 容易答应别人的要求　　　B. 说更多的话　　　C. 客气、友好
　　(3) 这里"说话"可以换成什么词？＿＿＿＿＿＿＿＿＿＿＿＿＿

好＋［verb］can be used to describe something or someone that is easy to deal with. Here, Zhao Yixin is saying that the people at the bookstore will be easier to negotiate with if a foreign person is present. In other contexts, you may describe a cellphone that is easy and convenient to use by saying 这个手机很好用 or describe a person who is easy to get along with by saying 我的室友很好相处(xiāngchǔ).

说话 in this phrase conveys more than its literal sense "talking". It has a similar function to 商量 or 沟通, meaning to talk in order to get another person to see or do things in your way.

4. 周丹锐觉得晚一点去书店的话更好,他们可以"顺便一起吃个晚饭"。
(1) 这里"顺便"可以用下面哪三个词替换?
   A. 正好   B. 顺带   C. 顺手   D. 顺路
(2) 假如你从北京坐火车去上海,去上海之前你要先在杭州玩一天,你可以怎么说? _____
(3)"吃个晚饭"里的"个"是指"一个"吗？你觉得周丹锐建议的晚饭是怎样的?
_____

The structure 顺便/顺带 + [action] can be used to state that an action can be conveniently performed while doing something else. Here Zhou Danrui is suggesting that they can take the opportunity of going to the bookstore together to dine out together. Both 顺路 and 顺便 indicate a sense of happening by coincidence which can also be expressed by 正好.

顺路 + [action] is used with actions that can be performed on one's way to do something else. Usually, this point is conveniently located on the person's way to a destination. Therefore, Zhou Danrui could also have used 顺路, indicating that they may dine together at a restaurant conveniently located on their way to the bookstore. In another context, you can say 我去上海的时候想顺路去杭州玩一天.

The structure 顺手 + [action] is used when the action in question is done by hand, e.g., 出去的时候请顺手关门. Note that 顺手 may also be used to say that things are working out smoothly. For example, when a person finds that he is getting more and more comfortable writing Chinese characters, he may comment 我写汉字越来越顺手了. We have come across this usage of 顺 in 2.2, where Zhou Danrui says 背过的句子,在用的时候倒是真的特别顺口.

In 吃个晚饭, the classifier 个 occurs between a verb and its object to casually indicate one instance of the action. This structure usually implies the briefness of the action. In the dialogue, Zhou Danrui is suggesting that they can have a quick meal together on their way to the bookstore or back from the bookstore. Here are some other contexts that use 个 in a similar way:

a. If your friend is waiting for you to go to a party together you may say 等一下,我洗个澡就走, indicating that you need to take a quick shower before you leave. Or if you need to quickly change your clothes before leaving, you could say 我换个衣服就走.

b. When you call a friend to suggest that you get together sometime, you may casually ask 你这周什么时候有空,我们见个面.

c. When dining out with friends, as you go to wash your hands, you may say 我去洗个手 or 我去个洗手间.

To sound less casual, you can replace 个 with 一下. For example, 洗一下澡, 换一下衣服, 见一下面, 洗一下手, 去一下洗手间.

4/4

(孙浩他们四人在校门口集合,准备上路去书店)

郑妮：　独立日快到了,我们组织同学们一起去金鸡湖边放烟花庆祝一下吧。

赵奕欢：独立日就相当于美国的国庆节吗?

周丹锐：可以这么说。独立日嘛,就是庆祝美国独立的节日。不过既然是在中国过节,我们是不是该组织一些不一样的活动来庆祝,比如志愿服务之类的?

孙浩：　我去请示一下苏大的老师和领导吧,说不定可以和校志愿队合作。

郑妮：　我们也去问问秦老师,看她有什么建议。

---

5. 国庆节/National Day

This is a Chinese national holiday when Chinese people celebrate the founding of New China in 1949. Many people turn out or tune in to watch the military parade in the Tian'anmen Square. This one-week holiday is often referred to as 黄金周 (the Golden Week). Transportation (especially train travel) during 黄金周 can be very crowded as many people take advantage of the long holiday to travel.

6. 关于独立日的庆祝活动,周丹锐有一个提议："我们是不是该组织一些不一样的活动来庆祝?"

(1) 听上去,周丹锐是不是特别希望组织一些不一样的活动? 实际上呢?

_____

(2) 为了表达他的提议,周丹锐还可以怎么说? _____

Chinese speakers often use question forms like 是不是(该)…… or 要不要…… to make indirect proposals, thus leaving more room for negotiation. Using 要不要…… makes the proposal sound more casual. For example, if you want to invite a friend to go to a museum with you but do not want to make your friend feel pressured, you may say 下午我打算去博物馆,你要不要一起去? In another context, a leader may make a proposal to a group by saying 我们是不是该开个会讨论一下……

7. 周丹锐提议组织志愿服务之类的活动,孙浩说:"我去请示一下苏大的老师和领导吧。"

（1）孙浩请示苏大的老师和领导的目的是什么？＿＿＿＿＿＿＿＿＿＿

（2）你觉得孙浩"请示"老师的时候会跟老师说什么？＿＿＿＿＿＿＿＿

（3）进同学的房间之前,是不是要"请示"他？如果不用"请示",应该怎么做？＿＿＿＿＿＿＿＿＿＿＿＿

Although the literal meaning of 请示 is asking for instructions or permission, it is only used when asking for an official approval from a superior. Therefore, to ask for your teacher's approval of an event proposal, you can use 请示, but to ask your classmate for permission to enter his room, you don't use 请示 unless you want to use sarcasm. Instead, you just 问 your classmate if you may enter.

🎧 体演文本

Review the sections of the dialogue assigned by your teacher by listening to the audio and role-playing with another Chinese speaker. Be ready to perform the assigned portion of the dialogue from memory in class.

💬 举一反三

Answer the following questions and think about how the dialogue can be adapted for different situations.

1. 孙浩说"学校是不会让那么多校外的人来校内参加活动的",学校为什么会有这样的规定？

2. 你怎么用简短的几句话跟中国人介绍美国的独立日？

3. 对话里的四个朋友讨论去书店的事时候,赵奕歆为什么提议周丹锐和郑妮也一起去？你觉得她的提议有道理吗？

4. 在说服别人和你一起做一件事的时候,一般有哪些技巧？

5. 如果你的美国朋友向你请教中国学校的学生会组织,你可以怎么向他们介绍？你觉得为什么每个学校都有这样的组织？中国人认为这么做的好处有哪些？

🎧 熟能生巧

Listen to the audio and perform the following drills until you feel confident with the items practiced.

☞ **Drill 1 Proposing a discussion**

Imagine you are in charge of planning cultural activities for your class. When asked by a classmate about plans for an upcoming activity, make a proposal that invites discussion about some aspects of the plans. The cues provide you with details that need to be discussed.

例：怎么搞

同学：下个星期我们是不是要搞文化活动？

郑妮：对，我们商量一下文化活动怎么搞吧。

1. 在哪儿搞
2. 去哪个社区
3. 表演什么节目
4. 怎么分组

☞ Drill 2 Politely rejecting a proposal

When your friend makes a proposal, politely reject it by first acknowledging the proposed advantage, and then pointing out a disadvantage of it. The illustrations provide the disadvantages you can mention.

例：

赵奕歆：我们请校外的人来参加活动吧，那样会很有意思。

周丹锐：有意思是有意思，可是学校不会同意。

1. $ $ $ $ 2.   3.   4.

☞ Drill 3 Pretending you remember something for the sake of maintaining a smooth conversation

When someone brings up a topic that you are expected to have heard about, try to continue the conversation even if you do not remember the specifics. You can first confirm with the speaker whether it is something famous and then ambiguously mention that you seem to have heard about it from the speaker.

例：

赵奕歆：那我们去秦老师上次跟我说过的那家书店怎么样？

周丹锐：那家很有名的书店吗？好像听你说起过……

1.   2.   3.   4.

Drill 4 Suggesting an unconventional activity

When your classmate proposes a discussion about your weekly cultural activity, suggest that you run the activity in an unconventional format. Each of the illustrations indicates the unconventional format you can suggest.

例：

孙浩：我们商量一下这周的文化活动怎么搞吧！
郑妮：不如我们一起把这周的文化活动搞成一个文化沙龙吧。

1. 英文讲座 2. 丹锐，生日快乐！ 3. 上海一日游 4. 成语比赛

Drill 5 Rejecting an invitation

When informally invited to participate in an activity which conflicts with your existing plans, politely turn down the opportunity by indicating that you have plans and proposing an alternative time. Depending on how interested you are in the activity, you may either propose a specific time to reschedule or suggest rescheduling without specifying when as Zhou Danrui does in the following example. Each of the illustrations indicates your existing plan and the happy/unhappy face indicates whether or not you are willing to participate in the activity.

例：

赵奕歆：今天晚上一起去唱卡拉OK吧？
周丹锐：我晚上约了一个朋友吃饭，要不改天吧？

1.   2.  3. 3. 4.

☞ **Drill 6 Making a modest suggestion**

When reminded that Independence Day is coming up, modestly suggest an activity using 是不是该…… or 要不要……. The cues provide you with the activities you can suggest.

例：

同学：很快就是美国独立日了。
郑妮：我们是不是该一起组织活动庆祝一下？

1.  2.  3.  4.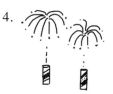

☞ **Drill 7 Making an analogy**

When your Chinese friend refers to a Chinese concept, ask her if it is analogous to a similar concept in American culture. The cues provide you with the analogies you may make.

例：国庆节 = 独立日？
赵奕歆：每年的十月一号是国庆节。
周丹锐：国庆节就相当于美国的独立日吗？

1. 七夕 = 情人节？
2. 中秋节 = 感恩节？
3. 春节 = 圣诞节？
4. 国家主席 = 总统？

☞ **Drill 8 Stating something obvious to a close friend**

When providing an obvious explanation to a close friend, you can use ……嘛, 就是……呀 to imply that the answer is so obvious that an explanation is in fact unnecessary.

In the following example, Zhou Danrui responds to his friend Zhao Yixin.

例：
赵奕歆：独立日是什么意思？
周丹锐：独立日嘛，就是庆祝美国独立的节日呀。
1.   2.   3.   4.

☞ Drill 9 Stating something obvious in a formal context

If the same questions in Drill 8 are raised by your audience at an oral presentation, you can use the idiom 顾名思义（gù míng sī yì），meaning "as the name implies", to indicate that the term is self-explanatory and avoid sounding too casual.

例：
李女士：独立日是什么意思？
周丹锐：独立日，顾名思义，就是庆祝美国独立的节日。
1.   2.   3.   4.

Narration

Narrate what happened in the dialogue from the perspective of one of the roles.

例：Miss Qin asks Zhao Yixin about their plans for the cultural event this week. Listen to the example carefully and learn how Zhao Yixin uses 一开始……，但是…… and 后来 to construct her narration.

秦老师：奕歆，这周的文化活动你们打算怎么搞？
赵奕歆：

昨天下课以后我和周丹锐他们一起商量了一下。	1) Describe the general background information;
一开始周丹锐提出想和校外的人一起讨论，但是我担心学校不同意让外面的人来校内活动。	2) State the original proposal (followed by a counter argument);
后来周丹锐想到了猫的天空之城。	3) Bring up the alternate suggestion;
那家书店确实经常举行文化沙龙活动，所以我们决定去那家书店和老板商量一下，一起把这次的文化讨论活动搞成一个文化沙龙。	4) State the final decision;
您觉得怎么样？	5) End the narration by inviting the other person's comment.

Now it's your turn!

Assume the role of Zheng Ni and tell Miss Qin your discussion about the July 4th celebration.

秦老师：郑妮，关于独立日的庆祝活动你们有想法了吗？

言外有意

Read the cultural notes below and prepare questions for further discussion with Chinese people.

1. 群策群力 (qún cè qún lì) Pool the wisdom and efforts of the masses.

Designing a meaningful cultural activity depends on the participation of everyone involved. At the beginning of a brainstorming session, you can encourage your team members by saying 只要大家群策群力,没有什么困难不能克服. After successfully carrying out the activity, you can report on the experience by saying 中美同学群策群力,把独立日的庆祝活动搞成了一次成功的志愿者服务活动.

2. 有朋自远方来 Friends from far away come for a visit.

Confucius once said 有朋自远方来不亦乐乎, meaning "to have friends come from far away, isn't that a joy". This sentence is frequently quoted by Chinese government officials when they welcome foreign visitors, as well as by ordinary Chinese people when they have the opportunity to host foreign friends. The respectful, hospitable treatment foreign guests generally experience in China is due in part to the fact that Chinese people view foreigners as friends from afar. This special treatment may mean that Chinese people overlook foreign behaviors that would be considered inappropriate for a Chinese person. As a result, a Chinese language learner who wants to develop deep, long-term relationships in China will need to take the initiative in learning how to function in ways that Chinese people truly find culturally coherent.

学而时习之

Before you actually do the field performances, rehearse doing them with a Chinese friend. The "Useful Expressions" box below provides you with some expressions you may use for these performances. For now, try saying them after the audio.

> **Useful Expressions**
> 1. 你好。请问外国人可不可以办市民卡?
> 2. 我是苏州大学的留学生。要在这里学习两个月。
> 3. 请问有什么适合我的公交卡吗?
> 4. 这几种卡有什么不同呢?
> 5. 用这种卡坐公交或者地铁有优惠吗?
> 6. 这种卡可以几个同学一起用吗?
> 7. 应该怎么申请呢?
> 8. 有没有申请费之类的?
> 9. 押金可以退吗?
> 10. 在哪里充值呢? 每次最少应该充多少钱?
> 11. 我发现中国的老师不喜欢学生上课的时候吃东西。
> 12. 你以前的老师都是这样的吗?
> 13. 如果学生……老师一般会怎么办?
> 14. 如果学生不同意老师观点,一般会怎么办?
> 15. 课程结束后,学生还会跟老师保持联系吗?
> 16. 我可不可以跟你们的负责人谈谈文化活动的事?
> 17. 我们可以借你们的地方组织文化活动吗?
> 18. 会有一些什么费用呢?
> 19. 你们一般用什么方式发布活动通知?
> 20. 我们项目希望能跟你们联合举办一次文化活动,不知道你们有没有兴趣?

Make it a habit to carry a notebook with you and take notes on your interactions with Chinese people.

☞ Performance 1 Saving on ground transportation

Visit an office that handles applications for bus passes to find out your options for saving on ground transportation.

____ Act 1: Greet the person at the information desk.

____ Act 2: State briefly your purpose of visit.

____ Act 3: Describe your resident status.

____ Act 4: Request your options for bus passes.

____ Act 5: Ask about the differences between the options (e.g., discounts, applicability).

____ Act 6: Express interest in one of the options.

____ Act 7: Ask about the requirements for application (e.g., personal identification, deposit, etc.).

____ Act 8: Ask about methods of renewal and if there is a minimum amount for renewal.

____ Act 9: Ask if and how unused money can be refunded.

____ Act 10: Tell the person your decision.

☞ **Performance 2 Comparing classroom etiquette**

Chitchat with a local student.

____ Act 1: Express your interest in classroom etiquette in China.

____ Act 2: Mention a classroom rule that you found unique in China.

____ Act 3: Ask if that rule applies to all classrooms in China.

____ Act 4: Talk about common problems students may have with their teachers.

____ Act 5: Provide examples of how those problems may be handled.

____ Act 6: Describe how a student may express an apology, a request or an objection to the teacher.

____ Act 7: Describe what a student may do to keep in touch with a teacher after a course ends.

____ Act 8: Discuss the cultural basis for the differences.

☞ **Performance 3 Organizing a cultural event**

Call and visit a local book caf or library and find out opportunities for co-organizing cultural events.

____ Act 1: Call to make an appointment with the person in charge.

____ Act 2: Formally introduce yourself to the person who is in charge.

____ Act 3: Explain the purpose of your call or visit.

____ Act 4: Describe your event (e.g., purpose, participants, activities, length, etc.).

____ Act 5: Describe possible benefits for the book caf or library.

____ Act 6: Ask what they can offer (e.g., space, dates available, free drinks, media device, etc.).

____ Act 7: Ask about the fees, if applicable.
____ Act 8: Negotiate for a waiver or a group discount.
____ Act 9: Explain that you will talk to your teacher and apply for the funds.
____ Act 10: Promise to keep in touch.

第三单元

饮食交友 Food and Friendship

3.1 朋友小聚

客随主便

投石问路

Listen to the five questions in the audio and answer them based on your own experience. Be ready to discuss these questions in class. You may write down some notes in the space provided below.

1.
2.
3.
4.
5.

边听边想

Listen to the audio and try to visualize the dialogue in your mind. Think about who the speakers are, the kind of social relationship they have, and what their intentions might be.

耳闻目睹

Listen to the audio again while following along in the printed text. As you listen, mark any place that you are unclear or have questions about.

客随主便

人物:周丹锐、孙浩、餐厅服务员

(辅导课刚结束,周丹锐和孙浩还在教室里)

周丹锐:听说十全街上有个"江南人家"很不错,我请你去那儿吃饭吧。

孙浩: 别客气,不用了,我去食堂吃就行了。

周丹锐:走吧,我来苏州半个月了,还没去十全街那边吃过呢。(1/4)

(孙浩和周丹锐到了"江南人家",坐下打算点菜)

周丹锐:你看看想吃点什么?

孙浩: 随便,你点吧,我不挑食。

周丹锐:那我们要清炒虾仁、鸡油菜心、莼菜汤,你能吃辣吗?

孙浩: 没问题。

周丹锐:那再来个水煮牛肉吧,两份米饭。

孙浩: 你很会点菜啊,有荤有素,有汤有主食。

周丹锐:没有没有,其实都是我们上课练过的。我们再要一瓶啤酒吧……

孙浩: 你今天能喝酒吗?明天不是有课吗?

周丹锐:嘿嘿,没事,就一瓶……(2/4)

(吃完饭,该买单了)

孙浩: 服务员,买单吧。

服务员:一共117块。

周丹锐:给你150。

服务员:不好意思,你有零钱吗?

孙浩: 我有,我来结账吧。

周丹锐:别、别,说好了我请的。20的能找开吗?再给张发票,谢谢。

服务员:不好意思,今天发票用完了,下次来再补给你们行吗?

周丹锐:这样啊。

孙浩: 要不你就少收我们点儿。

服务员:好吧,收你们115。这是找你们的钱。下次再来啊!(3/4)

(孙浩和周丹锐走出了"江南人家")

周丹锐:哇,刚才那算是砍价吗?又学了一招儿。(4/4)

知其所以然

The dialogue is broken down into sections below for explanation and analysis. Study

the notes and answer the questions for the underlined text.

1/4

（辅导课刚结束，周丹锐和孙浩还在教室里）

周丹锐：听说十全街上有个"江南人家"很不错，我请你去那儿吃饭吧。

孙　浩：　别客气，不用了，我去食堂吃就行了。

周丹锐：走吧，我来苏州半个月了，<u>还没去十全街那边吃过呢</u>。

---

1. 周丹锐想请孙浩吃饭："我来苏州半个月了，还没去十全街那边吃过呢。"

（1）为什么周丹锐这么一说，孙浩就接受邀请了？_____

（2）你陪一个中国朋友去了医院，那个朋友觉得麻烦你真不好意思，你可以怎么说让她不用那么不好意思？_____

还没［action］过 is used to state the fact that you haven't had the experience of performing an action. Usually both you and your listener would consider the action as worth a try. The final particle 呢 is added to indicate the speaker's request for the listener's attention to this fact. Here, by saying 还没去十全街那边吃过呢 Zhou Danrui is indicating that if Sun Hao accepted the invitation, he would actually be doing Zhou Danrui a favor. In this way, Sun Hao will feel better about accepting the invitation.

Stating yourself as the beneficiary of something you offer to do for the other person is a strategy you can use when you sincerely would like to offer to do something for a Chinese person. For example, when your Chinese friend expresses her apology for having you accompany her to the hospital, you may say 没事，我还没去过中国的医院呢，这次正好可以参观一下。

2/4

（孙浩和周丹锐到了"江南人家"，坐下打算点菜）

周丹锐：你看看想吃点什么？

孙　浩：　<u>随便，你点吧，我不挑食。</u>

周丹锐：那我们要清炒虾仁、鸡油菜心、莼菜汤，你能吃辣吗？

孙　浩：　没问题。

周丹锐：那再来个水煮牛肉吧，两份米饭。

孙　浩：　<u>你很会点菜啊，有荤有素，有汤有主食。</u>

周丹锐：没有没有，其实都是我们上课练过的。我们再要一瓶啤酒吧……

孙　浩：　你今天能喝酒吗？明天不是有课吗？

周丹锐：嘿嘿，没事，就一瓶……

---

2. 周丹锐请孙浩吃饭，他让孙浩点菜的时候，孙浩说："随便，你点吧，我不挑食。"

（1）假如你的朋友请你吃饭，让你点你喜欢吃的菜，你怎么说比较礼貌？
_____

假如你跟这个朋友是第一次一起吃饭,你习惯吃素,他让你点菜的时候你怎么做?
_____

(2) 朋友或者服务员问你:"有没有什么忌口的?"假如你不习惯吃辣的,你怎么回答? 如果你不能吃海鲜呢? _____

(3) 如果你听到一个中国妈妈对他的孩子说"不许挑食",你猜这个孩子想做什么? _____

The expression 我不挑食 ("I'm not a picky eater") is commonly used when you want to leave the decision of what food to order up to others. You could also say 我没有忌口的, which literally means that you don't have any foods you can't eat. This would also convey the message that you don't have a strong preference for ordering and will have no problem eating with what others may order. In China, when friends go out to have a meal together, it is considered rather lame if each person orders and eats his or her own dishes. Instead, food is usually ordered with the expectation that everyone will share what's on the table.

After ordering, the server may ask 有没有忌口的? If you have food allergies, this is your opportunity to alert the server by saying 我对 + [something] + 过敏, for example, 我对花生过敏. If you prefer to avoid eating something such as seafood or meat, you can directly inform others by saying 我不吃 + [something], for example, 我不吃肉.

3. 周丹锐点完菜,孙浩夸他:"你很会点菜啊,有荤有素,有汤有主食。"

(1) 右边这张照片是中国广西桂林的风景,你看着这张照片可以说:"桂林有(　　)有(　　),风景真美!"

(2) 你听别人说"老王这个人总是把故事讲得有声有色",说明老王这个人讲话_____。

A. 很夸张　　　B. 很生动　　　C. 很完整　　　D. 很严谨

The structure 有 X 有 Y can be used to point out either two complementing or contradictory qualities or characteristics. Typically, 有荤有素 is used to describe a balanced selection of food at a meal. 有山有水 describes natural scenery, while 有声有色 describes lively or effective presentations or activities. One can also use 有好有坏 to indicate an ambivalent attitude toward a topic under discussion.

3/4

(吃完饭,该买单了)

孙浩:　服务员,买单吧。

服务员:一共117块。

> 周丹锐：给你150。
> 服务员：不好意思,你有零钱吗？
> 孙　浩：我有,我来结账吧。
> 周丹锐：别,别,<u>说好了我请的</u>。20的能找开吗？再给张发票,谢谢。
> 服务员：不好意思,今天发票用完了,下次来再补给你们行吗？
> 周丹锐：这样啊。
> 孙　浩：要不你就少收我们点儿。
> 服务员：好吧,收你们115。这是找你们的钱。下次再来啊！

4. 当孙浩要跟周丹锐抢着付钱的时候,周丹锐说"说好了我请的"。

（1）中国人坚持要替朋友付钱的时候,他们一般都用什么理由？
_____

（2）你和好朋友约好了3点见面,但是他迟到了40分钟,你很生气,可以怎么说他？_____

（3）你和几个朋友计划好了吃饭以后一起去KTV唱歌,不过吃完饭后,一个朋友突然提出不去唱歌了,你有点不高兴,你可以怎么说？_____

The structure 说好了 + ［action］+ 的 can be used among peers to refute an undesired change of course by reiterating what has been agreed upon earlier, with an emphatic tone of voice. In the dialogue Zhou Danrui had planned to treat Sun Hao to dinner, and, when at the end of dinner Sun Hao offered to pay the bill, he protested, saying 别,别,说好了我请的. In another context, if someone is significantly late for an appointment, the one who has been waiting may express displeasure by saying 说好了3点见面的.

> **4/4**
> （孙浩和周丹锐走出了"江南人家"）
> 周丹锐：哇,刚才那算是砍价吗？<u>又学了一招儿</u>。

5. 发现在餐馆吃饭也可以砍价,周丹锐很兴奋,他说："又学了一招儿。"

（1）周丹锐说"学了一招儿"是跟谁学的？_____

（2）这"招儿"可以在什么时候用？_____

（3）下面哪两种情况下,你可以说"学了一招儿"？

　　A. 你跟老师谈话,老师介绍了一个阅读的方法,你觉得特别好。

　　B. 你在朋友家做客,你看朋友洗水果的方法很特别,觉得她的方法又快又干净。

　　C. 你在同学的房间注意到一些漂亮的垫子,她教你用旧T恤做了一个,方法很简单。

招儿 is a casual way to refer to a unique and clever way of doing something or a trick. It is generally used among friends. 学了一招儿 implies your interest in adopting the technique. It also conveys a lighthearted sense of humor. For example, after a friend teaches you a unique and simple way to make cushions out of old T-shirts, you can say 又学了一招儿.

体演文本

Review the sections of the dialogue assigned by your teacher by listening to the audio and role-playing with another Chinese speaker. Be ready to perform the assigned portion of the dialogue from memory in class.

举一反三

Answer the following questions and think about how the dialogue can be adapted for different situations.

1. 周丹锐和孙浩点菜的时候,孙浩说"随便,你点吧"。你认为他为什么会这样说呢,是不是客气话?

2. 你觉得中国人点菜的习惯是什么?(一般来说要怎么搭配?点几个菜?)

3. 周丹锐结账的时候没有零钱,孙浩说"我有零钱,我来结账吧"。在美国,你的朋友也会跟孙浩一样抢着帮你结账吗?

4. 服务员说"不好意思,今天发票用完了"。你觉得这个是真话还是借口?如果是借口,有可能是为什么不想给客人发票?

熟能生巧

Listen to the audio and perform the following drills until you feel confident with the items practiced.

☞ Drill 1 Insisting on an offer

When your Chinese friend declines your offer of treating hi[m/her], on presenting the activity as a fresh experience for [you,] indicates the offer on which you would like to

朋友:别客气,不用了,我去食堂吃㗎
周丹锐:走吧,我还没去十全街吃过饭

☞ **Drill 2 Deferring to the host**

In this drill, you are a guest at a meal. When your host asks you to order, politely allow your host to order by stating that you are fine with any dish. Use either 我不挑食 or 我什么都吃 to express your deference to the host's choices. Each of the illustrations will provide you with the role of the host you are dining with. Note that when talking with a superior you would avoid using 随便 to indicate your lack of preference.

例1：

周丹锐：你看看想吃点什么？
郑妮：随便，你点吧，我不挑食。

例2：

秦老师：你们看看，想吃什么就点什么。
周丹锐：秦老师，还是您点吧，我什么都吃。

1. 中国朋友   2. 赵奕歆的父母

3. 中文辅导老师   4. 周院长

☞ **Drill 3 Reassuring**

When your friend seems to be worried that your proposal to do something may bring you trouble, reassure her by indicating that what you propose to do is too trivial to cause problems. Think about the measure word for different items, although most of the time you can simply use 一次 to refer to something happening once.

例：

奕歆：你今天能喝酒吗？明天不是有课吗？

周丹锐：没事，就一瓶……

1.　　　　　2.　　　　　3.　　　　　4.

☞ **Drill 4 Insisting on paying the bill**

In this drill, imagine that you and a friend are disputing over who's going to pick up the tab for your meal. Insist on paying the bill by emphasizing that this arrangement was previously agreed upon. You will hear your friend referring to paying a bill in different ways.

例：

孙浩：这顿还是我来请吧。

郑妮：别，别，说好了我请的。

1.　　　　　2.　　　　　3.　　　　　4.

☞ **Drill 5 Confirming if something is what you think it is**

When someone tells you what he plans to do or has done, ask if it is what you think it is, using 算. The cues provide you with your judgments.

例：砍价

赵奕歆：我让他们再多送我一点赠品。

周丹锐：这算是砍价吗？

1. 毕业旅行
2. 实习
3. 你的午餐
4. 苏州特色

Note：Spoken with a disdainful tone (i.e., stress on 算), the same response in Drill 5 can convey contempt. For example, 这算是苏州特色吗？ would imply doubt that what your friend has described is a special feature of Suzhou.

Narration

Zhou Danrui is having small talk with his classmate Zheng Ni, who wonders what he meant by saying 学了一招儿. Assume Zhou Danrui's role and share the new strategy of negotiating the bill at a restaurant when the restaurant cannot provide a receipt.

郑妮：你刚才说"学了一招儿"是什么意思？

言外有意

Read the cultural notes below and prepare questions for further discussion with Chinese people.

1. 客随主便 (kè suí zhǔ biàn) A guest should allow the host to make decisions.

客随主便 defines a preferred host-guest practice that contrasts with the "make yourself at home" host-guest practice in American culture. In Chinese culture, the host has the "right" and responsibility to plan and make decisions for the guests, while the guest is expected to be a good sport who generally goes along with the plan. When a host presents a guest with options or asked about preferences, an appropriate response is 客随主便，你决定吧.

2. 被请客时点菜的特点

Related to the idea of 客随主便 is the expectation that when ordering dishes in a restaurant, a polite guest will try to let the host make decisions. The guest can say 您/你来点吧，客随主便. The host will often ask guests about their preference. When asked about what you like, it is fine to mention your allergies or strong preferences. For example, 我对海鲜过敏，不过你可以点 or 我习惯吃素. To avoid giving the impression that you are picky about food, you can name one of your favorite dishes instead of telling the host several things you do not like. The dish you mention should be a relatively common one with an affordable price. Also, guests should compliment some aspects of the meal, such as the environment of the restaurant, the tastiness of dishes or the quality of the service.

3. 苏菜特色

苏菜, also known as 苏帮菜, is one of the Eight Culinary Traditions (八大菜系) of China. Suzhou food is highly sought after throughout southern China. The freshness of ingredients is crucial in Suzhou cuisine. One of the most famous Suzhou dishes 清炒虾仁 was mentioned in the dialogue.

Another dish not mentioned in the dialogue is 松鼠鱼, which is popular throughout China. The dish is named after its special shape, just like the tail of a squirrel! This dish is sweet, sour and boneless, which adds to its popularity. As you may have discovered, 海鲜 (seafood) and 河鲜 (river fish) feature prominently in Suzhou cuisine.

3.2 家庭做客

礼轻情意重

🎧 投石问路

Listen to the five questions in the audio and answer them based on your own experience. Be ready to discuss these questions in class. You may write down some notes in the space provided below.

1.
2.
3.
4.
5.

🎧 边听边想

Listen to the audio and try to visualize the dialogue in your mind. Think about who the speakers are, the kind of social relationship they have, and what their intentions might be.

🎧 耳闻目睹

Listen to the audio again while following along in the printed text. As you listen, mark any place that you are unclear or have questions about.

礼轻情意重
人物：郑妮、赵奕歆、赵爸爸、赵妈妈

（赵奕歆带郑妮回家，赵奕歆的爸爸开门，妈妈也从厨房出来迎接）

赵奕歆：爸爸，妈妈，这就是我跟你们说的美国朋友，郑妮。郑妮，这是我爸、我妈。

赵爸爸：来了啊，快进来，快进来。

郑妮：叔叔阿姨好，给你们带了些水果。

赵妈妈：怎么还买东西来，真是乱花钱，奕歆，你怎么还让人家买东西啊？

赵奕歆：我没拦住她。

郑妮：阿姨，这是我的一点心意，本来说好了上次要来，结果学校临时有了别的安排。

赵妈妈：学校的事情重要，我们这里什么时候来都行。(1/4)

（过了一会，晚饭做好了，大家准备吃饭）

郑妮：阿姨您做了这么多菜，闻着好香啊。

赵妈妈：那就多吃点，尝尝我的手艺。

郑妮：以前就听奕歆说阿姨做菜特别好吃。

赵妈妈：就会做一些家常菜而已，也不知道合不合你的口味，快尝尝。

郑妮：真好吃，比外面做的好吃多了。

赵奕歆：是啊，我说我妈做饭好吃吧。(2/4)

……

赵爸爸：郑妮，多吃点多吃点。

郑妮：叔叔，我吃好了。

赵爸爸：再多吃一点啊，你阿姨烧汤最拿手，再喝一碗。

郑妮：好、好，我等一下自己来！阿姨您做的菜太好吃了，我明天都不用吃饭了。

赵妈妈：来阿姨家可要吃饱啊，别客气，以后想吃了就让奕歆带你来。(3/4)

（两个小时过去了，郑妮准备回学校）

郑妮：叔叔阿姨，今天真是谢谢你们了！让你们忙了那么长时间，真过意不去。

赵爸爸：别这么说，你能来我们也很高兴，我们老两口都喜欢热闹。

郑妮：有机会我一定会再来的。今天时间不早了，我就不打扰了，你们也早点儿休息。

赵妈妈：你们明天都要上课,我们也就不留你了,以后想来的时候,打个电话。
赵妮： 嗯,好的,叔叔阿姨我走了,再见啊!
赵爸爸：慢走啊!
赵妈妈：奕歆,替我们送送郑妮。(4/4)

知其所以然

The dialogue is broken down into sections below for explanation and analysis. Study the notes and answer the questions for the underlined text.

1/4

(赵奕歆带郑妮回家,赵奕歆的爸爸开门,妈妈也从厨房出来迎接)
赵奕歆：爸爸,妈妈,这就是我跟你们说的美国朋友,郑妮。郑妮,这是我爸、我妈。
赵爸爸：来了啊,快进来,快进来。
郑妮： 叔叔阿姨好,给你们带了些水果。
赵妈妈：怎么还买东西来,真是乱花钱,奕歆,你怎么还让人家买东西啊?
赵奕歆：我没拦住她。
郑妮： 阿姨,这是我的一点心意,本来说好了上次要来,结果学校临时有了别的安排。
赵妈妈：学校的事情重要,我们这里什么时候来都行。

---

1. 赵奕歆解释为什么郑妮带了水果来:"我没拦住她。"
(1) 赵奕歆说"我没拦住她",是因为郑妮走得太快了赵奕歆追不上她吗?
_____
(2) 这里可不可以换成"我没挡住她"? 为什么? _____
(3) 如果警察在路上"拦住"一辆车,一般会是什么原因? _____
(4) 在篮球对抗赛上,你想让队友阻止一位对方队员得分,可以说什么?
　　A. 快拦住他。　　　　B. 快挡住他。

拦住 and 挡住 share the meaning of stopping something or someone by blocking the way in front. However, 拦住 can be used in an abstract sense. For example, in the dialogue, Zhao Yixin does not physically block Zheng Ni's way and merely fails to prevent her course of action. Similarly, in (3), the policeman does not use his physical body to stop the car. However, in (4), the players will use their bodies to block the way and hold their rivals back. Therefore, 挡住 is more appropriate in (4). In another context, if a Chinese speaker wants his friend to get a cab, he may say 你去拦一辆出租车吧. Without 住, the action of blocking rather than the result of stopping is emphasized.

住 in the structure [verb] + 住 functions as a resultative complement indicating that the action was successful. The negative form of this structure is often associated with 没 and thus 没 + [verb] + 住 indicates that the action failed.

You may have noticed by now that, within the casual setting of home and in the context of close family relationships, Chinese people sometimes make a friendly fuss over something as a way of expressing closeness and heartfelt feelings. In the dialogue, Mrs. Zhao expresses her appreciation for Zheng Ni's hostess gift by fussing over her wasting money on them and "blames" her daughter for allowing that to happen. Zhao Yixin's reply follows in the same vein:"I wasn't able to hold her back!"

2. 郑妮解释为什么上次没有来赵奕歆家:"本来说好了上次要来,结果学校临时有了别的安排。"
(1) 郑妮告诉赵妈妈学校临时有了别的安排,这是真正的结果吗?
_____
(2) 如果去掉这里的"结果",语气会有什么不同?_____
(3) 你跟秦老师约好这个星期见面,但是她突然要去北京开会,不能见你。如果你的同学问你什么时候跟秦老师见面,你怎么回答?_____

本来 + [plan] + 结果 + [an unexpected obstacle] is commonly used to express one's disappointment at not being able to carry out a plan. For example, when asked if he did something fun recently, a Chinese person may disappointedly respond, 昨天晚上本来要去唱KTV 的,结果作业太多了, indicating that he was not able to go to KTV as planned due to having too much homework. In another context, to explain why he has not met with his teacher yet, he would say 本来这个星期要跟秦老师见面的,结果她突然要去北京开会.

2/4

(过了一会,晚饭做好了,大家准备吃饭)
郑妮: 阿姨您做了这么多菜,闻着好香啊。
赵妈妈: 那就多吃点,尝尝我的手艺。
郑妮: 以前就听奕歆说阿姨做菜特别好吃。
赵妈妈: 就会做一些家常菜而已,也不知道合不合你的口味,快尝尝。
郑妮: 真好吃,比外面做的好吃多了。
赵奕歆: 是啊,我说我妈做饭好吃吧。

---

3. 郑妮夸赵妈妈做菜好吃,赵妈妈谦虚地回答"就会做一些家常菜而已"。
(1) 赵妈妈这样说的意思是做家常菜_____
    A. 不容易。   B. 是很一般的事。
(2) 你的同学觉得你对苏州特别了解,问你是不是做了很多研究,你怎么告诉他你没做过特别的研究,只是在网上看过一些介绍?_____

（3）如果你的朋友夸你的书法写得好，但你觉得自己只是会写楷书，所以没什么特别的，你怎么谦虚地回应你的朋友？_____

（4）你带中国朋友去一家咖啡厅。看见你跟老板很熟的样子，中国朋友问你："你经常来这家咖啡厅吧？"但是，实际上你只去过一次。你怎么回答你的朋友？_____

[statement] + 而已 is used to minimize the importance of what is stated, indicating that it is simple and nothing special. It is often used in response to compliments to show modesty. In the dialogue, Zhao Yixin's mom is being modest by emphasizing that she only knows how to cook homestyle dishes. In other contexts, this structure may also be used to shift responsibility when blamed, indicating the speaker's indifference to the consequence. For example, if a boy is blamed by his teacher for making a girl cry, he may protest 我只问了她一个问题而已, indicating that he should not be blamed since all he did was asking the girl a question. A Chinese person may say 我就开个玩笑而已 when his friend takes a light-hearted comment too seriously.

而已 often co-occurs with expressions like 就, 不过 or 只是. For example, when your friend is surprised at your knowledge about Suzhou and infers that you must have done a lot of research about it, you may downplay what you've done by saying 只是在网上看过一些介绍而已. To modestly respond to a compliment on your calligraphy skills, you may say 我就会写楷书而已, indicating that you can only do the basic style. To tell your friend that you are not as frequent a customer at the café as he expected, you can say 我只来过一次而已.

4. 郑妮夸赵妈妈做菜好吃，赵妈妈客气地回答"也不知道合不合你的口味"。

（1）你的口味是怎样的？你喜欢清淡的菜，还是口味重一点菜？你喜欢甜的，还是辣的？

（2）你吃过的哪些中国菜比较合你的口味？_____

（3）如果郑妮觉得有一道菜太辣了，不太合她的口味，她应该怎么回答赵妈妈？_____

（4）如果你在逛商店时听到有人说"这件衣服不错，很合身"，这是什么意思？_____

When treating guests to a meal, Chinese hosts seldom ask 好不好吃 directly. Instead, they often choose a more euphemistic expression such as 合不合口味, asking whether the food is to one's taste. This grants guests more freedom in terms of how to respond. As a guest, you can simply say 很好吃 to give a positive answer. But if you find one dish too spicy, you can say 很好吃，但我不太能吃辣 to indicate that you cannot eat too much of that dish.

In addition to 合口味, 合 is also used in 合身 (fits one's size) and 合心意 (meets one's expectation/preference). Of course, how to handle situations that are 不合心意 is a challenge to everyone in every culture!

3/4

……

赵爸爸：郑妮，多吃点多吃点。

郑妮：　叔叔，我吃好了。

赵爸爸：再多吃一点啊，你阿姨烧汤最拿手，再喝一碗。

郑妮：　好、好，我等一下自己来！阿姨您做的菜太好吃了，我明天都不用吃饭了。

赵妈妈：来阿姨家可要吃饱啊，别客气，以后想吃了就让奕歆带你来。

---

5. 赵爸爸让郑妮多吃点，郑妮说"我吃好了"。

（1）这里郑妮如果回答"我吃完了"，好不好？为什么？_____

（2）如果你的主人不断给你夹菜，让你多吃，为了客气地拒绝，除了说"我吃好了"，你还可以怎么说？_____

吃好了 often denotes the completion of eating with enjoyment and satisfaction. Compared with 吃好了, 吃完了 simply announces that the eating is done and sometimes it may imply that though one has finished the served food, he or she is still not satisfied. Therefore, 吃完了 is seldom used when you intend to refuse the host's offer of more food. 吃饱了, on the other hand, indicates that you are full. Therefore, 我真的吃饱了 can be used to indirectly refuse the host's offer of more food. Another conventional way to politely refuse more food is to say to the host that you will take food yourself, like Zheng Ni does later in the dialogue. When asked to have one more bowl of soup, she replies to Mr. Zhao, saying 好、好，我等一下自己来！

6. 赵爸爸让郑妮再喝碗汤，他说"你阿姨烧汤最拿手"。

（1）"拿手"是什么意思？_____

（2）你会不会做菜？有没有什么"拿手菜"？_____

（3）这里的"拿手"可以换成"擅长"吗？为什么？_____

（4）如果别人问你什么运动玩得最好，你可以怎么回答？_____

Both 拿手 and 擅长 [shàncháng] denote that someone is especially good at doing something, but 拿手 also conveys a sense of confidence. That is to say, it is almost impossible for that person to fail. The dish you are best at cooking is your 拿手菜. Based on the dialogue, you may say 排骨汤是阿姨的拿手菜.

Depending on the flow of the discourse, the common structure for 拿手 can be either "[someone] + [action] + 很拿手" or "[action] + [someone] + 很拿手". For example, 我打篮球很拿手 or 打篮球我很拿手. Although similar in meaning, 擅长 is usually used as a verb in the structure [someone] + 擅长 + [action]. For example, 他很擅长打篮球.

7. 赵妈妈叫郑妮不要客气, 她说"来阿姨家可要吃饱啊"。
(1) 这里"可"的用法和下面哪两个句子类似？
    A. 这个作业可写可不写。
    B. 那我可得好好向你学习了。
    C. 你可别忘了带书, 明天上课我要用。
(2) 你去黄山旅游回来, 觉得黄山特别漂亮。你的一个朋友问你觉得黄山怎么样, 你很兴奋地告诉他你对黄山的印象：
    A. 黄山真漂亮。   B. 黄山可漂亮了。
    如果你知道这个朋友没去过黄山, 你怎么说？ _____
    如果这个朋友跟你一起去了黄山, 你怎么说？ _____

Here 可 is used to emphasize the statement 来阿姨家要吃饱 and is similar to the 可 in 我可得多向你学习了 encountered in 1.1. In another context, if you really need the book which your friend has promised to bring you the next day, as you depart, you may emphasize the importance of the matter by saying 你可别忘了带那本书.

The use of 可 for an emphasis implies the speaker's assumption that the listener is unaware of what is stated. It conveys the sense of "in case you did not know". A Chinese person would not say 我妈妈做菜可好吃了 to a friend who has tasted her mom's cooking before. Therefore, if your friend who has never been to Mount Huang asks your opinion about that place, you may say 黄山可漂亮了 to emphasize your positive impression of Mount Huang. If you know your friend has been to Mount Huang, you may say 黄山真漂亮 to communicate your positive impression of it.

4/4

(两个小时过去了, 郑妮准备回学校)

郑妮：　叔叔阿姨, 今天真是谢谢你们了！让你们忙了那么长时间, <u>真过意不去</u>。

赵爸爸：　别这么说, 你能来我们也很高兴, 我们老两口都喜欢热闹。

郑妮：　有机会我一定会再来的。今天时间不早了, 我就不打扰了, 你们也早点儿休息。

> 赵妈妈：你们明天都要上课，我们也就不留你了，以后想来的时候，打个电话。
> 郑妮：　嗯，好的，叔叔阿姨我走了，再见啊！
> 赵爸爸：慢走啊！
> 赵妈妈：奕歆，替我们送送郑妮。

8. 郑妮表达歉意："真过意不去。"

（1）郑妮为什么要表达歉意？_____

（2）下面哪四种情况下适合用"真过意不去"来表达歉意？

　　A. 你去上海旅游，你的朋友请了一天假带你逛。结束的时候，你说"耽误你一天的工作，真过意不去"。

　　B. 在中国，快回国之前，你的护照丢了，为了很快补办护照，你的老师找了很多他的朋友帮忙，你对老师说"给您添了这么多麻烦，我真过意不去"。

　　C. 在公交车上，你不小心踩了一下别人的脚，你说"踩到你的脚，我真过意不去"。

　　D. 在中国，晚上你突然病了，你的中国父母带去医院，你说"耽误你们休息，我真过意不去"。

　　E. 你在朋友家，不小心把他最喜欢的CD弄坏了，你说要买一个新的赔给他，他坚持说"没关系，不用了"，你没办法，只好说"把你最喜欢的CD弄坏了，我真过意不去"。

过意不去 is commonly used to emphasize an apology for troublesome behavior. In the dialogue, Zheng Ni uses this expression just to demonstrate her politeness, and to show her appreciation for Zhao Yixin's parents' hospitality. It is typically used when you have caused the other person loss of precious things such as time, money and "face"（面子）. Therefore, if you just stepped on a person's foot on the bus, saying 过意不去 would be overkill. Saying 真对不起 or 不好意思 is sufficient.

9. 赵爸爸欢迎郑妮常来他们家，他说："我们老两口都喜欢热闹。"

　　（1）这里"老两口"指的是谁？_____
　　（2）"小两口"是什么意思？_____
　　（3）一对夫妻加上一个孩子，这样的家庭一般被称为什么？_____

The phrase 老/小两口 is commonly used to refer to a couple, often a married one. 老两口 refers to an old couple, whereas 小两口 is used for young couples. The 口 here is a measure word for family members. A Chinese family with one child is referred to as 三口之家. To find out how many people there are in a person's family, one may ask 你家有几口人？

(1) 你觉得赵奕歆的父母是不是一定很喜欢去人多的地方玩？
_____
(2) 对你来说,怎么样算"热闹"？_____
(3) 如果你不喜欢经常请很多人来家里聚会,你可以说"我喜欢生活____一点"。
　　A. 冷清　　　　　　B. 清静

Here, 喜欢热闹 denotes that Zhao Yixin's parents enjoy having company. It does not necessarily mean that they like the hustle and bustle of a public place. Some people prefer solitude, and they may say 我们喜欢清静. However, what's 清静 (nice and quiet) to one person could be 冷清 (cold and quiet) in the eyes of another, depending on how much a person likes to be with people. While 清静 describes a solitary lifestyle, 安静 is used to describe an environment that is literally void of noise or a person who is silent. Therefore, to explain why you don't like to study at a café, you can say 咖啡厅太吵了,我喜欢在安静一点的地方学习.

体演文本

Review the sections of the dialogue assigned by your teacher by listening to the audio and role-playing with another Chinese speaker. Be ready to perform the assigned portion of the dialogue from memory in class.

举一反三

Answer the following questions and think about how the dialogue can be adapted for different situations.

1. 赵爸爸明明看见奕歆和郑妮进门了,为什么还问"来了啊"？你在什么其他场合听到过中国人问这种答案很明显的问题？
2. 赵妈妈对郑妮说她买水果"真是乱花钱"。她这样说会不会不礼貌？为什么？
3. 什么样的礼物算是"一点心意"？
4. 你在中国人家做客,如果主人说"也不知道合不合你口味",你可不可以回答"合我的口味,我什么都爱吃,不挑食"？为什么？
5. 郑妮夸奕歆妈妈做菜好吃的时候,奕歆说"我说我妈做饭好吃吧",你觉得合适吗？为什么？
6. 假如你在朋友家做客,差不多到了回去的时间,但朋友一家还很热情地招待你吃水果,你怎么礼貌地告辞？

熟能生巧

Listen to the audio and perform the following drills until you feel confident with the items practiced.

☞ Drill 1 Expressing disappointment over a failed plan

When asked if you were able to do something you planned to do, explain that you intended to do it yesterday, but you were prevented by an unexpected circumstance. The cues indicate the unexpected situations.

例：学校安排了文化活动

孙浩：你去赵奕歆家了吗？

郑妮：本来昨天要去的，结果学校安排了文化活动。

1. 商店关门了
2. 秦老师病了
3. 信息中心放假了
4. 复印机坏了

☞ Drill 2 Showing understanding to someone who missed an appointment

When someone apologizes to you for failing to keep an appointment because of another commitment, express your understanding by trivializing your appointment.

例：

郑妮：本来说好了上次要来，结果学校临时有了别的安排，真对不起。

赵爸爸：学校的事情重要，我们这里什么时候来都行。

1.   2.   3.   4.

☞ Drill 3 Responding modestly to a compliment

When praised by others, modestly respond that you can do nothing more than the basics. Each of the cues indicates the basic level of skill which you will claim to have.

例：家常菜

赵奕歆：以前就听说你做菜特别好吃。

郑妮：就会做一些家常菜而已。

1. 楷书
2. 练习曲
3. 蛙泳
4. 卡拉OK

☞ Drill 4 Apologizing for taking someone's time

When your friend reports having finished doing something for you, express your appreciation by apologizing for taking up so much of your friend's time. Each of the illustrations shows you how your friend has helped you.

例：

孙浩：你最爱吃的火锅做好了，来尝尝吧。
郑妮：让你忙了那么长时间，我真过意不去。

1.  2.  3.   4.

☞ Drill 5 Initiating the close of a visit

In this drill, you will initiate the interaction, explaining to your host why you need to leave. The illustrations provide you with the reasons for leaving.

例：

郑妮：今天时间不早了，我就不打扰了，我也还得回去写作业。
赵爸爸：你有事要忙，我们也就不留你了。

1.  2.  3.  4.

Narration

Zhou Danrui has received an invitation for dinner at Sun Hao's home. He has never eaten dinner with a Chinese family in their home, so he asks Zheng Ni for advice.

1. Assume the role of Zheng Ni and share your experience and some tips on responding politely when the host urges you to eat more.

周丹锐：孙浩邀请我明天去他家吃饭，你说我有没有什么要注意的？

2. Assume the role of Zheng Ni and share your experience and some tips on how to politely state that it's time for you to leave.

周丹锐：孙浩邀请我明天去他家做客，有什么要注意的吗？

📖 言外有意

Read the cultural notes below and prepare questions for further discussion with Chinese people.

1. 礼轻情意重(lǐ qīng qíngyì zhòng) It's not the gift that counts, but the thought behind it.

The idiom 千里送鹅毛,礼轻情意重 (Having travelled thousands of miles to give a goose feather, the gift is light but the feelings are weighty) is often used to lighten up a gift-giving situation when the gift is an ordinary item. In many cases, it is not just a conventional saying but actually how people perceive what has happened.

2. 主客礼俗

When you are invited to visit a friend's home in China, it is a good idea to bring a gift, for example, fruit, an American souvenir, or a bottle of Chinese liquor or wine. The host may refuse to accept your gift at first out of politeness just like Zhao Yixin's mother does in the dialogue, but you should insist on giving it to him or her. You can express humility about the gift you bring by saying 这是我的一点心意. You can address your friend's parents as 叔叔 and 阿姨, just as Zheng Ni does in the dialogue.

When eating at a Chinese person's home, you will want to use various ways to compliment the food. While it is perfectly acceptable to express your enjoyment of the food, too many compliments about a particular dish may result in your host's insisting that you take the leftovers home with you. In this case you should be prepared to politely refuse and give some reason to justify your refusal. You can also compliment the food by praising the cook's culinary skill: 您的手艺真好! Whatever you say, the host will likely respond to your compliment by urging you to eat more.

A dinner party at a Chinese home usually does not go past 10:00 p.m. Yet it is very unlikely the host will directly initiate the conclusion of the visit. Instead the guest is expected to sense when it is time to bring the visit to a close by saying 时间不早了,不打扰你们了 or (让)您忙了一天了. It is also customary for the host to see the guest off. If the host is preparing to accompany you outside, you can say 请留步,请留步. This phrase literally means "please save your steps" and is part of an offer-refusal exchange which will most likely end with the host accompanying you for a certain distance to see you off. Always pay close attention to what hosts do! When you host Chinese friends, remember to show polite reluctance when accepting gifts, urge your guests to eat more, and to see them off when they leave!

3. 不要说"我很喜欢"

Being a polite guest at a Chinese friend's home in China, you may want to comment on his or her belongings (e.g., decorations) as your host shows you around. It is polite to show interest in the things you are shown to by asking questions about their origins, authors, meaning, material, etc. For example, when shown a calligraphy work, you may ask about the artist (e.g., 这是谁写的？这位书法家在中国很有名吗？), the style (e.g., 这是什么字体？) or the content (e.g., 这幅字写的是什么？大概是什么意思？). Unless something is presented to you as a gift for you, try to avoid saying 我很喜欢, because if your host senses that you like something, he or she may feel obliged to offer it to you as a gift.

3.3 出席宴会

高朋满座

🎧 投石问路

Listen to the five questions in the audio and answer them based on your own experience. Be ready to discuss these questions in class. You may write down some notes in the space provided below.

1.
2.
3.
4.
5.

🎧 边听边想

Listen to the audio and try to visualize the dialogue in your mind. Think about who the speakers are, the kind of social relationship they have, and what their intentions might be.

🎧 耳闻目睹

Listen to the audio again while following along in the printed text. As you listen, mark any place that you are unclear or have questions about.

高朋满座

人物：秦老师、汪总经理、周丹锐、孙浩、郑妮、赵奕歆

（秦老师、周丹锐、孙浩、赵奕歆、郑妮受汪总经理邀请参观了他的公司。现在在宴会厅，汪总请大家吃晚饭。）

秦老师：汪总，你这么盛情地款待，真是太麻烦你了！
汪总：　哪里哪里，我们尽点地主之谊也是应该的嘛。各位请进，大家随便坐。(1/5)

……

周丹锐：随便坐？到底该坐哪儿？
孙浩：　反正别坐那个对着门的座儿，那是主人的位置，待会儿汪总会坐那儿。
周丹锐：这么说汪总左右两边也不能随便坐了。我还以为礼仪讲座讲的那些主陪、副陪、主宾、副宾什么的只是说说而已，不会那么当真的。
孙浩：　有些场合可能随意些。不过如果是政府或者商业宴请，基本上都还挺讲究的。
周丹锐：还真麻烦。
孙浩：　习惯了也没什么。反正这种场合就是说些该说的话，沟通一下感情。(2/5)

……

郑妮：　（小声地）我们这个位置真亏，你看什么新菜一上来都先转到秦老师那儿，最后才到我们这儿。
奕歆：　谁让我们坐在秦老师右边呢……哎，你现在最好别喝酒！
郑妮：　还真得等到该敬酒的时候才能喝啊？哎呀，太多规矩了……(3/5)

……

孙浩：　丹锐，那些主陪、副陪、主宾、副宾都各敬三杯了，你现在可以去露一手了。
周丹锐：好，我去试试……汪总，我以茶代酒，敬您一杯，我叫周丹锐，丹青的"丹"，精锐的"锐"，感谢您的盛情款待，祝您身体健康，工作顺利！(4/5)
汪总：　你中文说得很溜嘛，不过小伙子不喝酒没诚意啊！
周丹锐：是这样的，汪总，在美国我的年龄还不够喝酒的法定年龄。不过，虽然以茶代酒，但心意是一样的啊！
汪总：　哈哈，你真会说话！秦老师，你的这些学生真懂事，很了解我们中国文

化啊!

秦老师:过奖了,他们刚开始学,以后还得请你多指导指导他们!(5/5)

知其所以然

The dialogue is broken down into sections below for explanation and analysis. Study the notes and answer the questions for the underlined text.

1/5

(秦老师、周丹锐、孙浩、赵奕歆、郑妮受汪总经理邀请参观了他的公司。现在在宴会厅,汪总请大家吃晚饭。)

秦老师:汪总,你这么盛情地款待,真是太麻烦你了!

汪总: 哪里哪里,我们尽点地主之谊也是应该的嘛。各位请进,大家随便坐。

---

1. 秦老师感谢汪总的招待,汪总客气地回答:"我们尽点地主之谊也是应该的。"
(1)"地主"本来是什么意思?＿＿＿＿＿＿＿＿＿＿＿＿＿＿
(2)这里的"地主"指的是谁?＿＿＿＿＿＿＿＿＿＿＿＿＿＿
(3)你的美国同学到苏州来找你玩,你请他吃了个饭,这算不算"尽地主之谊"?
＿＿＿＿＿＿＿＿＿＿＿＿＿＿

In some contexts, 地主 (literally meaning the owner of the land) denotes the landlord who hires peasants to work for him, which now has a negative connotation due to the agrarian revolution in China. But in the phrase 地主之谊, 地主 refers to a local person or a person who has become familiar with the local community, as opposed to a person from outside of the area. Usually the locals are more familiar with the local situation and feel obligated to take good care of their guests. In other words, they feel they must 尽地主之谊 (fulfill their obligations as hosts). The phrase 尽地主之谊 is widely used by hosts to express their desire to make their guests feel comfortable to accept their hospitality.

2. 汪总叫大家不要客气,他说:"大家随便坐。"
(1)汪总让大家"随便"坐,那么大家是不是可以想坐哪儿就坐哪儿?
＿＿＿＿＿＿＿＿＿＿＿＿＿＿
(2)这里的"随便坐"可不可以换成"随意"?＿＿＿＿＿＿＿＿＿＿＿＿＿＿
如果你请朋友们到家里吃饭,开始吃饭时你作为主人可以说什么?
＿＿＿＿＿＿＿＿＿＿＿＿＿＿

(4)如果你和朋友一起先逛街然后看电影,逛完街你和朋友都很饿,可是电影马上就要开始了,你可以提议＿＿＿＿＿＿＿＿＿＿＿＿＿＿
    A. 我们随便吃点吧。   B. 我们随意吧。

Literally, both 随便 and 随意 mean "as you wish", or "in whatever way you find convenient". Even though a host may invite guests to do as they please, in reality guests still need to follow some unspoken rules, especially in formal settings. Here, Manager Wang could have said 大家随意, which is less direct and more formal than 大家随便坐.

随便 is often used between friends as a response to questions about one's preferences; it would be impolite to use it at a banquet when your host offers you options of drinks. In that situation, an appropriate response would be 都可以 or 不用麻烦了.

Unlike 随便, which can be applied to oneself and can take objects, 随意 is only used when you ask other people to do whatever they wish and it cannot be followed by an action or an object. For example, when you and your friend are both hungry, but you do not have enough time for a meal before the movie starts, you can propose 我们随便吃点吧. One would never say 我们随意 or 我随意 in any serious sense.

2/5

……
周丹锐：随便坐？到底该坐哪儿？
孙浩：　反正别坐那个对着门的座儿，那是主人的位置，待会儿汪总会坐那儿。
周丹锐：这么说汪总左右两边也不能随便坐了。我还以为礼仪讲座讲的那些主陪、副陪、主宾、副宾什么的只是说说而已，不会那么当真的。
孙浩：　有些场合可能随意些。不过如果是政府或者商业宴请，基本上都还挺讲究的。
周丹锐：还真麻烦。
孙浩：　习惯了也没什么。反正这种场合就是说些该说的话，沟通一下感情。

---

3. 孙浩确定他们不能坐对着门的座儿，所以他说："反正别坐那个对着门的座儿。"

（1）"反正"在这里表达孙浩什么样的语气？ _____

（2）如果你的朋友很喜欢你的一本字典，你想送给她，她又不好意思要，你可以怎么说，让她放心地拿走？ _____

（3）如果学校有一个聚会，你已经决定不去参加，但你的室友一直问你他是去好还是不去好，你有点不耐烦了。可以怎么说？ _____

反正 is used to firmly state one's decision or statement indicating a sense of certainty. For example, if your friend shows great interest in your dictionary, you may generously say 你拿走吧，反正我不用, reassuring her that you no longer need it. In another context, if your friend proposes several options for a trip and asks you which one you like best, you may say 随便，反正我有时间, reassuring her that you have enough time for any itinerary.

In some contexts, such certainty may convey indifference or impatience. For example, if your friend cannot decide whether or not to go to a party and keeps asking you about it, you may say 反正我不去 to indicate your indifference about the decision or your impatience with being asked about it repeatedly.

4. 周丹锐没想到人们真的遵守宴会礼仪："我还以为……只是说说而已，不会那么当真的。"

　　（1）这里"当真"的意思是＿＿＿＿＿＿＿
　　　　A. 真的按照礼仪讲座讲的要求去做。
　　　　B. 把主陪、副陪、主宾和副宾当成真的。
　　（2）根据"我跟小明开了个玩笑，结果他当真了"这句话，小明认为那是个玩笑吗？＿＿＿＿＿＿＿＿＿＿＿＿＿＿＿＿＿
　　（3）如果你听同学说明天不上课，想去跟老师确认一下，你可以怎么跟老师说？＿＿＿＿＿＿＿＿＿＿＿＿＿＿＿＿＿

当真, as a verb, is used to say that someone takes something seriously. In the dialogue, Zhou Danrui is surprised that people seriously follow the rules introduced at the lecture on banquet etiquette. For example, if, as a joke, you proposed to have a party at Xiaoming's house and Xiaoming actually gets his place ready for the party, you may say 小明把玩笑当真了.

当真 can also be used to modify a verb, especially in literary texts. For example, you might read or hear characters in a ancient Chinese drama 你当真相信他的话, asking if someone really believes what another person said. In daily conversation, however, people use 真的 instead of 当真. Therefore, to confirm with your teacher whether or not what you heard about classes being cancelled is true, you may say 老师，明天当真不上课吗？

5. 孙浩说政府或者商业宴请"基本上都还挺讲究的"。
　　（1）这里的"讲究"可以换成下面哪个词？＿＿＿＿＿＿＿
　　　　A. 注意　　　　B. 认真　　　　C. 仔细
　　（2）你觉得自己是一个"讲究卫生"的人吗？＿＿＿＿＿＿＿＿＿＿＿＿＿＿＿＿＿
　　（3）朋友跟你说"小明家布置得很讲究"，这大概是什么意思？＿＿＿＿＿＿＿＿＿

讲究 is used to describe a person who pays great attention to or is very picky about something. For example, in formal settings, Chinese people value abiding by social conventions and rules of etiquette, so we can say 中国人在正式场合很讲究礼节. In the dialogue, 讲究 may be replaced by 注意, which highlights the aspect of paying attention to etiquette rules.

讲究 can also be used to describe the fine appearance or high quality of something.

For example, when a Chinese person describes a friend's home as 小明家布置得很讲究, he is saying that Xiaoming's home is decorated exquisitely.

3/5

……
郑妮：　（小声地）我们这个位置真亏，你看什么新菜一上来都先转到秦老师那儿，最后才到我们这儿。
赵奕歆：　谁让我们坐在秦老师右边呢……哎，你现在最好别喝酒！
郑妮：　还真得等到该敬酒的时候才能喝啊？哎呀，太多规矩了……

---

6. 郑妮觉得她和赵奕歆坐的位置非常不好，她说："我们这个位置真亏。"
（1）郑妮坐在什么位置？ _____
（2）她为什么觉得坐在那个位置"亏"？ _____
（3）如果你的同学因为临时有事错过了一场好看的电影，你觉得很可惜，可以怎么跟他说？ _____
（4）如果你在砍价的时候，老板说"我已经是在亏本卖了"，老板的意思是他还可以便宜吗？ _____

亏 is used as an adjective here to express a feeling of being disadvantaged. For example, if a person finds out the event that he didn't attend but his friends attended turned out to be free and interesting, he may comment 我没去，真亏 or 我没去，真是太亏了.

Another common use of 亏 is 亏本 (lose money in business). Here, 本 refers to the capital that was invested in a business or product. When bargaining, you may hear a vendor say 再便宜我就要亏本了, indicating that he would be losing money if he granted a further discount, or 我已经是在亏本卖了, indicating he is already selling below cost. In another context, if a person lost $100,000 in a business venture, he may tell people 去年我亏了 10 万美元.

7. 郑妮没想到真要按礼仪讲座上讲的要求做，她说："还真得等到该敬酒的时候才能喝啊？"
（1）根据这句话，在宴会上喝酒的时候有什么规矩？ _____
（2）这句话的哪些部分表达出惊讶的语气？ _____
（3）如果以前孙浩告诉过你他不会用筷子，当时你觉得他是开玩笑。今天，你们一起吃饭的时候孙浩用勺子，不用筷子，你有些惊讶，可以怎么说？ _____
（4）你的朋友让你猜一个很少见的汉字"仝"的读音，你随便猜了一个读音"tóng"，结果你的朋友说你猜对了。你很惊讶，你怎么说？ _____

还真…… is used to express your surprise at something that you did not expect to be true that turns out to be true either in front of your own eyes or as a result of later developments. It implies your reluctance to believe something to be true. Here, Zheng Ni did not expect the rule she heard at the lecture (i.e., 得等到该敬酒的时候才能喝酒) to actually be observed at real banquets. In another context, your friend Sun Hao once told you that he couldn't use chopsticks, but you didn't believe him. Then one day when you notice him using a spoon instead of chopsticks, you may express your surprise by saying 你还真不会用筷子啊? Similarly, if your wild guess about the pronunciation of an unfamiliar character turns out to be correct, you may say 还真读"tóng"啊? indicating your surprise.

4/5

……

孙浩： 丹锐,那些主陪、副陪、主宾、副宾都各敬三杯了,你现在可以去露一手了。

周丹锐： 好,我去试试……汪总,我以茶代酒,敬您一杯,我叫周丹锐,丹青的"丹",精锐的"锐",感谢您的盛情款待,祝您身体健康,工作顺利!

---

8. 孙浩告诉周丹锐他可以去敬酒了,他说:"你现在可以去露一手了。"
(1) 这里的"手"指的是真正的手吗?如果不是的话指的是什么?
　　_____
(2) 孙浩让周丹锐去"露一手"是因为他觉得周丹锐很会敬酒吗?
　　_____
(3) 可不可以说"我来给大家露一手"?如果可以,什么情况下可以说?
　　_____
(4) 你刚到一个公司,在迎新宴会上,老板听说你很会唱歌,所以要你唱一首。为了不让大家扫兴,你答应了。在唱歌之前你可以怎么说表示谦虚?_____

Here 手 can be understood as 手艺, which has been explained in 2.1. Therefore, 露一手 is usually used to encourage someone to show something they are good at. In the dialogue, while encouraging Zhou Danrui to propose a toast, Sun Hao is also complimenting on his toasting skills. Usually a Chinese speaker would not use it about himself because saying 我来露一手 may be interpreted as bragging. However, it is okay to say 我来露一手 to close friends or family members.

To tell people that you are ready to give something a try in a humble way, you may say 我来献丑了 or 我来献个丑. In (4), when your boss invites you to sing in front of your new colleagues at a welcome party, you can modestly accept the invitation by saying 那我就献丑了。

> **5/5**
> 汪总： 你中文说得很溜嘛,不过小伙子不喝酒没诚意啊!
> 周丹锐： 是这样的,汪总,在美国我的年龄还不够喝酒的法定年龄。不过,虽然以茶代酒,但心意是一样的啊!
> 汪总： 哈哈,你真会说话!秦老师,你的这些学生真懂事,很了解我们中国文化啊!
> 秦老师： 过奖了,他们刚开始学,以后还得请你多指导指导他们!

9. 汪总夸奖周丹锐:"你中文说得很溜嘛。"

(1) "说得很溜"和"说得很好"有什么区别吗? _____

(2) 你看到一个人弹吉他弹得很好,你可以怎么称赞他? _____

Here, 溜 is pronounced as "liù". It is a rather colloquial way to describe the adeptness a person demonstrates in performing a skill. Here, Manager Wang is impressed by Zhou Danrui's fluent speech and appropriate language. Besides speaking, 溜 is also applicable to other skills like playing the guitar 你吉他弹得真溜, or using a computer 他电脑玩得很溜.

The same character 溜 is pronounced as "liū" when it is used as a verb. For example, the popular sport of ice-skating is 溜冰 in Chinese.

10. 汪总夸奖周丹锐:"你真会说话。"

(1) 汪总夸周丹锐"会说话"是因为他觉得周丹锐_____

　　A. 中文说得好。　　　　B. 用词很准确。　　　　C. 应答巧妙得体。

(2) 一个"很会做人"的人,在下面的情况下她会怎么做?

a. 她带领的小组任务完成得很棒,公司发给她一笔奖金,她可能怎么办?

_____

b. 在公司门口遇见部门经理和公司的总经理,她先跟谁打招呼?

_____

会 + [action] can be used to describe people who are skillful at something. As was the case with 好说话 in 2.3, 说话 is not limited to its literal sense. When Manager Wang says Zhou Danrui 会说话, he is saying that Zhou Danrui knows how to say things in a way that other people are pleased to hear. Similarly, if you say a person 会办事, you are saying that this person is good at grasping opportunities to give people a positive impression by saying the right thing at the right time or knows how to deal with interpersonal relationships in a way that prevents disputes.

The term 会做人 entails 会说话 and 会办事. If you say a person 会做人, you are saying that this person is skillful in dealing with interpersonal relationships and has the ability to say and do the right things at the right time. Therefore, if a person who receives an award for a group project uses the money to take her team members out for dinner, she may be thought of as 很会做人. If a person who is described as 会做人 would greet her department head first even though the general manager is also present. This way, she can avoid appearing snobbish to her department head while demonstrating to the general manager that the department head is respected by his subordinate.

From the connotation of these expressions, especially 会做人, you can see how much Chinese people value interpersonal relationships—to be a human（做人）is to handle interpersonal relationships effectively.

体演文本

Review the sections of the dialogue assigned by your teacher by listening to the audio and role-playing with another Chinese speaker. Be ready to perform the assigned portion of the dialogue from memory in class.

举一反三

Answer the following questions and think about how the dialogue can be adapted for different situations.

1. 为什么副陪坐主人对面？副陪有哪些任务？
2. 孙浩说：“反正这种场合就是说些该说的话,沟通一下感情。”你认为参加宴会的时候你应该说些什么样的话？
3. 在中国人们一般通过哪些活动"沟通感情"？在你的国家呢？
4. 秦老师为什么对汪总说"以后还请你多指导"？她真的希望汪总以后可以多指导吗？

熟能生巧

Listen to the audio and perform the following drills until you feel confident with the items practiced.

☞ **Drill 1 Politely deflecting compliments**

When your guest thanks you for your hospitality, deflect the compliment in an appropriate way by referring to your duty as a host. In the example, Manager Wang starts with an archaic phrase 哪里哪里. To sound less formal, you may use 别这么说 or 没有没有.

例：

秦老师：汪总,你这么盛情地款待,真是太麻烦你了！

汪总：哪里哪里,我尽点地主之谊也是应该的嘛。

1.　　　　　2.　　　　　3.　　　　　4.

☞ Drill 2 Expressing great surprise

When your friend indicates that your wild guess is confirmed or your random wish is granted, respond with great surprise.

例：
孙浩：你真厉害，那个字就是读 tóng。
郑妮：(那个字)还真读 tóng 啊？
1.　　　　　2.　　　　　3.　　　　　4.

☞ Drill 3 Confirming assumptions and pointing out exceptions

When your friend states that he thinks his assumption is always correct, first respond that he can be right sometimes. Then point out that in certain particular circumstance his assumption does not apply. Each of the illustrations will provide the particular circumstance where the assumption doesn't apply.

例：

周丹锐：我还以为现在聚餐都不会那么讲究呢。
赵奕歆：有些聚餐可能随意些。不过如果是商业宴请，基本上都还挺讲究的。

1. 　2. 　3. 　4.

☞ Drill 4 Proposing a toast

In this drill, you will initiate the interaction by delivering a complete toast. First give a particular reason for your toast, and then express your good wishes. Lastly state that you will drink up first to show your respect. The illustrations will show to whom you are going to propose a toast and the reason for doing it. Below are some common good wishes people express when toasting (Note the three categories below are not mutually exclusive, so feel free to combine items as appropriate):

> To a retired person：祝你身体健康
> To a professional： 祝你工作顺利,祝你事业成功
> To a student： 祝你学业有成
> To a family： 祝你们全家幸福
> To anyone： 祝你万事如意

例：汪总/盛情款待

郑妮：我敬您一杯,感谢您的热情款待,祝您工作顺利,万事如意,我先干为敬！
汪总：太客气了,招待不周,谢谢,干！

1. 徐校长/对项目的支持　　2. 赵爸爸和赵妈妈/热情款待　

3. 孙浩/帮助　　4. 秦老师/关心　

Narration

Assume the role of Zhou Danrui and explain the rules and procedures for a formal Chinese banquet to your Japanese friend Mari, who will be the main guest at a formal banquet hosted by an important Chinese client.

Mari：丹锐,我们合作单位的老板要请我跟他们公司的人吃饭,好像是个特别正式的宴席。饭桌上我有什么要注意的吗？

言外有意

Read the cultural notes below and prepare questions for further discussion with Chinese people.

1. 高朋满座 (gāo péng mǎn zuò) A great gathering of distinguished guests.

You will hear this idiom often at a relatively formal banquet or event. The host of the event will use the idiom to show respect to the guests and to express the happiness to have all the guests gathered. For example, the host will begin the event by saying 感谢各位领导、嘉宾拨冗

(bō rǒng, a formal way to say "find a time") 前来参加这次活动,今日真是高朋满座! However, this idiom is not used in the context of a casual get-together among friends or family.

2. 宴席座次

As mentioned in the dialogue, there is a traditional way in which guests and hosts are seated at an official banquet. Most importantly, the host sits across from the door, and the assistant to the host (for example, his driver or secretary) sits across from him, next to the door so that he or she can enter and exit the room easily. The most important guest sits to the right of the host, and the second-most important guest sits to the host's left. Guests ranked 3rd and 4th sit next to the assistant, and the rest are seated in the middle seats. Not all of these rules are always followed so closely, but the host and main guest seating arrangement is still usually observed.

3. 喝酒敬酒

Whether it is to seal a business deal or to strengthen a friendship, alcohol plays an important role in Chinese culture. Usually, Chinese people drink liquor, generically referred to as 白酒, but wine is now becoming more and more popular. 茅台酒 is a popular liquor from Guizhou Province and is often served at expensive banquets.

Toasting is an important part of banquet culture, and the main host usually makes the first toast to welcome guests. Then, the main guest will make a toast to thank the host for his or her generosity (this toast is referred to as 回敬). After some eating, the host may get up and toast people individually. During a toast, you may hear: 干杯! This means that others expect you to finish your shot (whether of liquor or of 王老吉). If you have proposed the toast, it is polite for you to end your toast with 我先干为敬 and finish your drink first. Also, when toasting, don't forget to hold your glass slightly lower than the other person's to show your respect!

Formal toasts usually begin with gratitude or admiration and end with good wishes. Here are some useful expressions that you can use in your toasts:

(1) 感谢您的盛情款待;
(2) 感谢您的帮助;
(3) 一定要好好向您学习;
(4) 有时间麻烦您多教教我;
(5) 我是新人,很多东西不懂,今后请多多指教;
(6) 祝您身体健康。

If you want to learn more about Chinese banquet culture, including toasting, check out *Eat Shandong: From Personal Experience to a Pedagogy of a Second Culture* by Eric Shepherd. Although this book focuses on eating and drinking culture in Shandong Province, many of the traditions are applicable across China.

学而时习之

Before you actually do the field performances, rehearse doing them with a Chinese friend. The "Useful Expressions" box below provides you with some expressions you may use for these performances. For now, try saying them after the audio.

> **Useful Expressions**
>
> 1. 你今天晚饭有什么计划吗?
> 2. 我听说XX餐馆很不错。今天晚上我请你去那儿吃吧。
> 3. 走吧。我还没去XX餐馆吃过呢。就算陪我吧。
> 4. 别客气,你看看喜欢吃什么就点什么吧。
> 5. 你有没有忌口?
> 6. 你有什么推荐的吗?
> 7. 你想喝点儿什么?
> 8. 我们再要一个汤吧?
> 9. 那我们先要这些。不够了再点吧。
> 10. 来,我以可乐代酒敬你一杯,谢谢你帮我这么多忙。
> 11. 你吃好了吗? 要不要再来点主食?
> 12. 你别掏钱。说好了我请你的。
> 13. 你帮了我这么多忙,请你吃顿饭是应该的。
> 14. 那好吧,谢谢。下次我来请。
> 15. 我不挑食,什么都吃。你随便点吧。
> 16. 我对海鲜过敏,不过你爱吃的话可以点。
> 17. 这是我的一点心意。
> 18. 这幅字是您自己写的吗? 这是什么字体?
> 19. 这位书法家在中国很有名吗?
> 20. 有什么我可以帮忙做的吗?
> 21. 谢谢你们的邀请,还有这么热情的款待。
> 22. 今天打扰了你们这么久,我真过意不去。

Make it a habit to carry a notebook with you and take notes on your interactions with Chinese people.

☞ Performance 1 Treating a Chinese friend to dinner

Invite a Chinese friend to whom you feel grateful to a dinner.

_____ Act 1: Ask about your friend's food preference.

____ Act 2: Mention a place where you would like to go for dinner and invite your friend to join you.
____ Act 3: Provide a reason why your friend should accept your invitation.
____ Act 4: Ask about your friend's availability for dining-out together.
____ Act 5: Insist on treating your friend to dinner.
____ Act 6: Express your gratefulness for your friend's help.
____ Act 7: Propose to treat your friend to something else (e.g., a movie, a show, a day trip, etc.).

☞ Performance 2 Being a nice host

Dine out with your Chinese friend.
____ Act 1: Invite your friend to order whatever he or she likes.
____ Act 2: Explain that you will pay your friend's bill.
____ Act 3: Ask your friend to recommend food, if applicable.
____ Act 4: Ask the server to recommend food.
____ Act 5: Make sure you have ordered enough food.
____ Act 6: Propose a toast to your friend and encourage him or her to eat more.
____ Act 7: Explain to your friend why you are paying his or her bill.
____ Act 8: Insist on paying repeatedly if necessary.

☞ Performance 3 Being a polite guest

Visit a Chinese friend's home for dinner.
____ Act 1: Obtain your friend's address and the directions to get there.
____ Act 2: Take public transportation to get to your friend's home.
____ Act 3: Arrive up to 10 minutes early.
____ Act 4: Greet the people in your friend's home and present your gift(s).
____ Act 5: Ask questions about items to show interest (Note: Avoid complimenting).
____ Act 6: Offer to help with preparation.
____ Act 7: Compliment the food and express your appreciation.
____ Act 8: Express your appreciation for the invitation and hospitality.
____ Act 9: Initiate the close of the visit.

第四单元

游山玩水 Sightseeing

4.1 团队游

走马观花

🎧 投石问路

Listen to the five questions in the audio and answer them based on your own experience. Be ready to discuss these questions in class. You may write down some notes in the space provided below.

1.
2.
3.
4.
5.

🎧 边听边想

Listen to the audio and try to visualize the dialogue in your mind. Think about who the speakers are, the kind of social relationship they have, and what their intentions might be.

耳闻目睹

Listen to the audio again while following along in the printed text. As you listen, mark any place that you are unclear or have questions about.

走马观花
人物：郑妮、赵奕歆、游客

（下课了，郑妮和赵奕歆在教室里。郑妮在看刚拿到的旅游安排）

郑妮： 奕歆，你看了这张旅游安排吗？我们下周要去好多地方呢，外滩、城隍庙、浦东的国际金融中心，我们只有两天，时间够吗？

赵奕歆： 应该没有问题吧，我们去的这些地方都在上海市区，而且花一样的时间和费用，多去几个景点多好啊。

郑妮： 我倒是希望我们去的景点少一点，在一个景点呆久一点。

赵奕歆： 可能老师想你们来一趟不容易，尽量让你们多看一些吧。

郑妮： 可是这样赶来赶去多累啊……(1/4)

（郑妮和赵奕歆在上海豫园景点入口，游人很多）

游客： 能和你拍张照吗？

郑妮： 哦，好的。

赵奕歆： 哇，你很受欢迎啊。

郑妮： 我在中国总是有很多人要来和我一起拍照。

赵奕歆： 他们看你金发碧眼，长得漂亮嘛。

郑妮： 唉，有的时候也挺烦的。现在想起来，我们那天在拙政园老拉着那位写书法的老爷爷照相，他可能也很烦我们。

赵奕歆： 大家都把对方看成是"异国情调"了。不过我倒没看出来他烦你，他可一直都是笑眯眯的。

郑妮： 那倒是。……(2/4)

游客： 我们再拍一张吧。

郑妮： 啊？这么多人……

赵奕歆： 不好意思，我们老师在前面催我们去听导游讲解了，我们要赶紧追上他们。(3/4)

（郑妮和赵奕歆终于追上了导游）

郑妮： 奕歆，你觉得导游说的有意思吗？

赵奕歆： 其实没什么意思，尽是陈词滥调，文绉绉的，不过这边风景还是挺美的。

郑妮： 风景是挺美的，就是垃圾有点多。

赵奕歆： 这个嘛……可能也是因为游客太多了吧。现在是旅游旺季，管理也有些跟不上……哎呀，我们又掉队了。

郑妮：　导游走得也太快了吧，都来不及拍照了……(4/4)

知其所以然

The dialogue is broken down into sections below for explanation and analysis. Study the notes and answer the questions for the underlined text.

1/4

（下课了，郑妮和赵奕歆在教室里。郑妮在看刚拿到的旅游安排）

郑妮：　奕歆，你看了这张旅游安排吗？我们下周要去好多地方呢，外滩、城隍庙、浦东的国际金融中心，我们只有两天，时间够吗？

赵奕歆：应该没有问题吧，我们去的这些地方都在上海市区，而且花一样的时间和费用，多去几个景点多好啊。

郑妮：　我倒是希望我们去的景点少一点，在一个景点呆久一点。

赵奕歆：可能老师想你们来一趟不容易，尽量让你们多看一些吧。

郑妮：　可是这样赶来赶去多累啊……

---

1. 赵奕歆提示郑妮这次旅游安排的好处，她说："花一样的时间和费用，多去几个景点多好啊。"

（1）这里"多好"如果换成"很好"，感觉会有什么不同？_____

（2）如果你的朋友的室友搬走了，他有点难过，因为他不喜欢一个人住，你可以怎么安慰他？_____

（3）你和朋友一起去逛街，朋友提议打车去，你觉得那样太贵，你可以怎么强烈地指出来？_____

[statement] + 多好啊 is often used to comfort/console others by pointing out an exciting aspect about something with a slight sense of admiration. 很好啊 would not convey this sense of admiration. Here Zhao Yixin is trying to make Zheng Ni feel more comfortable about the itinerary by pointing out that for the same amount of time and money, she will be able to visit more places. For example, if your classmate complains that his elder sister treats him like a child, you may say 有个姐姐多好啊, indicating that you would love to have an elder sister. In this structure, 好 may be replaced by other desirable aspects. For example, if a friend complains about having to live alone, you may comfort her by saying 一个人住多自由啊 or 一个人住多好啊，可以自由自在的, pointing out that living alone means having more freedom.

Note that 多……啊 may also occur with undesirable aspects like 多累啊, 多难吃啊, 多贵啊. In this case, the speaker is pointing out an undesirable aspect, which he or she believes the other person is not aware of it. These comments are emphatic. Later in this dialogue, Zhen Ni emphasizes her aversion towards the tight schedule by saying 这样赶来

赶去多累啊. In another context, if your friend proposes that you take a taxi, you may strongly point out the disadvantage of taking a taxi by saying 打车去多贵啊.

2. 郑妮不同意去太多的景点,她希望"去的景点少一点,在一个景点呆久一点"。
(1) 这里的"呆"可以换成"住"吗？为什么？_____
(2) "我们在上海呆了一天"和"我们在上海待了一天"有什么区别吗？
_____
(3) 如果你星期六哪儿也没去,在家休息了一天,晚上朋友发短信问你今天做了什么,你可以怎么回复？_____

Both 呆 and 住 refer to being at a place for a period of time. However, while 住 refers specifically to lodging, 呆 can be used in a broader sense, either referring to lodging or simply being there. Some people use the character 待 instead of 呆. When referring to staying somewhere, these two characters have the same meaning. In other contexts, 待 can refer to waiting as in the phrase 等待 (to wait), and 呆 can refer to not being mentally present as in 发呆 (to stare blankly).

3. 赵奕歆给郑妮解释老师的心意："可能老师想你们来一趟不容易,尽量让你们多看一些吧。"
(1) 这里"尽量"可以换成别的词吗？_____
(2) 如果朋友邀请你去他的生日派对,但是那天你有很多安排,你可以怎么回答他？_____
　A. 我尽量。　　　B. 我尽力。　　　C. 我尽可能。
(3) 老师对学生们说："作文最迟周四交,不过最好_____交给我,这样我周四晚上就可以批改完还给大家。"下面哪两个词合适？
　A. 尽量　　　B. 尽力　　　C. 尽快　　　D. 尽早

尽量 and 尽力 are quite similar in that they both denote that one tries one's best to do something. However, they are not interchangeable. Using 尽量, the speaker is more concerned about conditions, whereas when using 尽力, the person's own capability is the primary concern. If you are invited to a friend's party and whether or not you can make it mainly depends on your schedule, it's more appropriate to reply 我尽量. Note that this response could be interpreted as a kind of polite refusal. It implies that although you want to go, it's highly probable that you won't be able to because of matters beyond your control. In another context, if your friend keeps blaming himself for failing to help another friend although he has tried his best, you may comfort your friend saying 你已经尽力了,就别那么自责了.

尽 X is a useful pattern that means "as X as possible". For example, 尽早 (as early as possible) can be used interchangeably with 尽快 (as quickly as possible). For example, to promise expedited work, a Chinese person may say 我会尽快/尽早做好.

尽 in the 尽 X pattern (except for 尽量 and 尽力) can be seen as short for 尽可能. Therefore, 尽早 is short for 尽可能早地 and 尽快 is 尽可能快地. In each case, the former (i.e., the shortened form) sounds more formal.

4. 郑妮还是不太喜欢这个旅游安排,说:"可是这样赶来赶去多累啊。"
(1) 这里的"赶"可以换成"跑"吗? ＿＿＿＿＿＿＿＿＿＿＿＿＿＿＿
(2) 你有没有过"赶作业"的经历? 如果有,是在什么情况下? ＿＿＿＿＿＿＿
(3) 你会为了什么事情"跑来跑去"? ＿＿＿＿＿＿＿＿＿＿＿＿＿＿＿
(4) 在"那件事小明说来说去也说不清楚"这句话里面,"说来说去"是什么意思?
＿＿＿＿＿＿＿＿＿＿＿＿＿＿＿

Compared with 跑, 赶 here has the implication that something is done in a rush. For example, if you are doing some homework that requires more than one hour to complete but it is due in 50 minutes, 我在赶作业 will be more suitable than 我在做作业 in that the latter does not indicate that you are rushed.

The pattern V 来 V 去 indicates that the speaker is not particularly fond of a repeated or prolonged action being described. For example, you may visit many stores in order to find a pair of jeans you like. In that case, you can say 我跑来跑去,就为了找一条喜欢的牛仔裤.

Note that this pattern does not necessarily involve physical movement between places. For example, 说来说去 simply indicates that a person does a lot of ineffective talking.

2/4
(郑妮和赵奕歆在上海豫园景点入口,游人很多)
游客:　　能和你拍张照吗?
郑妮:　　哦,好的。
赵奕歆:　哇,你很受欢迎啊。
郑妮:　　我在中国总是有很多人要来和我一起拍照。
赵奕歆:　他们看你金发碧眼,长得漂亮嘛。
郑妮:　　唉,有的时候也挺烦的。现在想起来,我们那天在拙政园老拉着那位写书法的老爷爷照相,他可能也很烦我们。
赵奕歆:　大家都把对方看成是"异国情调"了。不过我倒没看出来他烦你,他可一直都是笑眯眯的。
郑妮:　　那倒是。……

---

5. 对于很多陌生人要跟她一起拍照的情况,郑妮觉得"有时候也挺烦的"。

(1) 这里的"烦"是什么意思？_____
    A. 烦人　　　　　　B. 烦恼
(2) 你的生活中有什么事或者什么人让你觉得很"烦人"吗？_____
(3) 你的生活中有什么事让你很"烦恼"吗？_____

烦 is usually short for either 烦人 or 烦恼. 烦人 refers to matters that are annoying, e.g., 老被人拍照很烦人, while 烦恼 refers to a troubled state of mind. For example, to tell your friend that you are bothered by the job-hunting process, you say 找工作的事让我很烦恼.

烦 + [a person/situation] denotes the state of being annoyed by something or someone. For example, 郑妮很烦老被游客拉着照相 and 郑妮不好意思老拉着写书法的老爷爷跟她拍照, 担心他会烦她.

6. 郑妮自己也曾经"在拙政园公园老拉着那位写书法的老爷爷照相"。
   (1) 你有没有"拉着"别人做过什么事？_____
   (2) 这里的"老"如果换成"一直"意思会有什么不同吗？_____
   (3) 如果你不明白为什么总是有陌生人找自己照相,你可以怎么问你的中国朋友？_____

While 拉 means "to pull/drag", 老拉着 + [person] + [action] refers to a repeated action of asking or dragging someone into doing something without considering how that person may feel.

Compared with 一直, 老 implies that the speaker finds the repeated action unpleasant. For example, if you want to complain to a friend about strangers asking to take photos with you, you can ask 为什么他们老找我照相？

7. 对于人们喜欢找外国人拍照的现象,赵奕歆解释说"大家都把对方看成是'异国情调'了"。
   (1) 你觉得苏州的哪儿最有异国情调？_____
   (2) 怎样的人算"有情调"的人？_____
   (3) 如果一个朋友的家里很有欧洲情调,他家的布置或者生活习惯可能是怎样的？_____

有情调 is used to describe a place or a person that has emotional appeal, especially if it evokes romantic or sentimental feelings. For example, if your friend tells you that he goes to the movies with his girlfriend every week, you may say 你(们)真有情调 or 你们的生活真有情调. In another context, when visiting a friend's apartment, you may compliment him or her on its warm or cozy atmosphere or its artistic interior decoration by saying 你家真有情调. If the decorative style of the apartment reminds you in positive ways of European culture, you may say 你家真有欧洲情调.

3/4

游客： 我们再拍一张吧。

郑妮： 啊？这么多人……

赵奕歆：不好意思，我们老师在前面<u>催</u>我们去听导游讲解了，我们要赶紧追上他们。

---

8. 赵奕歆找了个借口帮郑妮走开，她说："我们老师在前面催我们去听导游讲解了。"

（1）这里的"催"可以换成"让"吗？为什么？＿＿＿＿＿＿＿＿＿＿＿＿＿＿

（2）你觉得在什么情况下你会和别人说"你催他一下"？＿＿＿＿＿＿＿＿＿＿

（3）如果你在认真做作业，但室友一直跟你说该准备出门了，你觉得有点烦，可以怎么说？＿＿＿＿＿＿＿＿＿＿＿＿＿＿＿

In requesting or urging someone to do something, 催 conveys more impatience than 让. For example, you may say 你催他一下 to your friend because there is a third person who should show up but does not. As another example, when you ask a waitress why your dish has not been served after a long wait, she may respond 我帮你催一下吧. When you feel annoyed by someone who is constantly urging you to do something, you may say 别催了. This is a rather direct and impolite expression, so be careful not to say this to a person of a higher rank than you.

4/4

（郑妮和赵奕歆终于追上了导游）

郑妮： 奕歆，你觉得导游说的有意思吗？

赵奕歆：其实没什么意思，尽是<u>陈词滥调</u>，<u>文绉绉</u>的，不过这边风景还是挺美的。

郑妮： 风景是挺美的，就是垃圾有点多。

赵奕歆：这个嘛……可能也是因为游客太多了吧。现在是旅游旺季，<u>管理也有些跟不上</u>……哎呀，我们又掉队了。

郑妮： 导游走得也太快了吧，都来不及拍照了……

---

9. 赵奕歆觉得导游说的没什么意思，她说："尽是陈词滥调，文绉绉的。"

（1）赵奕歆说导游的话是"陈词滥调"，这说明她觉得导游说的话怎么样？

　　A. 太长。　　　　B. 太无聊。　　　　C. 太难。

（2）如果说一个人"文绉绉的"，一般是说这个人有怎样的特点？＿＿＿＿＿

（3）如果有人说你文绉绉的，你觉得他的意思是什么？

　　A. 表扬我。　　　B. 批评我。　　　　C. 很难说。

(4) 如果你想说一本书写得非常难懂,你可以怎么说?＿＿＿＿＿＿＿＿＿＿

陈词滥调 is an idiom for saying that the words someone says are hackneyed and boring. It has a very negative connotation.

文绉绉的 refers to expressions (spoken or written) which sound very bookish. For example, to say that a book is full of literary or sophisticated expressions, you can say 这本书写得文绉绉的 or 这本书里的语言文绉绉的. Even if being "bookish" is not always perceived as a bad thing, 文绉绉的 usually carries a slight negative connotation. A more positive counterpart would be 有书生气. For example, 那个人说话很有书生气. Note that 有书生气 can also be used to positively describe a person's appearance and manners.

10. 对于景点垃圾多的情况,赵奕歆解释说:"游客太多……管理也有些跟不上。"
(1) 赵奕歆说"管理有些跟不上",是指"跟不上"什么?＿＿＿＿＿＿＿＿＿＿
(2) 如果你觉得读写课很难,你学得有点儿累,你可以怎么跟老师说?
＿＿＿＿＿＿＿＿＿＿
(3) 如果你的朋友在上钢琴课,你听说很有意思,想知道现在参加能不能很快和大家进度一样,可以怎么问?＿＿＿＿＿＿＿＿＿＿＿＿＿

跟不上 is used to describe the situation where the subject is having difficulty keeping up with a certain pace. Here, Zhao Yixin is using it in an abstract sense, saying that the grounds crew at the scenic spot have not kept up with the litter problem. Similarly, a Chinese speaker who is considering joining a piano class after the term has begun may wonder 如果现在开始上钢琴课的话,我担心我会跟不上, or he may ask the teacher 我现在加入你们的钢琴课,不知道能不能跟得上? To give an affirmative response, the teacher may say 跟得上. To give a negative response, the teacher might say 跟不上.

In the exchange below, 跟上、跟不上 and 没跟上 are used in their literal sense. Xiaoming is having difficulty keeping up with his friends' walking pace.

朋友:小明,快!跟上。(asking Xiaoming to catch up)
小明:你们走得太快了,我跟不上。(complaining that his friends are walking too fast)

Later, when telling his teacher why he was left behind by his group, Xiaoming may say 他们走得太快了,我没跟上.

体演文本

Review the sections of the dialogue assigned by your teacher by listening to the audio and role-playing with another Chinese speaker. Be ready to perform the assigned portion of the dialogue from memory in class.

举一反三

Answer the following questions and think about how the dialogue can be adapted for different situations.

1. 你觉得为什么有的中国人喜欢跟外国人一起拍照？你可以怎么礼貌地拒绝要和你拍照的人？
2. 赵奕欤为什么说导游说的话"尽是陈词滥调,文绉绉的"？你听过中国导游讲解吗？你同意赵奕欤的看法吗？
3. 导游的解说词里一般包含哪些信息？你游览景点的时候关注那些信息吗？
4. 在中国旅游的时候,花一样的时间和费用,你愿意尽量多去一些景点吗？
5. 跟团有哪些好处和坏处？怎么跟旅行社协商可能遇到的这些问题？

熟能生巧

Listen to the audio and perform the following drills until you feel confident with the items practiced.

☞ Drill 1 Emphasizing the positive

When your friend complains about something, emphasizing what he or she complains about actually has a positive aspect. The cues provide you with the exciting aspects.

例：多看些景点

朋友：我们只有三天时间,怎么安排去这么多地方啊？

郑妮：多去几个地方多好啊,可以多看些景点。

1. 自由自在的
2. 凉快一点
3. 多练习说外语
4. 多在成都玩一天

☞ Drill 2 Pointing out disadvantages and proposing an alternative

When your friend makes a proposal, emphasize the disadvantages of the proposal, and then propose an alternative. Each of the illustrations provides your friend's proposal and the alternative that you propose.

例：

朋友：我们打车去沃尔玛吧。

郑妮：打车去多贵啊,还是坐公交去吧。

☞ **Drill 3 Justifying expressions of hospitality**

When your friend expresses his or her surprise at your excessive offer, explain that you are trying to help him or her make the best out of the experience.

例：
客人：哇,安排了这么多地方啊。
郑妮：你来一趟不容易,想尽量让你多去一些地方。
1.　　　　　2.　　　　　3.　　　　　4.

☞ **Drill 4 Refusing a request**

When a new acquaintance requests you to stay longer, politely refuse by explaining that you are pressed for time because someone else is expecting you to do something. Each of the illustrations will provide you with the activity you are supposed to do next and the person who is waiting on you.

例：

游客：我们再拍一张照片吧。
郑妮：不好意思,老师在前面催我了,我得赶紧去听导游讲解了。

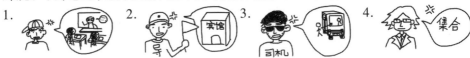

☞ **Drill 5 Acknowledging advantages and pointing out disadvantages**

When your friend brings up a positive aspect of a situation, acknowledge it and then mention a negative aspect to indicate your minor disappointment. Each of the illustrations will provide you with the negative aspect you can mention.

例：

赵奕歆：这里的风景挺美的。

周丹锐：风景是挺美的，就是垃圾有点多。

1.    2.    3.    4.

Narration

After they return from the study tour, Zheng Ni's Chinese friend is asking her how she liked the tour. Assume the role of Zheng Ni and make a reserved comment on the rushed pace of the busy itinerary. State your dissatisfaction while showing some understanding of the situation.

王林：郑妮，你们这次旅行怎么样啊？

言外有意

Read the cultural notes below and prepare questions for further discussion with Chinese people.

1. 走马观花(zǒu mǎ guān huā)

This idiomatic expression conveys the image of riding on a horse and looking at flowers, meaning "to look at something in a cursory fashion". It is often used when complaining about trips with travel agencies. For example, in the dialogue, Zheng Ni and Zhou Danrui may comment on their trip saying 每天都赶来赶去的，到每个地方都只是走马观花地看一下, indicating their discontent with the rushed itinerary. It can also be used to describe doing something in an extremely fast and careless manner. For example, 领导下基层搞群众工作，切忌走马观花.

2. 团队游 Group tour.

Traveling in China as a foreigner can take a lot of time to plan, so sometimes it is not a bad idea to find a travel agency. One advantage of taking part in a group tour, which is called 团队游 or 跟团游 in China, is that you don't have to spend time planning the trip. Since travel agencies can usually get discounts, travel with a group might cost less than traveling by yourself. However, a disadvantage is that you will have less freedom when traveling with a group. You will have to stay with the group most of the time and follow the tour guide's arrangements. Usually the tour guide will take the group to one place, introduce the history of the place, and then leave some time for travelers to take pictures and walk around. A lot of people do not like this type of travel due to its fixed and tight schedule. Nowadays, travel agencies provide a choice called 自由行(trip with freedom), which means the agency will only help arrange your flight tickets, hotels and, sometimes, entrance tickets for sightseeing places. Take a look at this travel agency's website (Ctrip, 携程) and see if there is anything that strikes you.

第四单元 游山玩水 Sightseeing

4.2 自助游

退而求其次

🎧 **投石问路**

Listen to the five questions in the audio and answer them based on your own experience. Be ready to discuss these questions in class. You may write down some notes in the space provided below.

1.
2.
3.
4.
5.

🎧 **边听边想**

Listen to the audio and try to visualize the dialogue in your mind. Think about who the speakers are, the kind of social relationship they have, and what their intentions might be.

耳闻目睹

Listen to the audio again while following along in the printed text. As you listen, mark any place that you are unclear or have questions about.

退而求其次

人物：周丹锐、孙浩、郑妮

（在教室，孙浩和周丹锐刚做完辅导）

周丹锐：孙浩，项目结束以后我和郑妮想去西藏看看，你觉得怎么样？

孙　浩：听说现在外国人去西藏都必须参加旅行团。

周丹锐：啊？那又会被催着不停地走马观花，连个喘息的工夫都没有。这次我们想轻松自在一点儿。

孙　浩：那你们就选别的地方啊。（1/4）

周丹锐：成都怎么样？听说附近也有很多可以看到藏族文化的地方。

孙　浩：成都是休闲美食之都，你那么爱吃，那个地方一定很适合你。去之前可以先在网上搜索一些旅游攻略。

周丹锐：我想坐火车去，正好体验一下在中国坐火车的感觉。

孙　浩：可以啊，现在的火车都提速了，又快又方便。不过现在是旅游旺季，你们最好提前把火车票买好。现在提前20天就能买了。

周丹锐：是吗，我听说现在火车票都是实名制，那外国人是不是只能在火车站买票啊？

孙　浩：不用去火车站，你们住的宾馆旁边就有个票务中心，里面也代售火车票。不过你可以先在铁道部网站上查一下。（2/4）

（周丹锐打开电脑，开始上网查车票）

周丹锐：网上显示15号的硬卧已经卖完了，只有软卧和硬座票。

郑　妮：软卧多少钱？

周丹锐：软卧735块5毛，硬座只要263块5毛。

郑　妮：哇，差这么多！不过坐硬座的话会不会太难受了？

周丹锐：硬座并不硬，就是不能躺着。而且那天老师不是说没坐过硬座就不算真正体验过中国的火车吗？（3/4）

郑　妮：要坐三十多个小时呢，太受罪了吧！我们还是坐软卧吧。

周丹锐：坐软卧的钱都可以坐飞机了。

郑　妮：要不就坐飞机好了，还可以多出一天去成都周边玩玩儿。那天奕歆告诉我有一个叫"去哪儿"的网站经常可以买到很低折扣的飞机票。

周丹锐：行，那我们再查查看吧。（4/4）

知其所以然

The dialogue is broken down into sections below for explanation and analysis. Study the notes and answer the questions for the underlined text.

1/4

（在教室，孙浩和周丹锐刚做完辅导）
周丹锐：孙浩，项目结束以后我和郑妮想去西藏看看，你觉得怎么样？
孙浩：　听说现在外国人去西藏都必须参加旅行团。
周丹锐：啊？那又会被催着不停地走马观花，连个喘息的<u>工夫</u>都没有。这次我们想轻松<u>自在</u>一点儿。
孙浩：　那你们就选别的地方啊。

---

1. 周丹锐不喜欢参加旅行团，因为"连个喘息的工夫都没有"。
（1）假如你的工作特别忙，老板从来不给工作人员任何休息时间。你可以怎么跟同事抱怨？_____
（2）在对话里"工夫"可以换成"时间"吗？_____
（3）如果你看见一个人特别快就把一瓶啤酒喝完了，很惊讶，跟朋友讲这件事的时候你可以怎么说？_____

工夫（gōngfu）is a colloquial term for time, especially the time for getting something done. For example, to metaphorically describe that a person drinks up a bottle of beer in the blink of an eye, you can say 一眨眼的工夫那人就把一瓶啤酒喝完了。

喘息的工夫 is a somewhat fixed expression and it refers to the time for breathing and a short break. Note that 工夫 here has nothing to do with martial arts, which has the same pronunciation but a different written form 功夫。

连……都…… is used to emphasize a statement with a sense of surprise or complaint. Usually the item following 连 is considered to be extreme in some way. Here Zhou Danrui is emphasizing his statement 没有喘息的工夫, complaining that on a group tour they do not even have a chance to breathe and rest for a while. For example, to complain about the lack of facilities at a hotel, a Chinese person may say 那个宾馆连枕头都没有, indicating that he thinks a pillow is a basic thing for a hotel to offer. To emphasize the rudeness of a child, he may say 那个小孩连自己的妈妈都骂, indicating that he thinks the last person one should scold is his own mother. In another context, if a person is surprised at the excessive facilities at a hotel, he may say 那个宾馆的房间里连冰箱都有, indicating that he thinks having a fridge in a hotel room is a luxury.

2. 项目结束后的旅游，周丹锐他们想玩得"轻松自在一点"。

（1）上课表演对话的时候你会不会感到不自在？_____

（2）如果你的中国家庭让你自己想做什么就做什么，你会有什么样的感觉？_____

自在 means feeling comfortable about oneself and one's surroundings. The word is often used in its negative form 不自在. For example，在陌生人面前我感到不自在. The positive form of the word is often used in combination of other words，such as 舒服自在，轻松自在 and 自由自在. For example，to describe the relaxed feeling at home，you may say 在家里我可以自由自在地做想做的事情.

2/4

周丹锐：成都怎么样？听说附近也有很多可以看到藏族文化的地方。

孙浩：　成都是休闲美食之都，你那么爱吃，那个地方一定很适合你。去之前可以先在网上搜索一些旅游攻略。

周丹锐：我想坐火车去，正好体验一下在中国坐火车的感觉。

孙浩：　可以啊，现在的火车都提速了，又快又方便。不过现在是旅游旺季，你们最好提前把火车票买好。现在提前20天就能买了。

周丹锐：是吗，我听说现在火车票都是实名制，那外国人是不是只能在火车站买票啊？

孙浩：　不用去火车站，你们住的宾馆旁边就有个票务中心，里面也代售火车票。不过你可以先在铁道部网站上查一下。

---

3. 孙浩觉得去成都不错，他说："成都是休闲美食之都。"

（1）根据孙浩的意思，成都在什么方面最出名？_____

（2）美国纽约是什么之都？_____

（3）你还知道哪些被称为"……之都"的地方？_____

The structure [place] + 是……之都 can be used to emphasize a particular quality or characteristic of a place, usually what the place is known for. For example, since Chengdu enjoys the reputation of being a fun city that has delicious food, people say 成都是休闲美食之都. Similarly, since Paris is famous for fashion, people say 巴黎是时尚之都. Big cities like New York may be called 时尚之都，美食之都 or 文化之都，depending on which aspect one wants to emphasize.

Another structure [place/thing] 有……之称 has similar functions but can also be applied for things in addition to places. For example, you can say 成都有"天府之国"之称 and you can also say 橄榄油有"液体黄金"之称（Olive oil is known as liquid gold）.

4. 夏天是旅游旺季，所以孙浩建议周丹锐"最好提前把火车票买好"。

（1）在中国，提前多久可以买火车票？_____

（2）你们的安排上写了出发时间是 10：00，但是老师通知说提前一个小时出发，现在你们的出发时间是几点？＿＿＿＿＿＿＿＿＿＿＿＿＿＿＿＿
如果推迟（tuīchí）一个小时出发是几点呢？＿＿＿＿＿＿＿＿＿＿＿＿＿＿＿＿
（3）你习惯提前完成作业吗？一般提前多久呢？＿＿＿＿＿＿＿＿＿＿＿＿＿＿＿＿

提前＋[action] expresses the idea of doing something ahead of time. For example，提前买火车票，提前出发，提前完成作业. The amount of time indicating how long in advance is inserted between 提前 and the action. For example，提前 20 天买火车票；提前一个小时出发；提前多久完成作业？

3/4

（周丹锐打开电脑，开始上网查车票）
周丹锐：网上显示 15 号的硬卧已经卖完了，只有软卧和硬座票。
郑妮：　软卧多少钱？
周丹锐：软卧 735 块 5 毛，硬座只要 263 块 5 毛。
郑妮：　哇，差这么多！不过坐硬座的话会不会太难受了？
周丹锐：硬座并不硬，就是不能躺着。而且那天老师不是说没坐过硬座就不算真正体验过中国的火车吗？

5. 硬座、硬卧、软卧

When purchasing a train ticket in China, you will choose among different types of seats. When taking conventional trains, you will choose among 软卧（soft sleeper），硬卧（hard sleeper），or 硬座（hard seat）. When taking 动车（semi-high speed train, or D trains）or 高铁（high speed train, or G trains），you will have to choose among 商务座（business seat），一等座（1st class seat）or 二等座（2nd class seat）. For long-distance travel, hard-sleeper tickets are most desirable because they are relatively cheap and comfortable. Therefore, they are the most difficult tickets to obtain.

It is better to do some research online and write down the train number and ticket type before going to buy tickets at the train station or ticket office. The ticket office 票务中心，usually charges a small transaction fee（手续费 shǒuxù fèi），but many people feel it is worth to save time traveling to the station and waiting in line.

6. 周丹锐想说服郑妮坐硬座去成都，他说："没做过硬座就不算真正体验过中国的火车。"
（1）周丹锐觉得"坐硬座"和"体验中国的火车"是什么关系？＿＿＿＿＿＿＿＿＿＿
（2）下面哪两个句子跟周丹锐说的意思一样？＿＿＿＿＿＿
　　A. 只有坐过硬座才算真正体验过中国的火车。
　　B. 要体验中国的火车就必须坐硬座。

C. 即使坐过硬座也不算真正体验过中国的火车。

D. 既然坐过硬座就算真正体验过中国的火车。

(3) 你和朋友在中国旅游,你特别想去长城,但是你的朋友不想去,你可以怎么劝她跟你去长城？_____

In the dialogue, Zhou Danrui tries to persuade Zheng Ni to take the hard-seat train to Chengdu, so he cites his teacher who stated 坐过硬座 as a prerequisite for being considered 体验过中国的火车. To express a prerequisite, the teacher used the double-negation emphatic structure 没［experience 过］就不算［statement］; you may also use 只有［condition］才［intended situation］or 要［intended situation］就必须［condition］. For example, to emphasize that typical Chinese cuisine is only available in China, you may say 只有在中国才能吃到地道的中国菜 or 要想吃地道的中国菜就必须去中国.

By contrast, the sentence with the 即使［condition］也［situation unchanged］structure would denote that even if you have traveled on a hard-seat train, you still cannot say that you have had the real experience of traveling by train in China. With the 既然［fact/situation］就［conclusion］structure, Zhou Danrui would be saying, "Now that you have taken a hard-seat train, you can say that you have had the real experience of traveling by train in China."

没［experience 过］就不算［statement］is used to emphasize an experience as a crucial component of what the person is already or will be engaged in. It is usually used to persuade people to have that experience. If you want to persuade your friend to visit the Great Wall, you can say 没到过长城,就不算真正到过中国, indicating that the Great Wall is a place every tourist should visit in order to say that they have visited China.

4/4

郑妮： 要坐三十多个小时呢,太受罪了吧！我们还是坐软卧吧。

周丹锐： 坐软卧的钱都可以坐飞机了。

郑妮： 要不就坐飞机好了,还可以多出一天去成都周边玩玩儿。那天奕歆告诉我有一个叫"去哪儿"的网站经常可以买到很低折扣的飞机票。

周丹锐： 行,那我们再查查看吧。

---

7. 郑妮不想坐那么长时间的硬座,她说:"要坐三十多个小时呢,太受罪了吧!"

(1) 郑妮说"太受罪了吧",她的语气是抱怨,还是商量？_____

(2) 郑妮建议坐软卧之后,周丹锐可以怎么告诉郑妮他觉得贵？_____

(3) 假如晚上12点多的时候你的室友想给老师打电话,你觉得老师可能休息了,所以想建议他别打。你可以怎么说？_____

受罪 means to suffer punishment or hardship. Obviously in Zheng Ni's mind, taking a hard seat for more than 30 hours in a slow train can be considered a punishment of sorts.

While the structure 太 + [adj.] + 了 is used to declare how the speaker feels about something. With 吧 in the end, the structure 太 + [adj.] + 了吧 denotes a sense of negotiation similar to "Don't you think it would be too…". In the dialogue, when Zhou Danrui suggests taking a hard seat train to Chengdu, Zheng Ni expresses her concern saying 太受罪了吧! and then goes on to suggest that they take the soft sleeper. In response to Zheng Ni, Zhou Danrui could have expressed his concern, saying 太贵了吧!

8. 周丹锐觉得软卧票太贵了,不值,他说:"坐软卧的钱都可以坐飞机了。"
（1）周丹锐这么说是想强调软卧票贵,还是飞机票便宜？_____
（2）如果你同学的手机坏了,修好要花 200 块钱,你觉得不值,因为他的手机新的也只要 220 多块,你可以怎么强烈建议同学别花钱修手机？_____

[Option 1]的钱都可以[Option 2]了 is used to reject someone's proposal for Option 1 by indicating that Option 2 would be preferred for the same amount of money. For example, if repairing a phone costs ¥1,000, which is approximately the price of a new phone, you could say 修手机的钱都可以买一部新的了, implying that it is not worth the money to repair the phone.

9. 郑妮觉得坐飞机更好,因为"还可以多出一天去成都周边玩玩"。
（1）这里"成都周边"可能指什么地方？_____
　　A. 成都附近。　　　B. 成都旁边。
（2）你去上海旅游一个星期的话,除了在市中心玩,还可以去哪儿玩？
_____
（3）苏州市周边有什么有意思的地方吗？_____

[place] + 周边 refers to the surrounding area of the place, similar to [place] + 附近. However, [place/person] + 旁边 is used to specifically indicate that two items are situated one next to another. For example, to say that you would like to visit places that are close to Shanghai, you can say 我想看看上海周边的景点. By contrast, to recommend a place for your friend to visit in Suzhou, you may say 金鸡湖挺不错的,旁边还有个摩天轮,可以鸟瞰金鸡湖.

10. 郑妮提议上"去哪儿"网买飞机票,丹锐说:"那我们再查查看吧。"
（1）根据这句话,周丹锐是接受还是不接受郑妮的提议？_____
（2）假如你的朋友给你推荐一本书,你不确定能不能读懂,你可以怎么告诉你的朋友你要先看一看再决定买不买？_____
（3）如果甜品店的老板给你推荐一种蛋糕,你不确定你会不会喜欢吃,你可以怎么告诉老板你要先尝了再决定买不买？_____

The structure [verb duplication] + 看 is used to indicate that the action will be performed casually before making a decision. In the dialogue, by saying 查查看, Zhou Danrui is saying that he will check and then make the decision as to whether they will go by plane. For example, if a Chinese suggests you buy a Chinese novel, you may respond 我先读读看. Similarly, if the bakery owner recommends you a kind of cake, you can say 我先尝尝看. Depending on the context, one can also use 试试看, 问问看, 听听看.

体演文本

Review the sections of the dialogue assigned by your teacher by listening to the audio and role-playing with another Chinese speaker. Be ready to perform the assigned portion of the dialogue from memory in class.

举一反三

Answer the following questions and think about how the dialogue can be adapted for different situations.

1. "旅游攻略"可以在哪些地方找到？有哪几种？读的时候哪些信息最重要？
2. 你在中国自助游,如果时间足够,你想去哪些地方？怎么去？为什么？
3. 非常喜欢自助游的人一般被称作什么？或者他们自称什么？（有很多有意思的名字,请你查一查）
4. 为什么不坐硬座就不算真正体验过中国的火车？你觉得还有哪些活动是中国文化里特有的？

熟能生巧

Listen to the audio and perform the following drills until you feel confident with the items practiced.

☞ **Drill 1 Emphasizing a negative comment**

When asked how you feel about something, make a negative comment and emphasize that the thing in question is lacking even some basic qualities. Each of the illustrations indicates the basic quality that's lacking.

例：赶

赵奕歆：你们上个周末的团队游怎么样？
周丹锐：特别赶,连喘息的工夫都没有。

1. 差  2. 糟糕

3. 小  4. 简单

☞ Drill 2 Recommending an option

When asked for your opinion about something, recommend it and indicate that you have taken your friend's interest into account. Each of the illustrations indicates your friend's interest.

例：美食

郑妮：项目结束以后我想去中国其他地方看看，你说成都怎么样？
孙浩：你那么喜欢美食，成都一定很适合你。

1.  2. 3. 4.

☞ Drill 3 Describing an incidental opportunity

When asked about your plans after the program, share your plan and mention an incidental advantage of that plan. Each of the illustrations will indicate your plan. The incidental advantage will be the experience you can gain from implementing that plan.

例：坐火车去成都
孙浩：项目结束后，你有什么打算？
郑妮：我想坐火车去成都，正好可以体验一下在中国坐火车的感觉。

1. 去海尔公司实习
2. 去育英小学教英文
3. 跟团去云南旅游
4. 在苏州大学读研究生

☞ **Drill 4 Persuading someone by reminding them of the importance of something**

When your friend refuses to try an experience, persuade him or her to try it by reminding him or her that the experience is a crucial part of what he or she is already engaged in, which in this case, is experiencing China.

例：

郑妮：坐硬座太难受了，还是算了吧！

周丹锐：没坐过硬座，就不算真正到过中国！

1.　　　　　　2.　　　　　　3.　　　　　　4.

☞ **Drill 5 Declining a proposal**

When your friend proposes buying something, decline by indicating that there is a better option for the same amount of money. The illustrations provide you with the better options.

例：

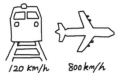

郑妮：我们坐软卧去成都吧。

周丹锐：坐软卧的钱都可以坐飞机了。

1. 　2. 　3. 　4.

Narration

1. When Zhou Danrui tells Zheng Ni that they had better go to Chengdu instead of Tibet, Zheng Ni is disappointed and wonders why. Please assume Zhou Danrui's role and tell Zheng Ni what you have learned from Sun Hao and try to convince her that Chengdu is a good alternative for Tibet.

郑妮：为什么啊？不是说好去西藏的吗？

2. When Zhou Danrui requests that Zhao Yixin book a flight for him and Zheng Ni on Qunar, Zhao Yixin wonders why they are not going to Chengdu by train as planned. Assume Zhou Danrui's role and tell Zhao Yixin how your discussion with Zheng Ni has led to the current decision.

赵奕歆：你们不是要坐火车去成都的吗？怎么改飞机了？

言外有意

Read the cultural notes below and prepare questions for further discussion with Chinese people.

1. 退而求其次(tuì ér qiú qí cì)

This idiomatic phrase is used when you have to go for a less preferred alternative. For example, in the dialogue, to visit Tibet, Zhou Danrui will have to join a tour group. Zhou Danrui does not want to go with a tour group, but he still wants to see Tibetan culture, so he chooses to go to Chengdu as an alternative. To narrate this situation, you may say 外国人去西藏必须跟团,可是周丹锐他们不想参加旅游团,所以只好退而求其次,改去成都. Similarly, Zhou Danrui really wants to take the hard-sleeper train, but there are no tickets available, so he has to choose hard seat as an alternative. To narrate this situation, Zhou Danrui may say 本来我想坐硬卧去成都,可是15号的硬卧卖完了,我只好退而求其次,买了硬座票. In another context, imagine that you want to buy a blue dress for your mom. The one that you really like in blue is sold out, but they have purple, which is your mom's second favorite color. If you decide to buy a purple dress instead, you can say 就退而求其次,买这条紫色的吧.

2. 实名制

Nowadays, the Chinese railway tickets are sold through a "real-name registration system", the so called "实名制(shímíng zhì)". Therefore, you will need to show your ID (identity) when purchasing train tickets.

3. 旅游攻略/路书/游记

When searching for travel information online, you will see these different terms. They are similar but provide slightly different information. 旅游小贴士 usually contains tips for traveling. It does not have to be destination-specific. 旅游攻略 is usually more detailed than 小贴士 and contains more specific information about a certain destination. A popular activity among Chinese young people is reading and sharing 攻略 online. 游记 usually consists of what people want to say about their trips. Its purpose is not necessarily to provide useful information for other travelers. 路书 is a new tool for creating digital 游记. This tool allows users to insert pictures, video clips, music recordings and share their travel experiences online.

4. 青年旅社

Youth hostels (青年旅社) are becoming more and more popular among young travelers in China, especially those traveling on their own or with a small group. Youth hostels are often run by locals who enjoy meeting foreigners and telling them about the local community, so talking to the youth hostel manager is a great way to find out what interesting

attractions are in the area. Hostels may even organize trips for you or help you buy discounted tickets to museums and other attractions. Since hostels in China are usually not very big, when trying to stay at a hostel, it is always better to call ahead or book a room online.

4.3 灵岩山

山不在高,有仙则名

🎧 投石问路

Listen to the five questions in the audio and answer them based on your own experience. Be ready to discuss these questions in class. You may write down some notes in the space provided below.

1.
2.
3.
4.
5.

🎧 边听边想

Listen to the audio and try to visualize the dialogue in your mind. Think about who the speakers are, the kind of social relationship they have, and what their intentions might be.

🎧 耳闻目睹

Listen to the audio again while following along in the printed text. As you listen, mark any place that you are unclear or have questions about.

山不在高，有仙则名

人物：秦老师、郑妮、导游、周丹锐、赵奕歆

（秦老师和同学们爬上了灵岩山，他们坐在山顶休息）

秦老师：这一路爬上来累坏了吧，不过我看你们体力真不错。

郑　妮：我在美国也常常去爬山。这山虽然不算太高，但风景真好！

秦老师：这就叫"山不在高，有仙则名"。

郑　妮：嗯，我终于明白这句话的意思了。一路上来都是各种形状的岩石，今天真是大饱眼福了。（1/5）

导　游：其实你说对了，灵岩山这个名字就是由山上多奇石而来的。又因为山上的石头颜色深紫，可以用来制作写书法用的砚台，从前的人将这座山命名为"砚石山"。（2/5）

周丹锐：刚才在路上听人说吴王为美女西施建造的宫殿就在这山上，是世界上最早的山上园林，这是真的吗？

导　游：对，那座宫殿叫作"馆娃宫"。据说现在的灵岩寺就是在宫殿的遗址上建的。至于这是不是最早的山上园林，学术界说法不一……（3/5）

周丹锐：马导，这些历史记载的东西你都记得住啊，也太厉害了吧。

导　游：哈哈，我可是靠这个吃饭的。好，现在我们一起进到寺庙里面去看看吧！（4/5）

（导游带着同学们来到了灵岩寺门前）

导　游：同学们，我们眼前的这座寺院就是吴中著名的灵岩寺，最初建于东晋末年，可惜原来的建筑除佛塔以外已经不存在了，现在我们看到的是清末和民国时期重建的……

郑　妮：到哪儿都有一大段讲解，我已经听不进去了。出来玩儿还跟上课一样，真累！

赵奕歆：俗话说，外行看热闹，内行看门道。如果不了解这些景点背后的故事，这些就只是普通的山水了。所以我们得争取当个内行啊！

郑　妮：我看当个外行也挺幸福的，我就坐在这井边好好享受一下这落日。

导　游：这边这口井，传说中是西施每天用来当镜子的。古人有诗云……

郑　妮：天哪，又来了……（5/5）

📖 知其所以然

The dialogue is broken down into sections below for explanation and analysis. Study

the notes and answer the questions for the underlined text.

1/5

(秦老师和同学们爬上了灵岩山,他们坐在山顶休息)

秦老师:这一路爬上来累坏了吧,不过我看你们体力真不错。

郑妮: 我在美国也常常去爬山。这山虽然不算太高,但风景真好!

秦老师:这就叫"山不在高,有仙则名"。

郑妮: 嗯,我终于明白这句话的意思了。一路上来都是各种形状的岩石,今天真是大饱眼福了。

---

1. 秦老师引用一个名句总结郑妮的看法:"这就叫'山不在高,有仙则名'。"

(1) 这句话的意思是一座山出名的主要原因是_____
   A. 它很高。   B. 风景好。

(2) 如果你问老师一个学期应该读几本书,老师说"读书不在多",她的意思是什么?_____

Chinese people often use a a famous saying to describe a situation. By quoting 山不在高,有仙则名, Miss Qin is saying that a mountain does not have to be high to be famous. For more details about the origin of this saying, you may refer to the 言外有意 section at the end of this lesson. The structure [something] + 不在 + [feature] communicates that the feature mentioned is not the most essential element of the thing under discussion. For example, a teacher may tell her students 读书不在多,而在精, indicating that reading books in large numbers is not as essential as reading books that are carefully selected. A father may tell his son, who is worried about not having as many friends as someone else, 朋友不在多,在于心, indicating that having more friends is not necessarily better and what matters is whether you treat each other sincerely.

这就叫…… is a typical pattern for introducing a Chinese idiom when making a generalization based on a few instances. If you are able to use this strategy appropriately when talking to Chinese people, you will definitely impress your Chinese interlocutors. You can always add 吧 at the end to soften the tone so that you won't sound arrogant as a foreigner.

2/5

导游:其实你说对了,灵岩山这个名字就是<u>由山上多奇石而来</u>的。又因为山上的石头颜色深紫,可以用来制作写书法用的砚台,从前的人将这座山<u>命名为"砚石山"</u>。

---

2. 导游解释"灵岩山"名字的来历说"这个名字就是由山上多奇石而来的"。

（1）根据导游的意思，灵岩山为什么叫"灵岩山"？＿＿＿＿＿＿＿＿＿＿

（2）如果你的中国朋友说他注意到明尼苏达州（Minnisota）有很多漂亮的湖，你可以怎么顺便告诉他这个州的别名"万湖之州"？＿＿＿＿＿＿＿＿＿＿

（3）如果你需要为你的大学写一篇中文简介，你怎么介绍学校名称的由来？＿＿＿＿＿＿＿＿＿＿

由……而来 is a formal way of explaining the origin of a name. Here, the tour guide is saying that the mountain is named 灵岩 after the numerous unique rocks. Alternatives of this structure include 由……而得名 or 因……而得名. Therefore, you may say 灵岩山就因山上多奇石而得名的. In a formal introduction to Standford University（斯坦福大学）, you may find 这所大学因它的创办者斯坦福夫妇而得名.

If your Chinese friend notices that there are lot of beautiful lakes in Minnesota, you may confirm his observation by saying 对，明尼苏达州就是因州内多湖泊而得名"万湖之州".

3. 导游介绍灵岩山的另一个名字："从前的人将这座山命名为'砚石山'。"
（1）这里的"将"和哪个字的用法很像？＿＿＿＿＿＿＿＿＿＿
（2）你有没有给什么东西起过名字？＿＿＿＿＿＿＿＿＿＿
（3）在给朋友介绍你的宠物狗时，可不可以说"我将它命名为小黑"？
＿＿＿＿＿＿＿＿＿＿

In this line, the expressions 从前，将，命名为 are all formal written-style expressions. Please match them with their casual or spoken-style counterparts from the right column below.

More written-style	More spoken-style
从前＿＿＿＿	A. 把
将＿＿＿＿	B. 叫作
命名为＿＿＿＿	C. 以前

If the tour guide were to rephrase this line in a casual manner, she would say 以前的人把这座山叫作"砚石山". Note that 把/将……命名为 is only used when someone officially names a place or a project. Therefore, when telling your friend your dog's name, it's more appropriate to say 我给它起名叫小黑 or simply 我叫它小黑.

3/5

周丹锐：刚才在路上听人说吴王为美女西施建造的宫殿就在这山上，是世界上最早的山上园林，这是真的吗？

导游：对，那座宫殿叫作"馆娃宫"。据说现在的灵岩寺就是在宫殿的遗址上建的。<u>至于</u>这是不是最早的山上园林，<u>学术界说法不一</u>……

4. 导游在回应周丹锐的第二个问题之前先复述了那个问题:"至于这是不是最早的山上园林……"

(1) 这里的"至于"可以换成什么别的词? ＿＿＿＿＿＿＿＿＿＿＿＿＿＿＿＿

(2) 如果你的朋友跟你说:"你就在中国工作吧,这样每天都可以吃到中国菜。"你可以怎么回答? ＿＿＿＿＿＿＿＿＿＿＿＿＿＿＿

Here, 至于 is used to introduce a topic that has been mentioned a little earlier. It can be replaced by 关于, which also indicates that "Now I am going to respond to the issue raised earlier". In the dialogue, Zhou Danrui raises a question that has two parts. After the tour guide has commented on the first part, she reintroduces the other part of the question to bring her listener's attention to her answer.

However, 至于 also differs from 关于 in that the former is usually used when you have something negative to say about the topic. For example, if your friend asks you if you would consider working in China since Chinese cuisine is so delicious, you may respond 中国菜我是很喜欢的,至于在中国工作,我倒是没考虑过, indicating that you have no interest in working in China.

5. 关于灵岩山是不是最早的山上园林,导游不能给出确定的回答,她说"学术界说法不一"。

(1) 导游接下来可能说什么? ＿＿＿＿＿＿＿＿＿＿＿＿＿＿＿＿

(2) 如果不用"说法不一",导游还可以怎么说? ＿＿＿＿＿＿＿＿＿＿＿＿＿＿＿＿

(3) 如果你和朋友一起做海报,你发现有一行里面的字有的大有的小,不好看,你可以怎么给朋友指出来? ＿＿＿＿＿＿＿＿＿＿＿＿＿＿＿＿

(4) 这里的"学术界"大概是指哪些人? ＿＿＿＿＿＿＿＿＿＿＿＿＿＿＿＿

(5) 你觉得自己算是"教育界人士"吗? ＿＿＿＿＿＿＿＿＿＿＿＿＿＿＿＿

(6) 你觉得哪些职业算是"体育界"的? ＿＿＿＿＿＿＿＿＿＿＿＿＿＿＿＿

The short phrase X 不一 is usually used to indicate a lack of consistency in terms of X, conveying a slight sense of disappointment. Following this phrase, the speaker might list a few different viewpoints. Although 不一 can be understood as 不一样 or 不同, if the tour guide had said 学术界说法各不一样 or 学术界有不同说法, the slight sense of disappointment about the lack of consistency would be lost. In other contexts, if you find that the size of some characters in one line of your friend's poster is not consistent, you may point it out by saying 这些字大小不一,不好看. In other contexts, you may encounter 长短不一 or 高矮不一.

［domain］+ 界 is a formal way to refer to a field encompassing several professions sharing some qualities or characteristics, such as 体育界, 教育界, 文艺界, 经济界, 学术界, etc. Consequently, ［domain］+ 界 + 人士 is a formal way to refer to people working in a specified field.

4/5

周丹锐： 马导,这些历史记载的东西你都记得住啊,也太厉害了吧。

导游： 哈哈,我可是靠这个吃饭的。好,现在我们一起进到寺庙里面去看看吧!

---

6. 周丹锐称赞了导游,导游幽默地回答:"我可是靠这个吃饭的。"

(1) "这个"指的是什么? ＿＿＿＿＿＿＿＿＿＿＿

(2) 这里的"吃饭"是指吃东西吗? ＿＿＿＿＿＿＿＿＿＿＿

(3) 如果你是作家,你可以说"我是靠＿＿＿＿吃饭的"。

靠……吃饭 is a colloquial way to tell people how one makes a living. It conveys a slight sense of humor. Usually, what can be inserted in this structure is someone's special trait or a distinct feature of an occupation. For example, 这个 in the dialogue refers to the tour guide's ability to memorize classic poems. For another example, a professional writer may say 我是靠写文章吃饭的 or 我是靠编故事吃饭的.

5/5

(导游带着同学们来到了灵岩寺门前)

导游： 同学们,我们眼前的这座寺院就是吴中著名的灵岩寺,最初建于东晋末年,可惜原来的建筑除佛塔以外已经不存在了,现在我们看到的是清末和民国时期重建的……

郑妮： 到哪儿都有一大段讲解,我已经听不进去了。出来玩儿还跟上课一样,真累!

赵奕歆： 俗话说,外行看热闹,内行看门道。如果不了解这些景点背后的故事,这些就只是普通的山水了。所以我们得争取当个内行啊!

郑妮： 我看当个外行也挺幸福的,我就坐在这井边好好享受一下这落日。

导游： 这边这口井,传说中是西施每天用来当镜子的。古人有诗云……

郑妮： 天哪,又来了……

---

7. 赵奕歆用一句俗话暗示郑妮听讲解的好处:"俗话说,外行看热闹,内行看门道。"

(1) 你知道哪些中文里的"俗话"? ＿＿＿＿＿＿＿＿＿＿＿

(2) 下面几句俗话可以在什么情况下引用? ＿＿＿＿

  A. 没有规矩,不成方圆。 B. 善有善报,恶有恶报。

俗话说 is used to make reference to a Chinese proverb or saying before using it to make a point about the situation. For example, if you are told a story in which an evil person was punished, you can start your comment by saying 俗话说,善有善报,恶有恶报,

and then elaborate on your point.

　　(3) 在这里,"外行"和"内行"分别指什么样的人? _____
　　(4) 你觉得自己在哪个方面是内行? _____
　　(5) "门道"在这里指的是什么? _____
　　(6) 你喜欢看热闹吗？怎么样算"看热闹"? _____

This is a widely used idiom in Chinese. 内行(nèiháng) and 外行(wàiháng) respectively refer to someone who is familiar with something and someone who is not. You can imagine that 内行 is someone who is "in" the field, whereas 外行 is "out of" the field. In the dialogue, 内行 refers to the people who know the background information about the scenic spots. 看热闹 refers to looking at something without any background knowledge about it, while 看门道 refers to having a more informed view of something.

　　8. 赵奕歆开玩笑说尽量多了解景点背后的故事:"我们得争取当个内行啊!"

争取(zhēngqǔ) + [situation] is used to encourage a person (including oneself) to try one's best to bring about a desirable situation. Here, Zhao Yixin encourages Zheng Ni to learn more about the places and become a 内行. In another context, if your friend asks you when you will finish a project, you may respond 争取今年之内做完, indicating that you will try your best to finish it by the end of this year.

体演文本

Review the sections of the dialogue assigned by your teacher by listening to the audio and role-playing with another Chinese speaker. Be ready to perform the assigned portion of the dialogue from memory in class.

举一反三

Answer the following questions and think about how the dialogue can be adapted for different situations.

　　1. 课文说中国人很喜欢引用诗文。你有什么例子吗?
　　2. 你爬过的哪些山给你"山不在高,有仙则名"的感觉?还有什么好的表达可以形容登山的感觉?
　　3. 你去过中国的寺庙吗?参观时候有什么要注意的?你觉得参观寺庙最有意思的是什么?
　　4. "外行看热闹,内行看门道",你同意吗?你在哪些方面是外行?哪些方面是内行?
　　5. 你觉得对话里的导游讲解的怎么样?在旅游时,你希望听导游介绍什么?

🎧 熟能生巧

Listen to the audio and perform the following drills until you feel confident with the items practiced.

☞ **Drill 1 Looking on the bright side**

When your teacher expresses concern that you may have a negative experience, acknowledge the difficulty, but mention that the negative impact is trumped by a positive aspect. Conclude your response with 还是挺值的 to reassure your teacher that you think the experience is worthwhile. The cues provide you with the positive aspects of the experience.

例：看到了好的风景

老师：这一路爬上来累坏了吧。

郑妮：累是有点累，但是看到了这么好的风景，还是挺值的。

1. 看了很多有名的景点
2. 认识了很多中国朋友
3. 学到了很多新东西
4. 中文水平提高了很多

☞ **Drill 2 Explaining the origin of a term**

When "tested" by a Chinese friend about the cultural origin of a certain term, explain it with the help of the cue.

例：山上多奇石

赵奕歆：你知道这座山为什么叫灵岩山吗？

周丹锐：这个名字是由山上多奇石而来的。

1. 邵逸夫先生
2. "仙灵所隐"的说法
3. 苏东坡
4. "日月光华，旦复旦兮"

☞ **Drill 3 Responding to a disputed issue**

When asked to give a definitive answer to a certain question, respond in a formal tone that the issue under discussion is currently under dispute.

例：

朋友："馆娃宫"是世界上最早的山上园林吗？

周丹锐：很难说，大家对"馆娃宫"是不是最早的山上园林还说法不一。

1.　　　　　　2.　　　　　　3.　　　　　　4.

☞ Drill 4 Summarizing with a Chinese idiom or a famous saying

When your friend mentions a situation, summarize it by referring to a Chinese idiom or a famous saying. Below is a list of idioms or famous sayings for you to select from. In the example, Zheng Ni selects "E. 山不在高,有仙则名" to summarize Zhou Danrui's comment about 灵岩山.

A. 自己动手,丰衣足食
B. 雪中送炭
C. 民以食为天
D. 熟能生巧
E. 山不在高,有仙则名

例:
周丹锐:这山虽然不算太高,但风景真好!
郑妮:这就叫"山不在高,有仙则名"。
1.　　　　　　2.　　　　　　3.　　　　　　4.

☞ Drill 5 Supporting your point with an idiom or famous saying

When your friend expresses confusion or a complaint about something, explain the rationale for doing it and support your point with an idiom or a famous saying. The cues provide you with idioms or famous sayings you may refer to, but it is up to you to elaborate on your point. In the following example, in response to Zheng Ni's complaint about having to listen to the tour guide's explanation, Zhao Yixin quoted 外行看热闹,内行看门道 and elaborated by talking about the importance of knowing the stories about places.

例:外行看热闹,内行看门道
郑妮:在中国旅游,到哪儿都有一大段讲解,真累。
赵奕歆:俗话说"外行看热闹,内行看门道"(如果不了解景点背后的故事,这些就只是普通的山水了)。

1. 货比三家不吃亏
2. 没有规矩,不成方圆
3. 礼轻情义重
4. 熟能生巧

Narration

Narrate an experience from its bright side. On the top of Mount Lingyan, Miss Qin is making a small talk with Zhou Danrui. Assume the role of Zhou Danrui and respond to Miss

Qin positively by telling her what you have learned from the trip to Mount Lingyan.

秦老师：怎么样，爬山累不累？

言外有意

Read the cultural notes below and prepare questions for further discussion with Chinese people.

1. 山不在高，有仙则名（shān bú zài gāo, yǒu xiān zé míng）

山不在高，有仙则名；水不在深，有龙则灵 is a famous quote from Liu Yuxi's（刘禹锡）"Inscription on My Simple Cottage（《陋室铭》）". What he is saying is that a famous mountain does not have to be high. As long as a fairy resides in it, it will be famous. A famous stream does not have to be deep. As long as a dragon resides in it, it will be famous. Following these lines, the author says 斯是陋室，唯吾德馨（This is a humble cottage. My virtue is what makes it not humble）.

2. 写山赞美山的诗歌传统

Chinese poetry often describes mountains and landscapes. Many lines from these poems are well-known and often quoted by Chinese people. For example, 一览众山小 is originally from a poem by Du Fu（杜甫）, who was one of the most famous poets in the Tang Dynasty. Du Fu used this line to describe his feeling after climbing Mount Tai: every other mountain seems to be small when you are on the top of Mount Tai. People now often quote this line to express the feeling of being on the top of a tall mountain. A lot of tall mountains in China have specific poems associated with them. For example, when people climb Mount Lu, they will likely quote the line 不识庐山真面目，只缘身在此山中 to describe its mystical scene. This is a line composed by the famous poet Su Shi（苏轼，1037–1101）. For smaller mountains, you can always quote Liu Yuxi's line.

3. 参观寺庙的禁忌和习惯

Temples, just like churches in Western countries, are everywhere in China. Some temples are Buddhist, and others are Taoist. People are expected not to talk loudly or wear revealing clothing when going to temples. Also, since monks are usually vegetarian, it is not polite to bring meat into the temple. Some religious practices in the temples might appear strange to you, but it is better to address the questions to your Chinese friends or teachers. If you are not a believer, you are not expected to participate in the religious practices. But if you want to participate and you are not absolutely sure about what to do, don't try without observing what the locals do!

学而时习之

Before you actually do the field performances, rehearse doing them with a Chinese friend. The "Useful Expressions" box below provides you with some expressions you may use for these performances. For now, try saying them after the audio.

Useful Expressions

1. 项目结束后我想去中国其他地方看看,你觉得去哪儿比较好?
2. 自助游太麻烦了,我在考虑要不要参加一个旅行团。
3. 你觉得在中国哪个旅行社比较好?
4. 你们跟旅游经纪人谈的时候一般要问些什么问题?
5. 我从来没有参加过旅行社组织的团队游。
6. 上次我们全家去欧洲旅游是找旅行社安排的,不过路线是我们自己定的。
7. 在中国,你可不可能只让旅行社安排交通和酒店,到一个地方以后自己旅游?
8. 请问你们有没有周末去黄山的旅游团?
9. 我喜欢玩得轻松自在一点的,不喜欢赶来赶去。
10. 这样的团一般是多少人?
11. 团费一个人多少钱?团费包括些什么?含不含餐费?含不含保险费?
12. 这个团有没有安排购物?
13. 一般是星期几发团?
14. 决定参团的话,要提前多久报名?
15. 报名的时候需要些什么材料?
16. 我跟几个同学一起参团的话还能有优惠吗?
17. 你能不能给我一份行程和报价,我跟同学商量一下再来报名?
18. 请问还有没有19号去成都的硬卧票?
19. 请问哪趟车最快?到成都大约要多长时间?
20. 快车和普通车的票价相差多少?上铺和中铺的票价相差多少?
21. (买快车和普通车的车票)手续费是一样的吗?

Make it a habit to carry a notebook with you and take notes on your interactions with Chinese people.

☞ Performance 1 Talking about trips

Have a conversation with a Chinese friend about traveling in China.

____ Act 1: Explain that you are interested in traveling to other places in China.

____ Act 2: Ask your friend for recommendations.

_____ Act 3: Request your friend to share personal travel experiences.

_____ Act 4: Ask about your friend's opinion of traveling with groups arranged by travel agencies.

_____ Act 5: Ask if your friend recommends any good travel agencies/websites.

_____ Act 6: Ask if your friend has tips for negotiating with a travel agent.

_____ Act 7: Share your experiences of traveling in other countries.

☞ Performance 2 Consulting a travel agent

Visit a travel agency and consult an agent about a group tour you are interested in.

_____ Act 1: Describe your purpose of visit.

_____ Act 2: Describe the type of tours you are looking for and ask for recommendations.

_____ Act 3: Ask about the average size of the groups.

_____ Act 4: Select an option and request a quote.

_____ Act 5: Ask what the fee covers (e. g., transportation, lodging, meals, admissions, insurance, etc.).

_____ Act 6: Ask about group discounts.

_____ Act 7: Ask about frequency of departures.

_____ Act 8: Ask about signup procedures.

_____ Act 9: Explain that you need to discuss it with your friend before you book the trip.

☞ Performance 3 Purchasing train tickets

Visit a railway ticket office and purchase train tickets for an upcoming trip.

_____ Act 1: Tell the ticket agent your destination, date of travel and number of tickets you want to buy.

_____ Act 2: Ask about the available types of trains and seats.

_____ Act 3: Request a comparison of the prices of different types of trains and seats.

_____ Act 4: Ask if any transaction fee is involved and how much it is.

_____ Act 5: Conclude the conversation.

☞ Performance 4 Talking with tourists

Visit a local tourist attraction (e. g., a temple, a historical site, a scenic spot, etc.) and engage in small talk with Chinese tourists to learn about why they are visiting that place, how they like the place, whether they are traveling with a travel agency and how they enjoy their trips so far.

Suggested acts? Come on! You know how to strike up a conversation with a stranger!

第五单元 解决问题 Solving Problems

5.1 钱包丢了

吃一堑，长一智

投石问路

Listen to the five questions in the audio and answer them based on your own experience. Be ready to discuss these questions in class. You may write down some notes in the space provided below.

1.
2.
3.
4.
5.

边听边想

Listen to the audio and try to visualize the dialogue in your mind. Think about who the speakers are, the kind of social relationship they have, and what their intentions might be.

耳闻目睹

Listen to the audio again while following along in the printed text. As you listen, mark any place that you are unclear or have questions about.

吃一堑，长一智

人物：周丹锐、秦老师、孙浩、出租车公司接线员

（孙浩和周丹锐刚买完东西回来，来到了秦老师的办公室）

周丹锐：秦老师，这些是活动部为周五的文化沙龙准备的零食，可以先放你这里吗？

秦老师：可以。一共多少钱？发票给我吧。

周丹锐：好的。（掏裤兜）哎呀，我钱包不会丢了吧？

秦老师：别着急，好好想想，你是不是放在别的地方了？

周丹锐：我身上没有别的口袋了。奇怪，我上车的时候钱包还在的。

孙　浩：会不会落出租车上了？钱包放裤子口袋里坐车的时候很容易滑出来的。

秦老师：下车的时候跟司机要发票了吗？得赶紧给出租车公司打电话联系司机。

孙　浩：发票在我这里，我来打电话吧。

周丹锐：我自己打吧，谁让我自己丢三落四的呢？(1/3)

（周丹锐给出租车公司打电话）

接线员：您好，强生出租车服务中心。

周丹锐：你好，我是苏州大学的留学生，刚才不小心把钱包落在你们公司的出租车上了，能不能麻烦你帮我联系一下司机？

接线员：好的。请问您有没有那辆出租车的车牌号？

周丹锐：有，是苏 E9527。

接线员：请您说一下具体的上车时间、地点和下车地点。

周丹锐：就是刚才。我大概两点半上车，从印象城坐到苏州大学本部校区。(2/3)

接线员：好的。您稍等，马上帮您联系司机。请您留个联系电话。

周丹锐：好，我的手机号码是 1836-622-1864。

接线员：请问是 183-6622-1864 吗？

周丹锐：对。

接线员：好的，先生怎么称呼呢？

周丹锐：哦，我姓周。

接线员：好的，周先生，您别着急。我们一有消息就会马上通知您的。

周丹锐：好的，谢谢。(3/3)

知其所以然

The dialogue is broken down into sections below for explanation and analysis. Study the notes and answer the questions for the underlined text.

1/3

（孙浩和周丹锐刚买完东西回来，来到了秦老师的办公室）

周丹锐：秦老师，这些是活动部为周五的文化沙龙准备的零食，可以先放你这里吗？

秦老师：可以。一共多少钱？发票给我吧。

周丹锐：好的。（掏裤兜）哎呀，我钱包不会丢了吧？

秦老师：别着急，好好想想，你是不是放在别的地方了？

周丹锐：我身上没别的口袋了。奇怪，我上车的时候钱包还在的。

孙　浩：会不会<u>落</u>出租车上了？钱包放裤子口袋里<u>坐车</u>的时候很容易滑出来的。

秦老师：下车的时候跟司机<u>要</u>发票了吗？得赶紧给出租车公司打电话联系司机。

孙　浩：发票在我这里，我来打电话吧。

周丹锐：我自己打吧，谁让我自己<u>丢三落四</u>的呢？

---

1. 周丹锐找不到钱包，孙浩提醒他：" 会不会落出租车上了？"

(1) 这里"落"怎么读？

　　A. là　　　　　　　B. luò

(2) 这里"落"可以换成下面哪个词？

　　A. 掉　　　　　　　B. 放　　　　　　　C. 滑

(3) 在宾馆退房的时候你想起来自己的手机还在房间里。你可以怎么跟朋友说？_____

(4) 你有把东西落在出租车上的经历吗？找回来了吗？_____

落（là）means to leave something behind unintentionally. It is often used in this pattern：把 + something + 落（在）+ place, as in 把手套落在公共汽车上了. Depending on the context, 掉 or 忘 can be used in place of 落 in this pattern. In the dialogue, since Zhou Danrui is not aware of leaving his wallet on the taxi, 掉 is a better alternative. In another context, as you and your friend are checking out at hotel, you realize that your cell phone is still in the hotel room, you may tell your friend 我把手机落在房间里了 or 我把手机忘在房间里了.

落 may also be pronounced as "luò", meaning to fall or descend. It can describe concrete objects, such as falling leaves 落叶 or the descent of an airplane 飞机降落, as well as abstractions such as responsibilities that fall on someone, e.g., 父母去世之后,照顾弟弟妹妹的重任就落在她身上了.

2. 秦老师给周丹锐出主意,她说:"得赶紧给出租车公司打电话联系司机。"
(1) 秦老师建议周丹锐怎么做?为什么要"赶紧"打电话?＿＿＿＿＿＿＿＿＿＿
(2) 如果你的同学突然生病了,你可以给他什么样的建议?＿＿＿＿＿＿＿＿＿＿
(3) 请选择合适的两个选项:
"请你＿＿＿＿＿＿把材料送来,有急用。"
A. 赶紧　　　　　　B. 赶忙　　　　　　C. 赶快

赶紧 means "quickly" and is used to describe doing something in a hurry. It is often used in an imperative sentence, to urge someone to act quickly. For example, a boss who wants a secretary to hurry and bring the documents can say 请你赶快把材料送来, or 请你赶紧把材料送来. In this case, 赶紧 can be used interchangeably with 赶快. Although 赶忙 also means "quickly" it can only be used to describe an action not to give a command or suggestion. Therefore, 赶忙 is seldom used following the pronoun 你.

3. 周丹锐决定自己来打电话,说:"谁让我自己丢三落四的呢?"
(1) 周丹锐说自己总是丢三落四,什么样的行为会被认为是丢三落四?你是一个丢三落四的人吗?＿＿＿＿＿＿＿＿＿＿＿＿＿＿＿＿＿＿＿
(2) 在对话里,除了说自己丢三落四以外,周丹锐还可以怎么说来表示类似的意思?

＿＿＿＿＿＿＿＿＿＿＿＿＿＿＿＿＿

This phrase describes someone who is absent-minded, often leaving things behind. Another common phrase to describe this kind of person is 马大哈. You can say 他做事总是不仔细,所以大家都叫他"马大哈" or 小李是个马大哈,这种事千万别交给他. While 丢三落四 usually specifically describes a person who fails to keep track of one's belongings, 马大哈 describes a more general personality trait in which someone has difficulty keeping track of more than just his/her belongings.

2/3

(周丹锐给出租车公司打电话)
接线员:您好,强生出租车服务中心。
周丹锐:你好,我是苏州大学的留学生,刚才不小心把钱包落在你们公司的出租车上了,能不能麻烦你帮我联系一下司机?
接线员:好的。请问您有没有那辆出租车的车牌号?

> 周丹锐：有，是苏 E9527。
> 接线员：请您说一下具体的上车时间、地点和下车地点。
> 周丹锐：就是刚才。我大概两点半上车，从印象城坐到苏州大学本部校区。

4. 周丹锐跟接线员说明打车的时间，他说："就是刚才。"

（1）如果周丹锐不说"就是刚才"，直接说"大概两点半上车"，表达的意思有什么不同？＿＿＿＿＿＿＿＿＿＿＿＿＿＿＿

（2）在去书店的路上，你的朋友问你要去买什么书，你可以怎么告诉他你要买的是刘老师推荐给你们俩的小说？＿＿＿＿＿＿＿＿＿＿＿＿＿

就是 is generally used to emphasize the information provided in response to an inquiry. In the dialogue, 就是刚才 is used to emphasize the immediate nature of the incident. In another context, when your classmate asks what book you are buying, to tell him that it is the book that your teacher recommended to the class earlier, you can say 就是上次刘老师推荐给我们的那本小说. Here, 就是 is used to connect the book in question with the one Miss Liu recommended. Here, it emphasizes that both speakers know the instance that Miss Liu recommended the book.

> **3/3**
> 接线员：好的。您稍等，马上帮您联系司机。请您留个联系电话。
> 周丹锐：好，我的手机号码是1836－622－1864。
> 接线员：请问是183－6622－1864吗？
> 周丹锐：对。
> 接线员：好的，先生怎么称呼呢？
> 周丹锐：哦，我姓周。
> 接线员：好的，周先生，您别着急。我们一有消息就会马上通知您的。
> 周丹锐：好的，谢谢。

5. 接线员向周丹锐询问个人信息："先生怎么称呼呢？"

（1）如果你不知道一个人的名字，你可以怎么礼貌地问他？＿＿＿＿＿＿＿

（2）"你叫什么名字"和"请问您怎么称呼"这两个问题有什么区别？应该怎么回答？＿＿＿＿＿＿＿＿＿＿＿＿

您怎么称呼 is a polite way to collect information about someone's name, similar to 您贵姓. Therefore, one could just respond with his or her last name, like Zhou Danrui says in the dialogue. The inquirer can then address the person by X 先生 or X 女士. They can also address the person using their official title like X 老师 based on the context. However, in a context where the speaker has no idea about the person's name or title and wants to know how the other person prefers to be addressed, 怎么称呼 is a more appropriate way of asking. For example, when picked up by a friend's friend at the airport, a Chinese visitor may ask that person 不好意思,请问我应该怎么称呼您? The person's response is likely to be 我姓周,你叫我小周就行 if the person is much younger than the visitor. If this is an elder person, he may respond 我姓周,你叫我周伯伯吧, indicating a sense of intimacy. Note that in the response, 叫 is used in the place of 称呼. 叫 is the informal counterpart of 称呼. Therefore, 你叫什么名字 is a casual way to ask a person's name and its response has to be one's full name or given name. In formal contexts, Chinese people generally consider it impolite to directly ask a person's full name or given name. This is why 请问您贵姓 and 请问您怎么称呼 are recommended.

体演文本

Review the sections of the dialogue assigned by your teacher by listening to the audio and role playing with another Chinese speaker. Be ready to perform the assigned portion of the dialogue from memory in class.

举一反三

Answer the following questions and think about how the dialogue can be adapted for different situations.

1. 如果周丹锐忘了拿发票,那他还能用什么办法找回钱包呢?
2. 你认为周丹锐为什么要自己给出租车公司打电话,不要孙浩帮忙?
3. 如果司机把钱包送回来了,周丹锐应该怎么感谢他? 在中国一般怎么感谢司机的这种行为?

熟能生巧

Listen to the audio and perform the following drills until you feel confident with the items practiced.

☞ **Drill 1 Predicting an unpleasant possibility**

When someone encounters a problem, such as when valuable things are missing, others may offer an explanation that tries to account for the situation. When Zhou Danrui discovers that his wallet is missing, Sun Hao suggests what may have happened in a way that shows his solidarity with and concern for his friend. Listen to the example and then respond to the situations you hear about using a similar approach. Each of the illustrations below shows the undesirable situation you think might have happened.

例:

周丹锐:(掏裤兜)钱包怎么找不到了。
赵奕歆:你的钱包不会丢了吧?

1. 　　2. 　　3. 　　4.

☞ **Drill 2　Comforting someone by proposing an alternative possibility**

When a friend suspects something unfortunate has happened, comfort him/her by proposing a positive possibility. In the example, when Zhou Danrui finds that he lost his wallet, Miss Qin comforts him and points out that maybe he left the wallet in a certain place.

例: 放在别的地方
周丹锐: 哎呀,我钱包不会丢了吧?
秦老师: 别着急,你是不是放在别的地方了?

1. 放在别的地方
2. 没电
3. 放在别的包里
4. 忘在房间里

☞ **Drill 3　Declining one's offer to help**

When your friend offers to help you do something, politely refuse by taking responsibility for the problem.

例:
赵奕歆: 你钱包是不是落出租车上了? 我帮你打电话问出租车公司吧。
周丹锐: 我自己打吧,谁让我自己落出租车上的呢。

1.　　　　2.　　　　3.　　　　4.

☞ **Drill 4　Retrieving a lost item**

Imagine that you accidentally left something in a public place and have gone back to retrieve it. When asked, explain what happened and request help from staff working there looking for your lost item. Each of the illustrations below shows what and where your lost item is.

例：

接线员：有什么事儿吗？

周丹锐：刚才不小心把钱包落在你们的出租车上了，能不能麻烦你帮我看一下。

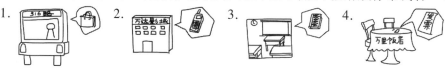

☞ **Drill 5 Reassuring by promising to notify someone as soon as information is available**

Imagine that you are a phone receptionist talking to a customer who is anxious to have his/her concern addressed as soon as possible. Reassure the customer by promising to contact him/her with information as soon as it is available.

例：

顾客：什么时候能有消息？

接线员：别着急，我们一有消息就会马上通知你的。

1.   2.   3.   4.

Narration

Zhou Danrui lost his wallet and was trying to get it back by calling the taxi company. Zhao Yixin heard about the incident and asked if he already got it back. Assume the role of Zhou Danrui and tell Zhao Yixin the story of how you lost your wallet and the effort you have made to get it back.

赵奕歆：丹锐，我听说你的钱包丢了？怎么回事儿啊，找回来了吗？

言外有意

Read the cultural notes below and prepare questions for further discussion with Chinese people.

1. 吃一堑，长一智（chī yī qiàn, zhǎng yī zhì）Learn from one's mistakes.

The idiom 吃一堑，长一智 is used to comfort a person who has just experienced a failure or a loss due to a mistake he or she made. In the dialogue of this lesson, Zhou Danrui put his wallet into his pant pocket, which caused him to lose it in the taxi （吃了一堑）. After this experience, he will not do that again because he has learned a lesson （长

了一智). In this context, Zhou Danrui could say 哎,吃一堑,长一智吧 to Miss Qin and Sun Hao to let them know that he is fine and will just take this as a lesson. On the other hand, if Zhou Danrui appears to be very upset, Miss Qin and Sun Hao can say the same to Zhou Danrui, encouraging him to view this as a learning experience.

2. 中国汽车牌照知多少 Facts about Chinese vehicle plates.

The taxi Zhou Danrui took has the plate number 苏 E9527. Chinese people who see this plate number can easily tell this car is from Jiangsu Province because of the character 苏, which represents 江苏省. Each province in China has its own single-character abbreviation, which is used on vehicle license plates. For example, 沪 is used for Shanghai while 浙 is used for Zhejiang Province. The selection and arrangement of letters and numbers on a license plate can also indicate which part of the province the vehicle is from and whether it is privately owned. As with cell phone numbers, certain numbers on a license plates are considered more auspicious than others. Purchasing a license plate with more 8s or 6s will cost more.

5.2 咨询前台

宾至如归

投石问路

Listen to the five questions in the audio and answer them based on your own experience. Be ready to discuss these questions in class. You may write down some notes in the space provided below.

1.
2.
3.
4.
5.

边听边想

Listen to the audio and try to visualize the dialogue in your mind. Think about who the speakers are, the kind of social relationship they have, and what their intentions might be.

🎧 耳闻目睹

Listen to the audio again while following along in the printed text. As you listen, mark any place that you are unclear or have questions about.

宾至如归
人物：郑妮、赵奕歆、前台服务员

（下课了，郑妮和赵奕歆在宿舍的房间里）

郑妮：　怎么还是连不上网啊？

赵奕歆：你们的网老这样吗？

郑妮：　也不是，平时就是速度比较慢，没有像今天这样彻底连不上。

赵奕歆：会不会是你们房间的端口出了什么问题？要不你给前台打个电话问一下。

郑妮：　也好，正好我还要问问收包裹的事。(1/4)

（郑妮给前台打电话）

郑妮　　你好。我是216房间的郑妮。我们房间的网络今天老是连不上，你知道是怎么回事吗？

服务员：是这样的，我们的服务器今天出了一点故障，技术人员正在抢修，估计下午四点以前就能恢复正常了。

郑妮：　噢，就是说现在楼里面哪里都连不上网吗？

服务员：对。你要是着急上网的话可以去图书馆。(2/4)

郑妮：　倒也没那么急。对了，顺便问一下，如果有人给我寄包裹的话，包裹是会送到前台吗？

服务员：这个要看是什么样的包裹了。如果是快递的话，他们会给你打电话，你要是不在，我们可以帮你签收。如果走的是邮局的话，你就得自己去邮政营业厅取。

郑妮：　哦，那邮政营业厅远吗？

服务员：不远，十梓街上就有。

郑妮：　好的，谢谢。

服务员：不用客气。(3/4)

（郑妮挂了电话）

赵奕歆：你家人要给你寄包裹吗？

郑妮：　不是，我打算在网上买一些书。

赵奕歆：噢，网购的东西一般都是走快递。

郑妮：　为什么？邮局不比快递公司便宜吗？

赵奕歆：寄平信或者明信片之类的是邮局比较便宜，但寄包裹还是走快递更划

算,又快又方便。打个电话他们就会上门来取。(4/4)

知其所以然

The dialogue is broken down into sections below for explanation and analysis. Study the notes and answer the questions for the underlined text.

1/4

(下课了,郑妮和赵奕歆在宿舍的房间里)

郑妮：　　怎么还是连不上网啊?

赵奕歆：你们的网老这样吗?

郑妮：　　也不是,平时就是速度比较慢,没有像今天这样彻底连不上。

赵奕歆：会不会是你们房间的端口出了什么问题? 要不你给前台打个电话问一下。

郑妮：　　也好,正好我还要问问收包裹的事。

---

1. 郑妮抱怨宾馆的网络:"怎么还是连不上网啊?"
(1) 这里的"连不上网"可以换成别的词吗? ＿＿＿＿＿＿＿＿＿＿＿＿＿＿＿
(2) 如果你在星巴克学习,想用他们的WiFi却用不了,你可以怎么问服务员?
＿＿＿＿＿＿＿＿＿＿＿＿＿＿＿＿＿
(3) "我今天连不上网"和"我今天上不了网"这两个意思有区别吗?
＿＿＿＿＿＿＿＿＿＿＿＿＿＿＿＿＿

The phrase 连(得)上/连不上 indicates whether a certain service, usually network-related, is usable. In the dialogue, Zheng Ni complains that she cannot use the Internet service. Similarly, when you are unable to connect to WiFi at a coffee shop, you can ask the staff 我怎么连不上WiFi 啊?

上不了网 also indicates the inability to use the Internet, however the reasons for this can be more varied than connectivity issues. For example, if someone does not have time to get on the Internet, he or she may say 今天我太忙了,上不了网.

2. 赵奕歆让郑妮给前台打个电话,郑妮说:"也好,正好我还要问问收包裹的事。"
(1) 为什么郑妮不直接说"好",而要说"也好"? ＿＿＿＿＿＿＿＿＿＿＿＿＿＿＿
(2) 如果你的朋友办了一个派对,可是要去的人不多,他说"人少点也好,不用做太多准备",这个"也好"表示怎样的心情? ＿＿＿＿＿＿＿＿＿＿＿＿＿＿＿
(3) "中国也好,美国也好,都面临着环境问题。"如果不用"也好",还可以怎么说? ＿＿＿＿＿＿＿＿＿＿＿＿＿＿＿

In the dialogue, 也好 denotes that Zheng Ni finds Zhao Yixin's suggestion a good idea. It indicates the realization of a positive benefit to some aspect of the situation and can be used to reassure oneself or someone else when something undesirable happens. For example, your friend, who does not get a lot of RSVPs to the party he is hosting, might reassure himself saying 人少点儿也好,不用做太多准备. The pattern X 也好, Y 也好……can be understood as "no matter X or Y…". Thus an alternative way to say 中国也好,美国也好,都面临着环境问题 is 不管中国还是美国,都面临着环境问题。

2/4

(郑妮给前台打电话)
郑妮： 你好。我是 216 房间的郑妮。我们房间的网络今天老是连不上,你知道是怎么回事吗?
服务员：是这样的,我们的服务器今天出了一点故障,技术人员正在抢修,估计下午四点以前就能恢复正常了。
郑妮： 噢,就是说现在楼里面哪里都连不上网吗?
服务员：对。你要是着急上网的话可以去图书馆。

---

3. 服务员向郑妮解释网络问题:"我们的服务器今天出了一点故障。"
(1) 这里的"故障"可以用下面哪两个词替换?
　　A. 问题　　　　　　B. 事故　　　　　　C. 毛病
(2) 如果你的朋友说"我的车出了点故障",那他的车可能怎么了?
_____
(3) 如果你的朋友说"我的车出了点事故",那他的车可能怎么了?
_____

　　In this context 故障 can be replaced by 问题 and 毛病 with slightly different connotations. 问题 is a very general term that covers all kinds of problems. 毛病 can be used in more casual situations to describe a small mechanical problem.
　　事故 is different as it refers to an external accident while 故障 denotes an internal problem which may or may not have caused an accident. For example, if a car has engine problems (发动机坏了), one can say 我的车出了点故障. If the car was rear-ended (车尾被撞了), one should say 我的车出了点事故.

4. 服务员解释现在的情况:"技术人员正在抢修。"
(1) "抢修"和"维修"有什么区别?_____
(2) 你看到新闻里说"市民抢购打折家电",这是什么意思?_____
(3) 在什么场合会看到人们进行"抢答"?_____
　　抢 in 抢修 denotes that the action is done in a hurry. In the dialogue, the technicians are trying to fix the Internet as soon as possible. The hotel receptionist's use of 抢修 instead of 维修 emphasizes the urgency with which the repair is being conducted. Similarly, 抢购

in 市民抢购打折家电 indicates that everyone is trying to buy the electrical appliances as soon as possible before they run out. You might hear 抢答 used on a quiz show（智力竞赛）when contestants are instructed to respond as quickly as possible.

5. 服务员告诉郑妮网络什么时候能修好："估计下午四点以前就能恢复正常了。"
   (1) 这里的"估计"可以换成"大概"吗？_____
   (2) 如果朋友问你身上的衣服多少钱，你只记得是100块左右，可以怎么说？
      A. 估计100块吧。　　　　B. 大概100块吧。
   (3) "我估计明天她不会来"和"我猜她明天不会来"有什么区别吗？
   _____

Here, both 大概 and 估计 can be used to make a reasonable guess, especially on the development of something in the future. For example, to predict that it's going to rain tomorrow, you can say 明天大概会下雨 or 明天估计会下雨. 大概 can also be used to indicate approximation. For example, when you can't recall the exact amount you paid for a shirt, you can say 大概100块吧. By contrast, to estimate the price of a shirt your friend presents to you, you say 估计要100块吧. 估计 indicates an informed guess, whereas 猜 can be used for either informed or wild guesses.

> **3/4**
>
> 郑妮：　倒也没那么急。对了，顺便问一下，如果有人给我寄包裹的话，包裹是会送到前台吗？
> 服务员：这个要看是什么样的包裹了。如果是快递的话，他们会给你打电话，你要是不在，我们可以帮你签收。如果走的是邮局的话，你就得自己去邮政营业厅取。
> 郑妮：　哦，那邮政营业厅远吗？
> 服务员：不远，十梓街上就有。
> 郑妮：　好的，谢谢。
> 服务员：不用客气。

6. 赵奕歆想顺便问一下收包裹的事情，她说："对了……"
   (1) 赵奕歆说"对了"的意思是什么？_____
   (2) 如果在这儿不说"对了"，还能怎么说？_____

In English, we use "by the way" to change the topic. In Chinese, 对了 serves the same function. This function of 对了 is not difficult to understand when Chinese people say it, but developing the habit of using it in your own speech may take time and practice. Your speech will sound more natural as you employ this common use of 对了 to change a topic. In many cases, Chinese speakers add a rising tone 诶（éi）before 对了 or just simply say 诶(éi) to indicate the change of the topic.

7. 服务员向郑妮解释包裹的事情:"如果走的是邮局的话……"
(1) 如果这里不用"走"的话还可以用什么词? _____
(2) 如果你的同学向你咨询寄包裹应该走快递还是走邮局,你可以怎么回答? _____
(3) 如果你听到别人说"这次准备走川藏线去西藏",那这个人是准备徒步去西藏吗? _____

You should already be familiar with the literal meaning of 走 (to walk). Here we introduce the metaphoric use of 走, which denotes the path of a certain action. Therefore, 走 in 这次准备走川藏线去西藏 indicates one's choice of route to Tibet rather than suggesting that he will walk all the way to Tibet. Similarly, 走邮局 is a colloquial way of indicating the choice of delivery service such as 邮局 and 快递. You can also say 用邮局, which is not as casual.

To compare delivery services, you may say 走快递比走邮局快 or 走邮局比走快递便宜. Note that although optional in this phrase, 的是 can affect the word order. Compare 他准备走川藏线去西藏 with 他去西藏走的是川藏线.

4/4

(郑妮挂了电话)
赵奕歆: 你家人要给你寄包裹吗?
郑妮: 　不是,我打算在网上买一些书。
赵奕歆: 噢,网购的东西一般都是走快递。
郑妮: 　为什么? 邮局不比快递公司便宜吗?
赵奕歆: 寄平信或者明信片之类的是邮局比较便宜,但寄包裹还是走快递更划算,又快又方便。打个电话他们就会上门来取。

---

8. 赵奕歆告诉郑妮网购的邮寄方式:"网购的东西一般都是走快递。"
(1) "网购"是通过什么买东西? _____
(2) 如果你经常通过邮局买东西,你可以怎么告诉别人这一点? _____
(3) 你听说过"代购"吗? 是什么意思呢? _____

This short phrase X 购 refers to the venue of buying something. The character 购 is a formal one denoting "buy" which you may have already encountered in 购物. 网购 refers to buying something through the Internet, 邮购 mail orders, and 代购 refers to purchases made through other people who have access to the goods. For example, to buy goods that are only sold in America, people in China have to use 代购 and pay the extra service fees (代购费).

体演文本

Review the sections of the dialogue assigned by your teacher by listening to the audio and role-playing with another Chinese speaker. Be ready to perform the assigned portion of the dialogue from memory in class.

举一反三

Answer the following questions and think about how the dialogue can be adapted for different situations.

1. 如果郑妮真的急着要用网络,而图书馆因为是周末也关门了,她还可以怎样跟酒店交涉让他们帮她解决问题？

2. 想象一下,如果那个酒店前台服务员的态度很冷淡,只是告诉你"网络有故障,什么时候修好还不知道",那你可以怎样跟她交涉以保证自己的权益？

熟能生巧

Listen to the audio and perform the following drills until you feel confident with the items practiced.

☞ **Drill 1 Contrasting typical and atypical situations**

When asked if a characteristic is typical of someone or something, explain that though the tendency does exist, it is usually not as bad as what the speaker has observed. For example, when Zhao Yixin asks whether the Internet at the hotel frequently has connectivity issues, Zheng Ni replies that although the connection speed is often very slow, she's always been able to connect. Each of the cues below indicates the characteristic that is typical of the person or situation.

例：网络/速度慢

赵奕歆：你们的网老是连不上吗？

周丹锐：平时就是速度比较慢,没有像今天这么彻底连不上。

1. 小李/话少
2. 马克/写作业粗心
3. 阅读作业/文章难
4. 饭店服务/上菜慢

☞ **Drill 2 Confirming the extent of a problem**

Each of the cues below indicates a problem with your hotel room which you have just reported to the front desk. Upon hearing the hotel receptionist's explanation, confirm your understanding of the extent of the problem. For example, when the hotel receptionist tells

Zheng Ni that the network connection in the building is down, Zheng Ni confirms whether this means there is no access to the Internet anywhere in the building.

例：

服务员：我们的网络服务器今天出了一些故障，现在正在抢修。

郑妮：噢，就是说现在楼里哪里都连不上网吗？

☞ Drill 3 Transiting to another question

After hearing the hotel receptionist accept your thanks for answering your first question, smoothly transit to your next question you have regarding the hotel facilities or services. The illustrations below indicate the services you want to ask about.

例：

前台：不客气。还有什么需要帮助的吗？

郑妮：对了，顺便问一下，酒店能代收包裹吗？

☞ Drill 4 Describing alternatives

Each of the illustrations below shows two alternatives that differ in price or time. When your friend Zheng Ni asks about local conditions, describe the two possible scenarios for the situation she is inquiring about. For example, when Zheng Ni asks how she can receive a package, the hotel receptionist explains that it depends on how the package is sent and describes two common scenarios.

例：

郑妮：别人给我寄了包裹，一般在哪里取？

服务员：这个要看是怎么寄的了。走邮局的话你要自己去邮局取，走快递的话他们会给你送过来。

Narration

After Zheng Ni calls the front desk about the broken WiFi, she runs into Zhou Danrui in the hotel hallway who is on his way to talk to the front desk about the broken WiFi. Assume Zheng Ni's role and tell Zhou Danrui what you have learned from the front desk about the situation of the hotel WiFi.

周丹锐：今天房间里一直连不上网，我都约好了跟我朋友视频的。我得去问问到底怎么回事儿！

言外有意

Read the cultural notes below and prepare questions for further discussion with Chinese people.

1. 宾至如归（bīn zhì rú guī）To make visitors feel at home.

This idiom is used in relatively formal contexts, such as giving instructions about hosting guests. For example, a hotel manager may tell his or her employees 我们的服务一定要给客人宾至如归的感觉。If you want to introduce a nice hotel to your friends, you can say 那个宾馆的工作人员特别友好，真的给人一种宾至如归的感觉。If you pay close attention, you may see signs with this idiom in restaurants and hotels.

2. 中国邮政与快递公司

China Post, 中国邮政, a government-owned enterprise, is the official postal service of China. Before the emergence of privately-owned express delivery companies, it was the only postal service available in China. Nowadays, Chinese people still use China Post's services to send regular letters, official documents, non-urgent packages or international packages. However, for urgent domestic packages and online products, people rely heavily on privately-owned delivery companies due to the lower price and high efficiency. Some of the commonly used delivery companies in China include 顺丰，申通，圆通，韵达。To use their services to send a package, all you need to do is give them a call, and they will usually come and pick up the package within hours.

Here are some expressions you will need for using the post office or delivery companies：

- 这个明信片寄平信的话大概几天可以到美国？
  How long does it take to send this postcard to America as a regular mail?

- 这个包裹寄海运和空运邮资差多少？

What is the price difference between sending this package by sea and by air?

- 我的运单号是47810340，可是不知道为什么在网上追踪不到我的包裹。

My tracking number 47810340, but for some reason I can't locate my package on the website.

5.3 空调病

寻医问药

投石问路

Listen to the five questions in the audio and answer them based on your own experience. Be ready to discuss these questions in class. You may write down some notes in the space provided below.

1.
2.
3.
4.
5.

边听边想

Listen to the audio and try to visualize the dialogue in your mind. Think about who the speakers are, the kind of social relationship they have, and what their intentions might be.

🎧 耳闻目睹

Listen to the audio again while following along in the printed text. As you listen, mark any place that you are unclear or have questions about.

寻医问药

人物：秦老师、郑妮、赵奕歆、医生

（早上，秦老师在房间接电话）

秦老师：喂？

郑　妮：秦老师，我是郑妮。我身体有点不舒服，今天上午的课能不能跟您请个假？

秦老师：你哪里不舒服？

郑　妮：我的头很晕，肚子很疼，感觉全身没有力气。

秦老师：怎么会这样？你现在在房间吧？我马上过来看看。

郑　妮：嗯。(1/5)

（两分钟后，秦老师到了郑妮的房间。郑妮开门）

郑　妮：秦老师好。

秦老师：你们的空调开得这么低啊！量体温了吗？

郑　妮：（递给老师体温计）这是我刚才量的……

秦老师：（读体温计）三十七度八，有点发烧。你咳嗽或者流鼻涕吗？

郑　妮：都没有。不过，昨天夜里吐了，还拉了几次肚子。

秦老师：吃药了吗？

郑　妮：吃了从美国带来的治拉肚子的药，但还是很难受。

秦老师：那去医院看看吧。(2/5)

（赵奕歆和郑妮在苏大附属医院一层大厅）

郑　妮：头晕、拉肚子应该看什么科啊？

赵奕歆：应该是内科。我们先去那边挂号。(3/5)

（15分钟后，郑妮在苏大附属医院普内一科诊室看医生，赵奕歆在旁边）

医　生：（对赵奕歆说）她这个啊，是空调病。

郑　妮：啊？空调病？

医　生：夏天得这病的人很多，不是大问题。长时间在空调房里呆着，空气不流通，或者睡觉时空调开得太低都可能导致你这些症状。(4/5)

郑　妮：那我还用打针吃药吗？

医　生：我给你开三天的消炎药和藿香正气胶囊，你按说明书上的要求吃就可以了。来，拿好这个单子，先去楼下交费，然后去药房取药。

赵奕歆：除了吃药以外还要注意什么吗？

医生： 天气热,别贪凉。房间里空调别开得太低,特别是晚上睡觉的时候,白天也别低于26度。另外,平时房间里要多通通风。少吃油腻辛辣的东西,多喝水。

郑妮： 好的,谢谢大夫。(5/5)

知其所以然

The dialogue is broken down into sections below for explanation and analysis. Study the notes and answer the questions for the underlined text.

1/5

(早上,秦老师在房间接电话)

秦老师：喂?

郑妮： 秦老师,我是郑妮。我身体有点不舒服,今天上午的课能不能跟您请个假?

秦老师：你哪里不舒服?

郑妮： 我的头很晕,肚子很疼,感觉全身没有力气。

秦老师：怎么会这样?你现在在房间吧?我马上过来看看。

郑妮： 嗯。

1. 秦老师听说郑妮身体不舒服,她说:"怎么会这样?"

(1) 秦老师问"怎么会这样",说明她对郑妮说的情况感到_____
   A. 怀疑。　　　　　B. 惊讶。

(2) 你听说中国和美国要打仗了,听到时会有怎样的反应?
   A. 怎么可能。　　　B. 怎么会这样。

(3) 你听说同学因为食物中毒去医院了,听到时会是怎样的反应?
   A. 怎么可能。　　　B. 怎么会这样。

When Chinese people hear bad news, 怎么会这样 and 怎么可能 are two natural responses. 怎么会这样 conveys surprise and concern and is used if you believe what you have heard is true. 怎么可能, on the other hand, shows dubiousness. It is used when you doubt the veracity of what you've heard. Therefore, depending on how much you believe the statements in (2) and (3), both answers are possible. Given that war between China and the US is unlikely, most people would respond with 怎么可能. The case of a classmate suffering from food poisoning, however, might elicit the more sympathetic response 怎么会这样.

> **2/5**
> （两分钟后，秦老师到了郑妮的房间。郑妮开门）
> 郑妮： 秦老师好。
> 秦老师：你们的空调开得这么低啊！量体温了吗？
> 郑妮： （递给老师体温计）这是我刚才量的……
> 秦老师：（读体温计）<u>三十七度八</u>，有点发烧。你咳嗽或者流鼻涕吗？
> 郑妮： 都没有。不过，<u>昨天夜里吐了，还拉了几次肚子</u>。
> 秦老师：吃药了吗？
> 郑妮： 吃了从美国带来的治拉肚子的药，但还是很难受。
> 秦老师：那去医院看看吧。

2. 秦老师看了看郑妮的体温计，她说："三十七度八。"
（1）这里的"三十七度八"应该是摄氏还是华氏？＿＿＿＿＿＿＿＿＿＿＿＿
（2）如果你量体温时显示的温度是 36.5，应该怎么读？这算发烧吗？
＿＿＿＿＿＿＿＿＿＿＿＿
（3）如果今天的气温是 36.5，应该怎么读？＿＿＿＿＿＿＿＿＿＿＿＿

Air and body temperatures that involve a decimal point are read differently. The number 36.5 on a thermometer is read as 三十六度五 when referring to body temperature and is read as 三十六点五度 when referring to air temperature. Both temperatures are expressed in Celsius. Normal body temperature averages around 37℃. A temperature above 38℃ is considered a fever.

3. 郑妮给秦老师描述自己的症状，她说："昨天夜里吐了，还拉了几次肚子。"
（1）感冒一般会有什么样的症状？＿＿＿＿＿＿＿＿＿＿＿＿
（2）过敏一般会有什么样的症状？＿＿＿＿＿＿＿＿＿＿＿＿
（3）如果你搬重物的时候，不小心腰受伤了，可以怎么跟医生说？
＿＿＿＿＿＿＿＿＿＿＿＿

When you see a doctor, you'll need to be able to describe your symptoms and discuss the cause of the problem. The chart below lists some common symptoms.

发烧	fever	咳嗽	cough
流鼻涕	runny nose	喉咙痛	sore throat
头痛	headache	胃痛	stomachache
拉肚子	diarrhea	吐	to vomit
浑身发痒	to itch all over	喘不上气	to have trouble breathing

续表

烫伤	to be burned	骨折	to have a broken bone
肿了	to be swollen	晕倒/头晕	to faint/to feel dizzy
扭	to sprain	闪	to strain (a muscle)

3/5
（赵奕歆和郑妮在苏大附属医院一层大厅）
郑妮： 头晕、拉肚子应该看什么科啊？
赵奕歆：应该是内科。我们先去那边挂号。

4. 郑妮询问赵奕歆应该看什么科，她说："头晕、拉肚子应该看什么科啊？"
赵奕歆说应该看内科，她说："我们先去那边挂号。"
(1) 在中国上医院看病第一步要做什么？_____
(2) 这里的"看"是什么意思？_____
(3) 这里的"看"还可以换成什么词？_____
(4) 如果你的同学骨折了，你陪他去医院，挂号时应该跟工作人员说什么？
_____

In China the first step toward diagnosis and treatment of any medical condition, mild or serious, is to go to a hospital or clinic to be examined by a doctor. Instead of making an appointment in advance, patients register upon arrival and are treated on a first-come first-served basis unless it is a medical emergency. Patients enter the hospital via its outpatient unit（门诊）or its emergency room（急诊）. To register（挂号）one must pay a fee and specify which category of medicine the condition falls under. The table below identifies some common terms for medical departments in a Chinese hospital：

内科	Internal Medicine	骨科	Orthopedics
外科	Surgery	神经科	Neurology
五官科	Eye, Ear, Nose & Throat	皮肤科	Dermatology

看 X 科（or 挂 X 科）is used when patients register at a hospital to indicate which department of medicine they wish to go to. Thus, to register for Orthopedics, you can tell the person at the registration window 我要看骨科 or 我要挂骨科. In the case of an acute illness, you should register for the ER by saying 我要挂急诊.

> **4/5**
>
> (15分钟后,郑妮在苏大附属医院普内一科诊室看医生,赵奕歆在旁边)
>
> 医生:(对赵奕歆说)她这个啊,是空调病。
>
> 郑妮: 啊?空调病?
>
> 医生: 夏天得这病的人很多,不是大问题。长时间在空调房里呆着,<u>空气不流通</u>,或者睡觉时空调开得太低都可能<u>导致你这些症状</u>。

5. 医生说得空调病的一个原因是"空气不流通"。
   (1) 你知道怎样可以保证空气流通吗? _____
   (2) 新闻里常常说"要促进商品流通",这是什么意思? _____
   (3) 把美元带到中国来算是"货币流通"吗? _____

In this phrase, 流通 can be understood as "flow". Thus, people usually open windows to ensure the flow of air. This word is also widely used in business to describe some abstract concepts, e.g., 商品流通 and 货币流通. Note that 商品流通 does not necessarily denote that commodities are shipped back and forth. Rather, it describes the constant trade of commodities. Similarly, simply bringing US dollars to China is not counted as 货币流通, but exchanging them for RMB and spending the money is.

6. 医生还列举了很多会导致空调病的原因,说:"……都可能导致你这些症状。"
   (1) 这里的"导致"还可以换成什么词吗? _____
   (2) 一位医生给病人解释缺乏运动的后果之一是肥胖,他可以怎么说?
   _____
   (3) 如果你的朋友问你你中文进步的原因,你可以怎么说? _____

Both 导致 and 造成 can be used to indicate the production of an undesirable outcome. For example, to explain that lack of exercises may cause obesity, one may say 缺乏运动会导致肥胖.

To express that something leads to positive results, you may use 有助于 or simply 让. For example, to say that watching news in Chinese leads to improvement in Chinese language ability, you could say 多看新闻有助于我的中文进步 or 多看新闻让我的中文有了很大进步.

> **5/5**
>
> 郑妮: 那我还用打针吃药吗?
>
> 医生: 我给你开三天的消炎药和藿香正气胶囊,你按说明书上的要求吃就可以了。来,拿好这个单子,先去楼下交费,然后去药房取药。
>
> 赵奕歆: 除了吃药以外还要注意什么吗?

> 医生：天气热,别贪凉。房间里空调别开得太低,特别是晚上睡觉的时候,白天也别低于26度。另外,平时房间里要多通通风。少吃油腻辛辣的东西,多喝水。
> 郑妮：好的,谢谢大夫。

7. 医生告诉郑妮一些注意事项,他说："天气热,别贪凉。"
（1）医生说"别贪凉"是让郑妮别做什么事？_____
（2）如果你的朋友经常因为乱吃东西而拉肚子,你可以怎么劝他别这样？
_____
（3）你听到别人劝你的朋友别"贪杯",这大概是什么意思？_____

Since 贪 denotes "to be greedy", the phrase 贪 X describes someone who does something excessively, often resulting in negative consequences. For example, 贪凉 refers to someone who goes to extremes to stay cool. The choice of words which can combine with 贪 are fixed by convention. For example, if someone often gets sick because he eats too much, his parent or close friend may admonish him by saying 别贪吃 or 别贪嘴. If someone drinks too much, you can say 别贪杯.

体演文本

Review the sections of the dialogue assigned by your teacher by listening to the audio and role-playing with another Chinese speaker. Be ready to perform the assigned portion of the dialogue from memory in class.

举一反三

Answer the following questions and think about how the dialogue can be adapted for different situations.

1. 在你的国家和在中国看医生有什么区别吗？请你说出其中最主要的三个。
2. 如果一个中国大夫告诉你少吃油腻辛辣的东西,多喝热水,别把空调开得太低,等等,你会听他的话吗？为什么？
3. 你在苏州有没有去看过医生？你的经历怎么样？

熟能生巧

Listen to the audio and perform the following drills until you feel confident with the items practiced.

☞ Drill 1 Describing symptoms to a doctor

Imagine that you need to see a doctor. When the doctor asks how you are feeling, describe your symptoms as indicated by illustrations below.

例：

医生：你哪里不舒服？
郑妮：我吐得很厉害，还有些头晕。

1.  2.   3.  4.

☞ **Drill 2 Asking for sick leave**

Imagine that you are feeling very sick and are not able to attend class this morning. Call your teacher to ask permission for skipping the activity scheduled for the morning. The cue indicates the activity you want to skip and the illustration indicates your major symptom.

例：课

秦老师：有事儿吗？
郑妮：老师，我今天不太舒服，烧得很厉害，今天上午的课能不能跟您请个假？

1. 讨论会  2. 文化沙龙

3. 社区活动   4. 比赛

☞ **Drill 3 Registering at the hospital**

Imagine you are registering at a hospital. State your illness and ask the nurse under which department you should register. The illustrations indicate your symptoms.

例：

护士：挂什么科？
郑妮：拉肚子应该挂什么科啊？
护士：内科。

1. 2. 3. 4.

☞ Drill 4 Asking for additional advice on how to keep healthy

After the doctor gives you his instructions for treating your illness, ask if there is anything else you should pay attention to in order to facilitate recovery. The illustrations below show the doctor's initial instructions.

例：

医生：你要按时吃药。
郑妮：除了吃药以外还要注意什么吗？

1. 2. 3. 4.

Narration

The next day, Zheng Ni meets her Chinese friend Sun Hao, who is concerned about her sickness. Assume Zheng Ni's role, reassure him that you feel much better and tell him your experience of getting sick and seeing a doctor.

孙浩：听说你昨天生病了，现在好点了吗？

📖 言外有意

Read the cultural notes below and prepare questions for further discussion with Chinese people.

1. 寻医问药 (xún yī wèn yào) Look for good doctors and medicines.

寻医问药 is not included as an item in a traditional idiom dictionary, but it has been used in written Chinese as an idiom. There is a website in China called 寻医问药网. Can you guess what the function of that website is?

2. 在中国看病的流程

Visiting a doctor in a Chinese hospital is not a simple task, but knowing what to expect can help you feel more prepared to handle it. Although the process may vary depending on the hospital and the nature of your illness, the following steps outline the general process.

Step 1 挂号 Registration

You will need to present identification, such as a passport, when you register. At the registration window, you will be asked to specify which department you need to visit. If you are not sure, you can ask. The basic registration fee is usually around ￥20, but it can cost up to ￥300 to see certain specialists. After submitting your registration form, you will be given a piece of paper telling you which room to go to, a card containing your personal information, and a blank booklet for recording your medical records. If you're not sure which wing or floor of the hospital to go to find the doctor you've been assigned, ask for directions before you leave the registration desk.

Step 2 看门诊 See a doctor

Sometimes there is a machine outside the doctor's office which is used to log into the system. Insert your card into the machine to claim your place in line and wait for your name to be called. Most young doctors can speak English. Writing down your symptoms or the tests you think you may need can help facilitate communication.

Step 3 打印病历 Print medical records

If your doctor writes medical records in the blank booklet, you can skip this step. Otherwise, ask the doctor where to print the records.

Step 4 付费 Pay for the examination/medicine

If no further tests are needed, proceed to the payment window. Present your card and medical records or booklet at the payment window and pay for the examination. Then proceed to Step 6. If further tests were required before the doctor could make a diagnosis and prescribe treatment, proceed to Step 5.

Step 5 检查 Medical tests

Proceed to the testing station and show the technician your evidence of payment. After completing the test, take the results back to the doctor. (Typical wait time for a blood test is 20-30 minutes.) After the doctor has reviewed the results of your tests, you will receive a diagnosis and prescription. If these are not written in your booklet, ask where to go to print your medical records.

Step 6 付费取药 Pay for the medication and get your medication from the pharmacy

The pharmacy is usually near the registration window. Show your evidence of payment and collect your medicine. If you cannot figure out how to take the medicine, go back to the doctor to ask for clarification. Make sure you have your passport and all your medical records before you leave the hospital.

3. 中国医生的常见建议

The doctors you see in China, regardless of where they have received their professional training, are likely to give you some suggestions that are based on traditional Chinese medicine. One important idea in Chinese medicine is 长期调理, translated as long-term recuperation, which is concerned with the patient's daily routine. For example, in our dialogue, the doctor suggested that Zheng Ni circulate the air in her room, set the air conditioner at a moderate temperature, avoid spicy or greasy food, and drink more hot water. These are the most common suggestions a Chinese doctor will give to a patient, especially for colds or stomach issues. Some doctors might also give you some suggestions that you have never heard of, such as drinking ginger soup. When this happens, show your respect for the suggestions and decide later if you want to try them or not.

学而时习之

Before you actually do the field performances, rehearse doing them with a Chinese friend. The "Useful Expressions" box below provides you with some expressions you may use for these performances. For now, try saying them after the audio.

> **Useful Expressions**
> 1. 你好！是第四教室楼管师傅吗？
> 2. 我是俄州大暑期班的学生，就在第四教室上课。
> 3. 冯院长让我打电话过来报修。
> 4. 教室里的空调突然不好用了/停电了/一直连不上网。
> 5. 能尽快请人来看看吗？
> 6. 预计多长时间能修好？
> 7. 最快什么时候能来修一下？
> 8. 你知道还有别的网络能临时用一下吗？
> 9. 能不能麻烦你帮我……
> 10. 方便留个您的电话吗？
> 11. 我想咨询一下看病的流程。
> 12. 我需不需要验血？/ 需要打针吗？
> 13. 挂完号是不是直接去三楼内科？
> 14. 请问在哪儿交费取药？
> 15. 这附近有没有比较好的药房？

Make it a habit to carry a notebook with you and take notes on your interactions with Chinese people.

☞ Performance 1 Reporting a problem over the phone

Call any of these persons to report a problem, such as the malfunction of certain facilities, and seek solutions: 1) a person at the front desk of your hotel, 2) a maintenance person on campus, or 3) a campus guard.

_____ Act 1: Greet and confirm that you have reached the right person.

_____ Act 2: Introduce who you are (and where you found the person's contact information).

_____ Act 3: Report what the problem is and how it consequently affects you.

_____ Act 4: Ask if a solution can be provided and how long it will take to solve the problem.

_____ Act 5: If it's an emergency, ask what's the earliest time someone can start working on it.

_____ Act 6: Ask if there's a backup plan.

_____ Act 7: Confirm that the person has the crucial information (e.g. the name of the building with electronic shortage).

_____ Act 8: Express your gratitude.

☞ **Performance 2 Requiring service (lost items/locked door)**

Talk to any of these person to require a certain service you need, for example, to retrieve a lost item or to open a locked door: 1) a person at the front desk of your hotel, 2) a maintenance person on campus, or 3) a campus guard.

_____ Act 1: Greet and introduce yourself to the person.

_____ Act 2: Explain the problem you need assistance with.

_____ Act 3: Request service from the person.

_____ Act 4: Provide additional information needed (e.g. when, where and what you lost).

_____ Act 5: If your request can't be attended to immediately, ask when the service will be provided.

_____ Act 6: Exchange contact information for future updates.

_____ Act 7: Express your gratitude.

☞ **Performance 3 Visiting a Chinese hospital**

Go to a general hospital and collect information at the information desk about the general procedures of seeing a doctor in China.

_____ Act 1: State that you have some questions about the procedures of seeing a doctor.

_____ Act 2: Describe your symptoms and ask what department you need to visit.

_____ Act 3: Ask if you will need medical tests (e.g., blood test).

_____ Act 4: Ask about the price for registration.

_____ Act 5: State your assumptions about the procedures (e.g., where to go after registration) and seek confirmation.

_____ Act 6: Ask where to pay for the examination/medication and where the pharmacy is.

_____ Act 7: Ask for a recommendation of a nearby pharmacy.

第六单元 社会活动 Social Engagements

6.1 到社区去

一回生，两回熟

投石问路

Listen to the five questions in the audio and answer them based on your own experience. Be ready to discuss these questions in class. You may write down some notes in the space provided below.

1.
2.
3.
4.
5.

边听边想

Listen to the audio and try to visualize the dialogue in your mind. Think about who the speakers are, the kind of social relationship they have, and what their intentions might be.

🎧 耳闻目睹

Listen to the audio again while following along in the printed text. As you listen, mark any place that you are unclear or have questions about.

一回生，两回熟
人物：秦老师、王主任、郑妮、李阿姨、周丹锐、孙大爷

（大家刚参观了龙桥社区，现在在社区的活动室跟居民代表联谊）

秦老师：同学们，这位是龙桥社区的王主任。感谢王主任帮助我们组织今天的活动，下面我们欢迎王主任给我们介绍社区的情况。

王主任：好的。大家好，首先欢迎美国朋友们来到我们龙桥社区。我们这个小区呢现有常住人口7000多人，1500多户……大家刚才走进来的时候看到的就是我们的居民楼，这里呢是我们社区的活动室，居民经常会在这里搞一些社区活动，具体的我就不多说了，接下来的时间呢美国朋友们可以直接跟我们的居民代表交流一下……（1/4）

（郑妮旁边的阿姨招呼郑妮）

李阿姨：姑娘，来这边坐。

郑妮：哎，阿姨好。

李阿姨：来，来，吃桔子。小姑娘你是美国来的吧？跟你商量点事儿啊，阿姨想请你周末来给我儿子辅导辅导英语。他快高考了，英语成绩啊不太跟得上……

郑妮：是这样的，阿姨，我愿意是愿意，但是我们这个项目有特别多社会服务还有文化活动，都安排在周末，恐怕……

李阿姨：不用每周都来，你什么时候有空来就行了。

郑妮：要不然我留一个电子邮箱给您吧，如果您儿子有问题可以给我写邮件。

李阿姨：噢，噢，那也好……（2/4）

（15分钟过去了，大家在为表演做准备，周丹锐在调吉他）

孙大爷：小伙子，弹吉他啊。

周丹锐：诶，大爷您好！

孙大爷：我年轻的时候也经常拉拉二胡，搞搞乐器什么的。

周丹锐：那太好了，我对中国的民族乐器也很感兴趣，您坐您坐。大爷，贵姓啊？

孙大爷：免贵姓孙。（3/4）

周丹锐：噢，孙大爷！我叫周丹锐，丹青的丹，精锐的锐。您今年多大岁数了？

孙大爷：我72了。

周丹锐：一点都不像啊，我看您也就60岁左右。

孙大爷：哈哈，真会说话！我呢，平常喜欢运动，身板硬朗得很呢。

周丹锐：我等会要表演个节目，得抓紧时间把吉他调一下，您帮我先听听。
孙大爷：好啊！(4/4)

知其所以然

The dialogue is broken down into sections below for explanation and analysis. Study the notes and answer the questions for the underlined text.

1/4

（大家刚参观了龙桥社区，现在在社区的活动室跟居民代表联谊）

秦老师：同学们，这位是龙桥社区的王主任。感谢王主任帮助我们组织今天的活动，下面我们欢迎王主任给我们介绍社区的情况。

王主任：好的。大家好，首先欢迎美国朋友们来到我们龙桥社区。我们这个小区呢现有常住人口 7000 多人，1500 多户……大家刚才走进来的时候看到的就是我们的居民楼，这里呢是我们社区的活动室，居民经常会在这里搞一些社区活动，具体的我<u>就</u>不多说了，接下来的时间呢美国朋友们可以直接跟我们的居民代表交流一下……

---

1. 王主任介绍完社区的大概情况，他说："具体的我就不多说了。"
(1) 王主任为什么不继续说具体的情况？_____
(2) 如果你在做口头报告的时候，来不及仔细报告一些具体细节，可以怎么说？
_____
(3) 上课发言的时候，如果不想重复别人已经说过的，你可以怎么提出自己的看法？_____

Here, 就 is used to indicate a natural consequence under certain circumstance or condition. Having introduced the general information about the community, Director Wang wants to save the time for the local residents and the American students to communicate individually. In another context, if you don't have enough time to give details in your presentation, you can explicitly say 由于时间关系，具体的我就不多说了. During a class discussion, to avoid repeating the points that has been brought up, you can begin with 刚才大家说过的我就不多说了 and then make a transition to express your own idea.

2/4

（郑妮旁边的阿姨招呼郑妮）

李阿姨：姑娘，来这边坐。

郑妮：　哎，阿姨好。

> 李阿姨：来,来,吃桔子。小姑娘你是美国来的吧? <u>跟你商量点事儿啊</u>,阿姨想请你周末来给我儿子辅导辅导英语。他快高考了,英语成绩啊不太跟得上……
>
> 郑妮： <u>是这样的</u>,阿姨,我愿意是愿意,但是我们这个项目有特别多社会服务还有文化活动,都安排在周末,恐怕……
>
> 李阿姨：不用每周都来,你什么时候有空来就行了。
>
> 郑妮： <u>要不然</u>我留一个电子邮箱给您吧,如果您儿子有问题可以给我写邮件。
>
> 李阿姨：噢,噢,那也好……

2. 社区的李阿姨想让郑妮帮个忙,她说:"跟你商量点事儿啊。"

(1) 李阿姨说她的请求以前,为什么先说"跟你商量点事儿啊"? _____

(2) 如果你下课后想跟朋友一起去吃饭,会不会说"跟你商量点事儿啊,我们一起去吃饭吧"? _____

(3) 如果你身体不舒服想跟老师请假,可不可以跟老师说:"跟您商量点事儿啊,我今天可以请假吗?" _____

(4) 这里的"商量"可以换成"说"吗? 为什么? _____

跟你商量点事儿 is used when you want to make a request which would require quite some effort from the interlocutor. This colloquial phrase softens the tone, making the request less abrupt. It is often used between people of roughly the same social status, but is rarely used when talking with someone of a higher status. This phrase would not be used either when proposing to eat together with a friend, since eating a meal together is not a difficult request. When you want to make a request of a teacher or superior, address him or her first and then say 有件事情想跟您商量一下 instead of 跟你商量点事儿.

跟你说点事儿 carries a quite different meaning, indicating that one is about to give information, rather than making a request.

3. 郑妮委婉地拒绝李阿姨,她说:"是这样的……"

(1) 郑妮说了"是这样的"之后做了什么? _____

(2) 如果你的客户想让你帮他一个忙,可是这违反了公司规定,你可以怎么拒绝? _____

When offering a reason for making a refusal, 是这样的 can be used to soften the tone, followed by the explanation that the decision is out of one's control. For example, a client is asking for a favor which is against the rules. To politely refuse the client, you can start by saying 是这样的,李总。我很愿意帮你,但是…… and continue to give the reason.

第六单元　社会活动 Social Engagements

Generally speaking, this phrase is only used as a response to a rather serious or formal request.

4. 郑妮解释说项目里有很多活动,她说:"文化活动都安排在周末,恐怕……"
（1）郑妮在"恐怕"后面可能会说什么？_____
（2）为什么郑妮不把话说完？_____
（3）如果你被朋友邀请去参加他的生日宴会,可是你有别的安排,你怎么回答比较好？
　　A. 我大概去不了。　　　　　B. 我恐怕去不了。
（4）"恐怕晚上没时间吃饭了"和"我怕晚上没时间吃饭"意思上有什么区别吗？
_____

恐怕 is often used to indicate potential difficulty or trouble. When offering a reason for a refusal, you can just say 恐怕 to indicate the difficulty in accepting the request and your interlocutor should be able to understand your meaning. If you are talking with someone you are unfamiliar with, this strategy could cause embarrassment. Compared with 大概, 恐怕 denotes that you are unable to do something, although you are willing to. Both 恐怕 and 我怕 can be translated as "I'm afraid that", but 我怕 shows more of a genuine concern, whereas 恐怕 is more of a speculation based on the current situation.

5. 郑妮提出了别的解决方法,她说:"要不然我留一个电子邮箱给您吧。"
（1）"要不然"还可以用什么词代替？_____
（2）如果你和朋友准备去看电影,你想星期五去,可是你的朋友星期五有事,你可以怎么说？_____
（3）如果你作业没有及时做完,老师下课后跟你说:"明天一定要把作业交给我,要不然……"你觉得他可能想说什么？_____

要不然 is often used in negotiation. When one option is considered impossible, one can use 要不然 to raise another option, which is usually not as good as the previous one, but more applicable. As Zheng Ni says here, although it is impossible for her to tutor Li's son, she can provide some help by email. 要不然 can also be used to issue a warning, usually to point out the negative consequences of not following a specific course of action.

3/4

(15分钟过去了,大家在为表演做准备,周丹锐在调吉他)
孙大爷：小伙子,弹吉他啊。
周丹锐：诶,大爷您好!
孙大爷：我年轻的时候也经常拉拉二胡,搞搞乐器什么的。

> 周丹锐：那太好了,我对中国的民族乐器也很感兴趣,您坐您坐。<u>大爷,贵姓啊</u>?
>
> 孙大爷：免贵姓孙。

6. 孙大爷跟周丹锐说自己年轻时候的事儿:"我年轻的时候也经常拉拉二胡。"

（1）如果孙大爷说他年轻时经常"拉二胡",意思有什么不一样? _____

（2）如果别人问你平常有空时喜欢做什么,你可以怎么回答? _____

（3）"我星期六一般不做什么,就在家里_____。"

　　A. 睡觉睡觉　　　　　　B. 睡睡觉

The duplication of a verb usually denotes that this action is conducted in a casual way. When 孙大爷 says 我年轻的时候经常拉拉二胡, he indicates that *erhu* was just a hobby, not how he earned a living. If he had said 我年轻的时候经常拉二胡, then perhaps he used to have a job of playing *erhu*, or at least practiced it seriously. To duplicate the verb in verb-object phrases such as 睡觉 only repeats the verb (e.g., 睡睡觉).

7. 周丹锐问孙大爷姓什么,他说:"大爷,贵姓啊?"

大爷回答说:"免贵姓孙。"

如果这里不用"贵姓啊",周丹锐还可以怎么问?孙大爷会怎么回答?

_____

(您)贵姓 is a very formal and respectful way of asking a person's last name, and 免贵姓 + last name is the paired response. This exchange usually happens upon first meeting in a relatively formal situation, such as a business setting or an academic conference. An alternate way of asking someone's name was introduced in 5.1: 大爷,您怎么称呼啊? A response to this question might be 我姓孙,你就叫我孙大爷吧.

> **4/4**
>
> 周丹锐：噢,孙大爷!我叫周丹锐,丹青的丹,精锐的锐。<u>您今年多大岁数了</u>?
> 孙大爷：我72了。
> 周丹锐：一点都不像啊,我看您也就60岁左右。
> 孙大爷：哈哈,<u>真会说话</u>!我呢,平常喜欢运动,身板硬朗得很呢。
> 周丹锐：我等会要表演个节目,得抓紧时间把吉他调一下,您帮我先听听。
> 孙大爷：好啊!

8. 周丹锐问孙大爷的年纪:"您今年多大岁数了?"

（1）在这里还可以怎么问孙大爷的年纪? _____

（2）如果是问一个上小学的小朋友的年龄,可以怎么问? _____

(3) 如果是问一个看上去和你同龄的人呢？＿＿＿＿＿＿＿＿＿＿＿＿＿＿＿＿

Expressions for asking a person's age vary. To ask a senior person, you can either say 您今年多大岁数了 or 您多大年纪了. To ask a small child, you can say 你多大了 or 你几岁了. For other age groups, it's more appropriate to ask the person's year of birth 你哪年的, or to ask the zodiac of the person's year of birth 你属什么的. When an adult Chinese asks another adult's age, he or she is usually ready to compliment the other person on his or her youthful appearance or early achievement.

9. 周丹锐称赞孙大爷看上去年轻，他说："我看您也就 60 岁左右。"
(1) 如果这里不用"也就"，还可以怎么说？＿＿＿＿＿＿＿＿＿＿＿＿＿＿＿＿
(2) 如果你的中文老师告诉你她 40 多了，你可以说什么话让她高兴？
＿＿＿＿＿＿＿＿＿＿＿＿＿＿＿＿
(3) 如果你朋友让你猜一双鞋的价格，你觉得不会超过 200 块，可以怎么说？
＿＿＿＿＿＿＿＿＿＿＿＿＿＿＿＿

也就 +［a range of number］is normally used to provide a ceiling for an estimation the speaker would like to make. For example, if your teacher tells you that she's in her 40s but she looks young for her age, to compliment her younger looking, you may say 我看您也就 30 岁左右.

最多 can also be used to introduce the highest estimation, yet the estimation can't be a range (number +左右). Therefore, an alternative way of saying 我看您也就 60 岁左右 is 我看您最多 60 岁. In another context, when asked by a friend to guess the price of a pair of shoes that you think worth no more than ￥200, you can say 这双最多 200 块吧.

10. 周丹锐说孙大爷看上去年轻，孙大爷挺高兴，他说："哈哈，真会说话。"
(1) 孙大爷说周丹锐"真会说话"，这是在夸他吗？＿＿＿＿＿＿＿＿＿＿＿＿＿＿＿＿
(2) 如果你在看电影时觉得一个演员演得特别好，你可以怎么说？
＿＿＿＿＿＿＿＿＿＿＿＿＿＿＿＿
(3) 可以把这里的"真会说话"换成"真能说"吗？＿＿＿＿＿＿＿＿＿＿＿＿＿＿＿＿

真会 +［action］is used to praise someone for being really good at something. This kind of compliment may carry a tone of slight exaggeration, but generally conveys a positive tone. The structure 真能 +［action］, on the other hand, does not necessarily have a positive connotation. For example, 真能说 indicates that someone is talking too much or has been talking for a long time. The verbs used in this structure usually only consist of one character, such as 真能吃, 真能写 and 真能睡. For example, if a student filled all the space on his exam paper while others only wrote a few lines to answer the same question, one might describe the first student by saying 这个人真能写！

体演文本

Review the sections of the dialogue assigned by your teacher by listening to the audio and role-playing with another Chinese speaker. Be ready to perform the assigned portion of the dialogue from memory in class.

举一反三

Answer the following questions and think about how the dialogue can be adapted for different situations.

1. 通常什么样的居民会作为居民代表被邀请到这个活动中？
2. 如果你现在被邀请到苏州大学附近的一个社区去交流，你想和那儿的居民交流什么话题？你有什么节目可以带给他们？
3. 如果一个阿姨请你教她的孩子英文，但是你不想答应她，你可以用什么办法礼貌地拒绝她？你有没有碰到过这种情况？
4. 你有没有遇到过"很会说话"的人？什么样的事让你觉得他很会说话？

熟能生巧

Listen to the audio and perform the following drills until you feel confident with the items practiced.

☞ **Drill 1 Politely requesting help**

Initiate the conversation by politely making a request to someone. In the example, Sun Hao asks Zhou Danrui to tutor English for his cousin. In the following drills, you initiate the conversation by making a request to Sun Hao. Each of the illustrations provides you with the activity you need help with.

例：给我表弟辅导英语

赵奕歆：跟你商量点事儿啊，我想请你给我表弟辅导英语。
周丹锐：好啊，没问题。

1. 帮我练习采访问题

2. 教我包饺子

3. 帮我搬家 　　4. 帮我修改作文

🔲 Drill 2 Politely refusing someone in an indirect way

Upon hearing a request or invitation from Sun Hao, politely refuse by stating your other obligations. Use 恐怕…… to avoid making him uncomfortable. Each of the illustrations provides the reason you have to decline Sun Hao's request or offer.

例：

孙浩：我想请你这个周末辅导我表弟英语。
郑妮：这个周末我有很多活动,恐怕……

🔲 Drill 3 Politely refusing someone due to circumstances out of your control

In this drill, upon hearing a request or invitation from Sun Hao, politely refuse by stating that as much as you would like to, you are unable to for good reasons. Each of the illustrations provides the reason why you have to decline Sun Hao's request or offer.

例：

孙浩：我想请你这个周末给我表弟辅导英语。
郑妮：我愿意是愿意,但是这个周末我们有很多活动。

🔲 Drill 4 Asking someone's surname

In this drill, initiate the conversation by asking about a stranger's family name. Upon hearing the response, greet him or her properly. Each of the illustrations shows information about your interlocutor based on which you can decide how to address him/her.

例：

郑妮：大爷，您贵姓啊？
孙大爷：免贵姓孙。
郑妮：孙大爷您好！

1.   2.   3.   4.

☞ **Drill 5 Suggesting an alternative**

When someone makes a suggestion, propose an alternative option and explain the reason. Each of the illustrations shows your alternative suggestion or reason for it.

例：

李阿姨：你留一个电话号码给我吧。
周丹锐：要不然我留一个电子邮箱给您吧，我查邮件更方便。

1.   2.    3.   4.

Narration

Practice narrating the general procedure of the cultural event at Longqiao Community from the students' perspectives.

1. Assume Zheng Ni's role and tell Sun Hao about your experience at Longqiao Community.

孙浩：郑妮，你们昨天下午的文化活动去哪儿参观了？有意思吗？

2. Assume Zhou Danrui's role and tell Zhao Yixin about your experience talking to Uncle Sun at Longqiao Community.

赵奕歆：丹锐，你们昨天下午去哪儿搞活动了？

言外有意

Read the cultural notes below and prepare questions for further discussion with Chinese people.

1. 一回生,二回熟 (yīhuí shēng, èrhuí shú) Strangers at the first meeting, friends at the second.

This idiom is used to say that friendships and relationships will be naturally established through socialization. For example, if your friend is reluctant to go out and meet some new friends, you can encourage him or her by saying 一回生二回熟嘛. Or, after hosting a get-together at your place, you can show friendliness to your new friends by saying 一回生二回熟,以后多来玩. In some areas in China, you may feel that people treat you as a 熟人 after your first meeting. In other contexts, this idiom is used to express the idea that the first time to do something is always the hardest, but it will get easier if you keep trying.

2. 中国人对外国人的态度 Common Chinese reactions to meeting a foreigner.

Some Chinese people you meet, especially in smaller cities, will have had little opportunity to interact with foreigners. As a result, they may feel uncomfortable talking with you because they are not sure what to say, or they may ask a lot of obvious questions to satisfy their curiosity. Some people will approach you because they want to practice their English. Even though your goal is to speak Chinese, you can use this as an opportunity to meet more Chinese people. Most people will be more than willing to help you with your Chinese. Since most Chinese are proud of their hometown, saying something positive about it is an easy way to initiate a conversation and make more friends.

Traditionally, in China it is considered culturally appropriate to ask a stranger questions about their age, income, family background, or marital status. In business settings today, however, people are more careful about asking these kinds of personal questions. Nevertheless, you should be prepared for such questions when you are socializing with Chinese people in an informal setting.

3. 中国人对陌生人的称呼 How Chinese address strangers.

In the dialogue above, before 孙大爷 knows Zhou Danrui's name, he calls him 小伙子. Both 小伙子 and (小)姑娘 are common ways for the older generation to address younger men and women. There is regional variation of the terms younger people use to address older people. Depending on where you are in China you may hear 大爷, 爷爷, 老伯 or 大伯 used to address older men and 阿姨, 大妈, 婆婆 used to address older women. Using correct terms of address in Chinese is an art. Pay close attention to which terms people around you use and note how this varies depending on their communicative intentions.

6.2 志愿服务

意在言外

🎧 投石问路

Listen to the five questions in the audio and answer them based on your own experience. Be ready to discuss these questions in class. You may write down some notes in the space provided below.

1.
2.
3.
4.
5.

🎧 边听边想

Listen to the audio and try to visualize the dialogue in your mind. Think about who the speakers are, the kind of social relationship they have, and what their intentions might be.

耳闻目睹

Listen to the audio again while following along in the printed text. As you listen, mark any place that you are unclear or have questions about.

意在言外

人物：周丹锐、孙浩、敬老院工作人员、郑妮

（星期一中午，刚下课，孙浩叫周丹锐一起去吃饭）

孙浩： 丹锐，听说你们想去敬老院做义工，要不要找青志协的会长帮你们联系一下？

周丹锐： 不用不用，也不是所有同学都参加，我们几个自己联系一家就行了。

孙浩： 可能以学校的名义联系会比较保险，一群留学生直接打电话说要去做义工，对方恐怕不会轻易接受吧。

周丹锐： 没事儿，先让我们自己试试吧。（1/4）

（周丹锐和郑妮给幸福之家敬老院打电话，一位工作人员接电话）

工作人员：喂，你好。

周丹锐： 您好，请问是幸福之家敬老院吗？

工作人员：对，你是哪里？

周丹锐： 您好，我叫周丹锐，是苏州大学的留学生。我和几个同学想问一下您这儿需不需要志愿者？

工作人员：噢，留学生？外国人啊……你们是从哪个国家来的？

周丹锐： 我们都是从美国来的，在美国都有很丰富的志愿服务经验。两周以前我们还刚和苏州大学的青志协一起到农民工子弟小学做过义工。（2/4）

工作人员：这样啊……你们这个献爱心的热情我很敬佩，也谢谢你们对我们敬老院的关注……

周丹锐： 您过奖了，能够尽自己一份力我们也觉得很荣幸。不知道您那儿什么时候方便我们可以过来商量一下详细情况……

工作人员：噢，这个……是这样的……现在我们这边呢暂时没有公开招募志愿者的计划。要不这样吧，你先留个电话，以后有机会我再联系你们。

周丹锐： 噢，好的。我的电话是18366221864，我姓周，丹青的丹，精锐的锐。

工作人员：好，谢谢。再见。

周丹锐： 再见。（3/4）

（周丹锐挂了电话）

郑妮： 他们怎么说？这周末能开始吗？

周丹锐： 说是现在不对外招志愿者，让我留了个联系方式，说以后再联系。

郑妮： 以后是什么时候呀……看来还是得找青志协帮我们联系一下。(4/4)

知其所以然

The dialogue is broken down into sections below for explanation and analysis. Study the notes and answer the questions for the underlined text.

1/4

（星期一中午，刚下课，孙浩叫周丹锐一起去吃饭）
孙浩： 丹锐，听说你们想去敬老院做<u>义工</u>，要不要找青志协的会长帮你们联系一下？
周丹锐：不用不用，也不是所有同学都参加，我们几个自己联系一家就行了。
孙浩： 可能<u>以学校的名义</u>联系会比较保险，一群留学生直接打电话说要去做义工，对方恐怕不会轻易接受吧。
周丹锐：没事儿，先让我们自己试试吧。

---

1. 下课了，孙浩问周丹锐文化活动的事，他说："听说你们想去敬老院做义工？"
(1) 这里的"义工"可以换成"志愿者"吗？_____
(2) 你是否做过义工？如果做过，是怎样的工作？_____
(3) 如果你做演讲时提了一个问题，希望有人举手回答，你可以怎么问？
_____

Both 义工 and 志愿者 are nouns that refer to people who volunteer at NGOs, charities and other orgnizations. You can describe their participation in the volunteer work as 做义工 or 参加志愿活动. Note that while in English "volunteer" can be used as both a noun and a verb, and it can also be used in situations where one volunteers to do something, in Chinese people usually go with a verb phrase "愿意 + verb". For example, during a presentation you ask a question and look for someone who volunteers to answer the question, you can say 有人愿意回答吗?

2. 孙浩觉得通过学校联系比较好，他说："可能以学校的名义联系会比较保险。"
(1) 孙浩是让周丹锐在打电话的时候告诉对方自己在哪个学校吗？
_____
(2) "以"可以用哪个字代替？_____
(3) 如果你和朋友准备晚上出去吃饭，需要打电话订位，你可不可以跟朋友说"你以我的名义给饭店打个电话吧"？为什么？_____

Originating from classical Chinese, 以 has many different usages. Here, it resembles 用 in modern Mandarin. The phrase 以 X 的名义 is a formal way of saying "to do something in the name of X" where X is generally a person or an organization. 名义 is a formal term, referring to the names of people or organizations that are powerful or influential. Sun Hao recommended that Zhou Danrui work through official channels to contact the retirement center because someone speaking on behalf of the university would be more likely to be accepted than an individual student. However, in a casual context this structure would be too formal. For example, when you ask a friend to book a restaurant for dinner, simply say 用我的名字订个位子吧.

（4）这里的"保险"可以换成"安全"吗？_____

（5）如果你正在写一篇一周后要交的作文，你的同学看到后觉得你不需要这么早写，你可以怎么回答他？_____

（6）保险还有什么意思？你买过保险吗？_____

When used as an adjective or adverb, 保险 is usually used to express that (by taking a certain method) the expected outcome is ensured. For example, though you are not sure whether or not student ID is needed to buy a train ticket, you still bring it with you to make sure you will get the ticket no mater what. You can say 我还是带着比较保险. When used in this way 保险 is not interchangeable with 安全. 安全 refers to physical and financial safety. Therefore, you can either say 钱放在银行比较安全 or 钱放在银行比较保险. When used as a noun, 保险 refers to insurance.

2/4

（周丹锐和郑妮给幸福之家敬老院打电话，一位工作人员接电话）

工作人员：喂，你好。

周丹锐：　您好，请问是幸福之家敬老院吗？

工作人员：对，你是哪里？

周丹锐：　您好，我叫周丹锐，是苏州大学的留学生。我和几个同学想问一下您这儿需不需要志愿者？

工作人员：噢，留学生？外国人啊……你们是从哪个国家来的？

周丹锐：　我们都是从美国来的，在美国都有很丰富的志愿服务经验。两周以前我们还刚和苏州大学的青志协一起到农民工子弟小学做过义工。

---

3. 敬老院的工作人员接电话，他问："你是哪里？"

（1）工作人员是问周丹锐在什么地方吗？_____

（2）如果周丹锐是给青志协会长的手机打电话，这里的"哪里"还可以换成什么词？_____

你是哪里 is a common way of inquiring about a caller's identity on the phone, mostly used by receptionists from institutions. 哪里 here refers to one's name, title and especially the organization that the person is associated with. When answering a call from a private phone, one can say 你是哪位 which is still a polite way of finding out who is calling.

> **3/4**
>
> 工作人员：这样啊……你们这个献爱心的热情我很敬佩,也谢谢你们对我们敬老院的关注……
>
> 周丹锐：您过奖了,能够尽自己一份力我们也觉得很荣幸。不知道您那儿什么时候方便我们可以过来商量一下详细情况……
>
> 工作人员：噢,这个……是这样的……现在我们这边呢暂时没有公开招募志愿者的计划。要不这样吧,你先留个电话,以后有机会我再联系你们。
>
> 周丹锐：噢,好的。我的电话是18366221864,我姓周,丹青的丹,精锐的锐。
>
> 工作人员：好,谢谢。再见。
>
> 周丹锐：再见。

4. 工作人员回应周丹锐的请求,他说:"你们这个献爱心的热情我很敬佩。"
  (1) 这里的"敬佩"可以换成什么词?
      A. 羡慕　　　　　　B. 佩服
  (2) 在你的生活中,有没有过让你很敬佩的人? _____
  (3) 你有没有喜欢的名人? 他们身上有没有什么特点让你很羡慕?
  _____
  (4) 在学校里你对哪些人应当表现出尊敬? _____

There are many words in Chinese that can be interpreted as "admire", but they often have some slight differences in connotation. 羡慕 denotes admiration for others' physical features or mental abilities which you yourself lack but would like to have. For example, 我很羡慕他的身材, or 我很羡慕他乐观的性格. By contrast, 佩服 refers only to admiration for personality traits or mental capacities, such as 我很佩服他刻苦学习的精神. 敬佩 adds a sense of respect to 佩服 and thus is often used to refer to people who have made a great sacrifice to achieve something worthwhile.

5. 周丹锐想知道什么时候可以商量下详细情况,他问:"不知道您那儿什么时候方便……"
  (1) 如果去掉"不知道",语气上会有什么变化? _____
  (2) 如果你想和老师约一个时间讨论作业,你可以怎么说? _____
  (3) 如果你在家等快递,过了说好的时间一个小时之后,包裹还是没来,你给快递公司打电话时可以怎么问? _____

The phrase 不知道…… used in front of a question softens the tone of the inquiry, increasing the level of politeness. It's often used when you want to discuss something or ask for a favor. For example, to request an appointment with your teacher, you may say 不知您

什么时候有空 or 不知您什么时候方便. In another context, when you get impatient with a delayed delivery and call the delivery service, you can intentionally drop 不知道 and make your tones sound harsher：包裹什么时候能送到？

（4）你的同事提出他可以开车送你去机场,但是你的航班特别早。在你接受同事的好意之前,可以怎么客气一下？＿＿＿＿＿＿＿＿＿＿＿＿＿＿＿

（5）如果你要出差,想请同事帮你照顾自己的小狗,可以怎么说？＿＿＿＿＿＿

The phrase 什么时候方便 in the dialogue is used to ask politely the availability of someone to set up a meeting. 方便 here refers to the convenience of doing something, especially for the sake of others. It is polite to double check if something is convenient for someone before accepting his or her help or hospitality. For example, if you have a very early fight to catch in the morning and a colleague offers to drive you to the airport, before accepting the generous offer, it is polite to ask 那么早方便吗？方便 can also be used when asking for a favor. For example, to ask a colleague if he or she can take care of your pet dog while you are away, you may say 跟你商量个事儿啊,不知道方不方便帮我照顾一下小狗.

4/4

（周丹锐挂了电话）

郑妮： 他们怎么说？这周末能开始吗？

周丹锐：说是现在不对外招志愿者,让我留了个联系方式,说以后再联系。

郑妮： 以后是什么时候呀……看来还是得找青志协帮我们联系一下。

---

6. 郑妮问周丹锐打电话的结果如何,她说:"他们怎么说？"

（1）"他们怎么说"里的"他们"指的是谁？＿＿＿＿＿＿＿＿＿＿＿＿＿＿＿

（2）接电话的只有一个人,为什么郑妮要用"他们"？＿＿＿＿＿＿＿＿＿＿

（3）郑妮问"他们怎么说"是想知道什么？

　　　A. 对方说的决定是什么。　　　　B. 对方是怎么表达决定的。

（4）如果有人请你简单介绍下你就读的大学,你可以怎么说？＿＿＿＿＿＿＿

By now you should be very familiar with the use of 怎么说 in "XX 中文怎么说". 怎么说 can also be used to inquire about results or final decisions. In the dialogue Zheng Ni asks Zhou Danrui about the response from the retirement home regarding the volunteer work. In another situation in which a group of friends agreed to get together for a meal during the weekend, but has not yet made a final decision about place and time, someone might ask 周末吃饭怎么说？

Since Chinese people tend to regard an organization as a mass of people, 他们 can be used in conversation to refer to an organization. Likewise in Chinese when referring to the institution you belong to you should use 我们 + [institution], such as 我们学校 and 我们

公司. You may also encounter 我校 as an abbreviation of 我们学校 in formal contexts such as a news report or a public speech.

🎧 体演文本

Review the sections of the dialogue assigned by your teacher by listening to the audio and role-playing with another Chinese speaker. Be ready to perform the assigned portion of the dialogue from memory in class.

💬 举一反三

Answer the following questions and think about how the dialogue can be adapted for different situations.

1. 孙浩在得知周丹锐他们想去敬老院做志愿者的时候,有什么提议？为什么会那样提议？
2. 你觉得那个敬老院还会联系周丹锐吗？
3. 工作人员说的那些话是什么意思？为什么他那么敬佩周丹锐？
4. 你觉得周丹锐在跟敬老院交流这件事上,哪些做得比较成功,哪些比较失败？

🎧 熟能生巧

Listen to the audio and perform the following drills until you feel confident with the items practiced.

☞ **Drill 1 Doing something in the name of an institution or a recognized individual**

When asked if something can be done on your own behalf, suggest doing it in the name of an institution or a recognized person to better achieve the goal. Each of the illustrations shows the institution or person under whose auspices you propose to work.

例：保险

周丹锐：我们自己联系敬老院行吗？
赵奕歆：可能以学校的名义联系会比较保险。

1. 保险　2. 便宜　3. 方便　4. 容易

☞ **Drill 2 Politely refusing an offer to help**

When a friend offers to help, politely refuse by pointing out that the task is not beyond your reach.

例：麻烦

赵奕歆：我请青志协的会长帮你联系吧。

周丹锐：不用不用，也不是特别麻烦，我们自己联系就行了。

1. 严重
2. 远
3. 麻烦
4. 重

☞ Drill 3 Priming a rejection

In this drill, you have the chance to practice a strategic way of hinting rejection on behalf of an organization. Following the example, assume the role of the staff member and express your appreciation of one's enthusiastic offer to work in order to prime the following rejection. Each of the illustrations provides the organization you work for and the quality you admire.

例：

周丹锐：我们这个周末就可以开始志愿服务。

工作人员：你们这个献爱心的热情我很敬佩，也谢谢你们对我们敬老院的关注。

☞ Drill 4 Responding to appreciation

When your supervisor thanks you for volunteering at the organization and compliments on your devotion to a collective endeavor, respond formally. In the example, Zhou Danrui uses 荣幸 to indicate that he feels honored to be of help. Besides 荣幸, you can also use 自豪 (pride), 开心 or 高兴.

例：荣幸

敬老院负责人：非常感谢你们这段时间的辛勤工作，你们献爱心的热情我很敬佩。

周丹锐：能尽自己的一份力，我们也觉得很荣幸。

1. 荣幸

2. 自豪
3. 开心
4. 高兴

☞ Drill 5 Expressing mild annoyance

In this drill, practice conveying that you are mildly dissatisfied by someone's vague response. In the example, Zheng Ni questions when exactly the Retirement Home will call them.

例：
周丹锐：人家说现在不对外招募志愿者,以后再跟我联系。
郑妮：以后是什么时候呀……

1.　　　　　2.　　　　　3.　　　　　4.

Narration

Zhou Danrui and Zheng Ni tried to reach out to the Retirement Home to set up a volunteering work against Sun Hao's suggestion that they should do so in the name of Soochow University. The next day Miss Qin asks them how did it go. Assume Zhou Danrui's role and elaborate on the misunderstanding occurred during the negotiation when what was meant to be a refusal was initially taken as an approval.

秦老师：我听孙浩说你们几个同学想去敬老院做义工,联系得怎么样了?

言外有意

Read the cultural notes below and prepare questions for further discussion with Chinese people.

1. 意在言外(yì zài yán wài) The meaning is implied between the lines.

When communicating with Chinese people, keep in mind that there are some meanings and intentions that are usually expressed indirectly or left unsaid. 意在言外 is used to describe this phenomenon. For example, a refusal in Chinese often takes an indirect form. This is known as 婉言谢绝 (wǎnyán xièjué) "to refuse with indirect and kind words". In the dialogue, the staff member at the Retirement Home said 你们这个献爱心的热情我很敬佩……现在我们这边呢暂时没有公开招募志愿者的计划. This is an example of 意在言外 as well as 婉言谢绝. The idiom 意在言外 is not often used in daily conversation except when talking about communication techniques.

2. 单位/中间者的重要性

In our story, Zhou Danrui was trying to contact the Retirement Home to do some volunteer work but did not succeed. Would the result have been different if the phone call had been made by the 青志协? Very likely! In China, the trust between two business partners usually provides a basis for their institutional relationship. When dealing with foreigners, some institutions tend to be extra cautious. If Zhou Danrui had mentioned that he works with the 苏大青志协 or had mentioned the names of some teachers that were known to the people working at the Retirement Home, the outcome might also have been different. In other words, when introducing yourself, don't forget to mention what institution you are from or who introduced you to the interlocutor.

3. 献爱心,不求回报

The phrase 献爱心 is widely used in public service announcements in China, usually to encourage people to contribute or donate to rural or disaster areas. The idea of 献爱心 is closely associated with the mindset of 不求回报 or not seeking a reward. This phrase is often used to praise charitable thoughts and acts, as in our dialogue. However, it can also be used sarcastically to describe actions or investments with no return. For example, if your close friend keeps making bad business decisions, you can tease him by saying 你到底是在做生意呢,还是献爱心呢? Or if you want to complain about an unbalanced relationship, you could say 他/她根本不懂付出,我总不能一直献爱心吧?

6.3 参加会议

毛遂自荐

🎧 投石问路

Listen to the five questions in the audio and answer them based on your own experience. Be ready to discuss these questions in class. You may write down some notes in the space provided below.

1.
2.
3.
4.
5.

🎧 边听边想

Listen to the audio and try to visualize the dialogue in your mind. Think about who the speakers are, the kind of social relationship they have, and what their intentions might be.

耳闻目睹

Listen to the audio again while following along in the printed text. As you listen, mark any place that you are unclear or have questions about.

毛遂自荐

人物：秦老师、郑妮、周丹锐、张经理

（星期五快下课的时候，秦老师来教室通知一件事）

秦老师：明天上午我们要去西交国际会展中心参加一个苏州美食节的会议，是关于"绿色有机食品"的。这可是一个参与中国比较正式的专业会议的好机会。你们还可能有机会和很多大企业的领导和专家交流交流。

郑妮：我们到那里具体要做些什么？

秦老师：他们可能会问你们对本地美食的看法，你们自己也可以想一些相关的问题，今晚好好准备准备。还有，到时候要是听不懂或者觉得没意思，也不要东张西望或打瞌睡，注意别让人看到你很无聊的样子。(1/4)

周丹锐：要是能早点通知我们就好了，我都约好了明天上午和几个中国朋友一起踢球。

秦老师：没办法，我也是昨天晚上才收到外办送来的请柬。明天上午八点半我们直接在西交国际会展中心的正门集合，不要迟到。(2/4)

（星期六，在国际会议中心。会间休息的时候，郑妮在会场门口遇到会上发言的张经理）

郑妮：张经理，您好！刚才听了您关于转基因食品的发言。我觉得您说的那个大众消费心理特别有道理。我在大学也是学习营养学的，对这个话题很有兴趣。

张经理：是吗？你是哪个大学的？

郑妮：美国俄亥俄州立大学。(3/4)

张经理：哦，你们学校的营养学专业排名很靠前啊。我两年前去那边参加过一次学术研讨会。

郑妮：那真是太巧了。张经理，您要是有机会再来哥伦布，一定要联系我，我可以给您当向导。我叫郑妮，这是我的电子邮箱。我能不能也留一个您的联系方式，以后有什么问题可以多多向您请教。

张经理：好的好的。这是我的名片。

郑妮：谢谢张经理，很高兴认识您。(4/4)

知其所以然

The dialogue is broken down into sections below for explanation and analysis. Study

the notes and answer the questions for the underlined text.

1/4

（星期五快下课的时候，秦老师来教室通知一件事）

秦老师：明天上午我们要去西交国际会展中心参加一个苏州美食节的会议，是关于"绿色有机食品"的。这可是一个参与中国比较正式的专业会议的好机会。你们还可能有机会和很多大企业的领导和专家交流交流。

郑妮：我们到那里具体要做些什么？

秦老师：他们可能会问你们对本地美食的看法，你们自己也可以想一些相关的问题，今晚好好准备准备。还有，<u>到时候</u>要是听不懂或者觉得没意思，也不要<u>东张西望</u>或打瞌睡，注意别让人看到你很无聊的样子。

---

1. 秦老师跟同学们说一些注意事项，她说："到时候要是听不懂或觉得没意思……"

（1）这里秦老师说的"到时候"是指什么时候？ _____

（2）假如你是秦老师，有的学生明天要一块儿出去旅游。你怎么提醒学生不要忘带护照？ _____

到时候 refers to a previously mentioned time. Using this expression may cause confusion if no time was mentioned previously. It may sometimes refer to a vague point of time, usually in the future, chosen by the speaker. For example, 到时候你自然明白 means "you will understand in due course". Another common usage of 到时候 can be seen in 到时候再说/到时候再看/到时候再决定吧, indicating "you play something by ear".

2. 秦老师提醒学生不要表现出无聊的样子，他说："……也不要东张西望或打瞌睡。"

（1）你觉得一个人如果东张西望，会给人一种什么感觉？ _____

（2）如果你在商场里听到一个妈妈在严厉地对孩子说"手不要东摸西摸的"，你觉得那个妈妈的意思是什么？她为什么要这么说？ _____

（3）如果你听到一个人抱怨说"这几年一直东奔西跑忙工作，真想彻底放一年假，好好歇歇"。你觉得这个人可能做什么样的工作？ _____

东张西望 means to glance around. The verb 张望 means "to look around". There are several other common patterns which use the pattern 东 X 西 Y, to convey the meaning of doing something without a particular goal or plan. For example, a journalist may complain that his job forces him to 东奔西跑 (bustle about/run around here and there). The manner of talking randomly without a clear topic may be described as 东拉西扯, e.g., 他东拉西扯地讲了半天，我完全不知道他想说什么. Since X and Y in this pattern are usually characters that are very similar in meaning, in certain contexts, they can be the same characters. For example, to keep her child from playing with goods that she is not going to buy, a mother may warn the child 手不要东摸西摸的.

2/4

周丹锐：<u>要是能早点通知我们就好了</u>，我都约好了明天上午和几个中国朋友一起踢球。

秦老师：没办法，我也是昨天晚上才收到外办送来的请柬。明天上午八点半我们直接在西交国际会展中心的正门集合，不要迟到。

---

3. 周丹锐觉得秦老师通知得有点晚，他说："要是能早点通知我们就好了。"
（1）这里如果周丹锐说"为什么不早点通知我们呢"好吗？为什么？
_____

（2）星期六早上安排了去参观社区，你不太想去，可以怎么跟你的朋友抱怨一下？
_____

We've encountered the conditional 要是 several times in previous units. Here, the pattern 要是 + ［condition］ + 就好了 is used to express mild complaint about a current situation. It's a strategic way of hinting that certain arrangements are inconvenient without necessarily opposing them directly. For example, to complain about having to attend an event on Saturday morning, you can say 要是礼拜六不用去参观社区就好了.

3/4

（星期六，在国际会议中心。会间休息的时候，郑妮在会场门口遇到会上发言的张经理）

郑妮：　　张经理，您好！刚才听了您关于转基因食品的<u>发言</u>。我觉得您说的那个大众消费心理特别有道理。我在大学也是学习营养学的，对这个话题很有兴趣。

张经理：是吗？你是哪个大学的？

郑妮：　　美国俄亥俄州立大学。

---

4. 郑妮称赞张经理的发言，她说："刚才听了您关于转基因食品的发言……"
（1）"发言"和"演讲"有什么区别？什么场合你会发言？_____
（2）如果你的老师给你第一周的课堂评语是"发言不够积极"，你觉得老师的意思是？_____
（3）项目开学典礼上，苏州大学国际汉语学院的老师说："下面请周院长_____。"
　　A. 发言　　　　B. 讲话　　　　C. 演讲　　　　D. 报告

（4）项目开学典礼上，苏州大学国际汉语学院的老师说："接下来请学生代表周丹锐同学＿＿＿＿＿＿＿。"

　　A. 发言　　　　　B. 讲话　　　　　C. 演讲　　　　　D. 报告

发言 emphasizes expressing one's opinion, for example, in a meeting（会议发言）or in class（课堂发言）. 演讲 refers to giving a speech on formal occasions which is well scripted, usually around a theme or topic, such as 乔布斯在清华大学的演讲. If someone of a superior status（领导）gives a talk, it is referred to 讲话, not 发言. For example, at program-opening ceremony a talk by the dean would be referred to as 讲话, while one by a student representative would be referred to as 发言. Typically 报告 refers to presentations that report on the results of investigation or research.

5. 郑妮很赞同张经理的观点，她说："我觉得你说的那个大众消费心理特别有道理。"

　　（1）如果你的同事说公司的某项规定"完全没有道理"，你觉得他支持不支持那项规定？＿＿＿＿＿＿＿＿＿＿＿＿＿＿＿＿＿＿＿＿＿＿＿

　　（2）如果郑妮不说"有道理"，她还可以怎么夸张经理的发言？＿＿＿＿＿＿＿

有道理 means that something makes sense, implying that you agree with the logic of the statement. Here Zheng Ni thinks Manager Zhang has made good points in her talk. Alternatively, she could have said 你说的那个大众消费心理让我很受启发, indicating that she had found Manager Zhang's ideas inspiring. Saying 有道理 after someone explains an idea or a point of view can show that you support what they said. If you want to politely disagree with someone's point you can say 有道理，不过…… and follow with your own opinion or reason that conflicts with what the speaker has said.

4/4

张经理：哦，你们学校的营养学专业排名很靠前啊。我两年前去那边参加过一次学术研讨会。

郑妮：　那真是太巧了。张经理，您要是有机会再来哥伦布，一定要联系我，我可以给您当向导。我叫郑妮，这是我的电子邮箱。我能不能也留一个您的联系方式，以后有什么问题可以多多向您请教。

张经理：好的好的。这是我的名片。

郑妮：　谢谢张经理，很高兴认识您。

---

6. 张经理夸郑妮的大学，她说："你们学校的营养学专业排名很靠前啊。"

　　（1）选择大学的时候，你觉得排名靠前重要吗？为什么？＿＿＿＿＿＿＿＿

　　（2）上课或者听讲座的时候，你喜欢坐靠前的座位还是靠后的座位？为什么？

＿＿＿＿＿＿＿＿＿＿＿＿＿＿＿＿＿＿＿＿＿＿＿

（3）坐飞机的时候，你喜欢坐靠窗的座位，还是靠过道的座位？为什么？
_____

（4）摆放家具的时候，你喜欢写字台靠窗，还是靠墙？ _____

靠前 literally means to be leaning towards the front. In the context of the dialogue (排名很靠前), it is indicating that the nutrition major at Ohio State University ranks towards the top of the list. Sometimes 靠前/靠后 can also be used in a more literal sense to describe physical location. For example, when taking a group photo, you may be asked to 靠前站. When attending a class or lecture, some people may prefer to sit closer to the front, i.e., 有的人喜欢靠前的座位 or 有的人喜欢靠前坐.

🎧 体演文本

Review the sections of the dialogue assigned by your teacher by listening to the audio and role-playing with another Chinese speaker. Be ready to perform the assigned portion of the dialogue from memory in class.

💬 举一反三

Answer the following questions and think about how the dialogue can be adapted for different situations.

1. 如果你的一个美国同学要在中国参加一个跟他专业有关的学术研讨会，你可以给他什么样的建议？

2. 你有过在中国参加专业会议的经历吗？你有哪些收获？

3. 如果郑妮回美国以后还想跟张经理联系，并且想明年夏天去张经理的公司实习，你觉得她应该怎样发邮件给张经理？

🎧 熟能生巧

Listen to the audio and perform the following drills until you feel confident with the items practiced.

☞ **Drill 1 Emphasizing the benefit of participating in an activity**

Encourage your interlocutor to participate in a cultural activity by pointing out the opportunity it provides to expand the knowledge of a certain field. Each of the illustrations provides the type of knowledge one is likely to gain from the experience.

例：

周丹锐：我们明天都要去参加这个会议吗？
孙浩：这可是一个了解中国的专业会议的好机会。

☞ Drill 2 Giving advice about behavior to avoid

When asked by a Chinese student who is new to your university in the U. S. and is worried about what to pay attention to at an important event tomorrow, suggest that the student avoid inappropriate behaviors even if what he worries about happens. The illustrations indicate the inappropriate behaviors to be avoided.

例：

孙浩：明天的讲座我担心我会听不懂,怎么办啊？
郑妮：到时候要是听不懂,也不要打瞌睡。

☞ Drill 3 Asking for contact information

Imagine that you are about to conclude a small talk with a person you meet for the first time. Request the person's contact information and modestly explain the reason why you wish to keep in touch. Each of the illustrations shows who you are speaking with and the cue indicates the reason why you want to stay in touch.

例：多多向你请教

周丹锐：我能不能留一个你的联系方式,以后可以多多向你请教。
张经理：好的好的。这是我的名片。

1. 多多向您学习 　　2. 一起出去玩

3. 有问题可以联系你   4. 多多向您请教

☞ Drill 4 Showing hospitality by showcasing your city

Show hospitality by inviting a new acquaintance to contact you if he ever visits your city. Look at the prompts and initiate an offer to take your friend to see or do something that the city is well-known for. The illustrations indicate the places you come from and the activities or famous places you want to take your friend to.

例：

郑妮：您要是有机会来哥伦布，一定要联系我，我带你去参观俄亥俄州立大学。
张经理：谢谢！

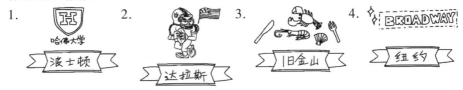

Narration

The American students attended a conference on organic food at Suzhou Xijiao International Convention Center. On their way back to school, Miss Qin asks the students what they think about conference. Assume Zheng Ni's role and tell Miss Qin how the experience turned out to be valuable.

秦老师：郑妮，你觉得今天的文化活动怎么样，有收获吗？

言外有意

Read the cultural notes below and prepare questions for further discussion with Chinese people.

1. 毛遂自荐 (Máo Suì zìjiàn) To recommend oneself.

This idiom is usually used to describe people who offer their services to a superior with confidence that he or she is capable of the job. For example, at the beginning of a new semester when the teacher asks if anyone wants to serve as the class monitor, if Zhou Danrui recommends himself for the position, you can say 周丹锐向老师毛遂自荐当班长。

In the dialogue, when Zheng Ni approaches the speaker at the conference, her agenda is to establish contact and keep in touch with the speaker for networking purposes. In that sense she offers her services to the speaker if she ever needs her help in the future.

2. 中国人对食品安全的关注

Concern about the cleanness of food is certainly not a new topic in China. The widespread use of social media such as Weibo（微博）, has brought China's system of food production, distribution and consumption to people's attention by exposing abuses in the system. Even though many people may not know exactly what genetically modified food（转基因食品）is or the difference between organic food（有机食品）and green products（绿色食品）, more and more people are paying attention to issues of food quality and safety. However, some Chinese people might not feel comfortable talking about topics such as food safety or pollution with foreigners, so try to avoid initiating conversations about such topics.

3. 你会说客气话吗？

For advanced-level Chinese language learners, being able to recognize Chinese people's 客气话（polite expressions）is an important skill to develop. Learners should also work on being able to use those expressions just as Chinese people do. In our dialogue, Zheng Ni apparently did a good job by saying 张经理，你要是有机会再来哥伦布，一定要联系我，我可以给你当向导。Although Manager Zhang is unlikely to take this as a serious invitation, Zheng Ni will definitely leave a positive impression as a result of her effective use of 客气话。Manager Zhang might describe Zheng Ni as 懂事 indicating that she understands the right thing to say or do in a given situation.

第六单元　社会活动 Social Engagements

学而时习之

Before you actually do the field performances, rehearse doing them with a Chinese friend. The "Useful Expressions" box below provides you with some expressions you may use for these performances. For now, try saying them after the audio.

> **🎧 Useful Expressions**
> 1. 宝宝真可爱,他几岁啦?
> 2. 我也有个小侄女,今年三岁。正是最可爱的时候。
> 3. 不好意思,你这件球衣是在哪儿买的?很特别啊。
> 4. 我也是XX队的铁杆球迷。今年他们表现太好了。
> 5. 除了足球你还看什么别的体育比赛?
> 6. 留个联系方式吧,有机会一起看比赛。
> 7. 你参加过志愿者活动吗?
> 8. 中国比较常见的志愿服务有哪些?
> 9. 在大学里这些志愿者活动一般是谁发起的?
> 10. 大学生组织义工活动,一般是以个人名义还是以学校的名义联系?
> 11. 刚才听了您关于……的报告,受益匪浅。
> 12. 我也对……非常感兴趣,现在我正在XX大学读YY专业,我的研究方向是……
> 13. 去年夏天我在北京参加了……项目……
> 14. 大三的时候我在XX公司的YY部门实习过……
> 15. 方便留一下您的联系方式吗?
> 16. 不知道您最近什么时候有空,我想跟您约个时间讨论一下……

Make it a habit to carry a notebook with you and take notes on your interactions with Chinese people.

☞Performance 1　Making small talk with strangers

When given the chance, for example, when the maintenance person is in your room to fix the air conditioner or when sitting on a shared seat with someone on a long bus ride, initiate a pleasant chat.

　　____ Act 1: Start the conversation by either mentioning the obvious or making a compliment.

　　____ Act 2: Exchange hometown information.

　　____ Act 3: Give a brief self-introduction and reveal something about you (e.g., who you are and why you are here).

_____ Act 4: Engage the other person by asking open-ended questions about the person's interests, jobs, or the surroundings.

_____ Act 5: If you think the conversation is going well, exchange contact information and propose to meet again.

_____ Act 6: End the conversation politely.

☞ **Performance 2 Discussing volunteer activities**

Talk to a Chinese friend about the volunteer activities he or she has participated in and the common procedure of reaching out to a local organization to arrange such an activity.

_____ Act 1: Ask your Chinese friend if he or she has participated in any volunteer activities.

_____ Act 2: Follow up by asking what the common types of volunteer work in China are.

_____ Act 3: Tell your own experiences and introduce the common types of volunteer work in the US.

_____ Act 4: Ask your friend about the common procedure of organizing a volunteer activity in Chinese universities (e.g., who is usually the organizer).

_____ Act 5: Introduce the common practices in the U.S. based on your own experience.

_____ Act 6: Comment on the similarities and differences between the two countries.

_____ Act 7: Propose to participate in a volunteer activity together in the future.

☞ **Performance 3 Elevator speech: self-introduction**

Introduce yourself to a person of importance (e.g., a professor, a senior manager in the organization you are interested in) and succinctly describe your interests, goals and skills in a couple of sentences. Select the most relevant pieces of information about yourself based on your goals for meeting this person.

_____ Act 1: State how you come to know the person (e.g., you heard the talk he/she gave).

_____ Act 2: Introduce your name, institutional affiliation, major and year at college.

_____ Act 3: State your personal interests in a certain field related to the person.

_____ Act 4: List one or two relevant experiences, for example, a recent internship or job in the field, or transferrable skills developed through a student club.

_____ Act 5: Ask if this person will be available in the near future for discussing a topic of interest.

_____ Act 6: Exchange contact information.

_____ Act 7: Express appreciation.

第七单元 调查研究 Research

7.1 确立话题

有的放矢

投石问路

Listen to the five questions in the audio and answer them based on your own experience. Be ready to discuss these questions in class. You may write down some notes in the space provided below.

1.
2.
3.
4.
5.

边听边想

Listen to the audio and try to visualize the dialogue in your mind. Think about who the speakers are, the kind of social relationship they have, and what their intentions might be.

耳闻目睹

Listen to the audio again while following along in the printed text. As you listen, mark any place that you are unclear or have questions about.

有的放矢

人物：秦老师、郑妮

（上午在教室，刚下课，郑妮想跟秦老师约个时间面谈）

郑妮：　秦老师，关于这次的研究，我想了两个话题，但是不确定哪个更好，我能不能跟您约个时间，请您指点一下？

秦老师：当然可以，今天下午三点到五点我都会在办公室，你随时都可以来。

郑妮：　太好了。那我三点来办公室请教您。(1/4)

（下午，郑妮来到了秦老师办公室）

郑妮：　秦老师好。

秦老师：你好。来，坐吧。你想研究的话题是什么？

郑妮：　一个是关于中国人移民到国外的，一个是中国人对环境问题的看法。您看哪个更好？

秦老师：都是很有意思的话题。但是考虑到我们这次活动希望大家从中国人普遍关心的问题入手，所以，第二个话题可能更符合活动的目的。

郑妮：　好的，那我就做关于环境问题的研究。(2/4)

秦老师：不过如果你只说"环境问题"，话题太大，你能不能说得更具体一点。

郑妮：　其实我主要想了解中国人怎么看雾霾跟经济发展的关系。

秦老师：嗯，这样具体一些。你为什么想研究这个话题呢？

郑妮：　我觉得随着近些年中国经济的高速发展，环境污染越来越严重，生活环境好像成了经济发展的代价，我想知道中国人怎么看。(3/4)

秦老师：你说的中国人是谁呢？

郑妮：　啊？就是我要去采访的那些普通中国人啊。

秦老师：你觉得他们的看法会是一致的吗？

郑妮：　可能不一定。噢，我明白了。您的意思是我应该把研究对象按身份背景分类，然后有针对性地对一些人群进行采访，对吗？

秦老师：对。这样你才能了解到不同身份背景的人看问题的视角有什么不同，他们的表达方式有什么特点。

郑妮：　好的。谢谢老师，现在我对这个研究活动的目的和方法都清楚多了。……(4/4)

知其所以然

The dialogue is broken down into sections below for explanation and analysis. Study

the notes and answer the questions for the underlined text.

> **1/4**
> （上午在教室，刚下课，郑妮想跟秦老师约个时间面谈）
> 郑妮：　秦老师，关于这次的研究，我想了两个话题，但是不确定哪个更好，我能不能跟您约个时间，请您指点一下？
> 秦老师：当然可以，今天下午三点到五点我都会在办公室，你随时都可以来。
> 郑妮：　太好了。那我三点来办公室请教您。

1. 郑妮要确立研究话题，她想请教秦老师："……请您指点一下？"
（1）你不太确定你的研究论文的结构是不是合理，你可以怎么请你的老师给建议？＿＿＿＿＿＿＿＿＿＿＿＿＿＿＿＿＿＿＿＿＿
（2）你设计了一张文化沙龙的海报，你可以怎么向懂设计的教授寻求改进建议？
＿＿＿＿＿＿＿＿＿＿＿＿＿＿＿＿＿

The saying 指点一下 is frequently used to politely request comments or suggestions on something you are working on. It indicates humbleness on your part by placing the addressee on a higher status with obvious expertise. For example, a student could very politely ask for his teacher's comments on the organization of his research paper by saying 老师，能不能请您指点一下我论文的结构? Similarly, to ask for a design expert's suggestions on a poster you are designing, you may politely say 李教授，我设计了一张文化沙龙的海报，能不能请您指点一下? 一下 here adds a sense of politeness, implying that it will only take a short time for the person to give the necessary directions or instructions.

2. 郑妮跟秦老师约好了三点去办公室，她说："那我三点来办公室请教您。"
（1）如果你要跟教授约一个时间讨论自己的论文，教授告诉你他周二下午一点半有空，你可以怎么礼貌地确认那个时间你会来见他？＿＿＿＿＿＿＿＿＿＿＿＿＿＿＿＿
（2）假如你在读一首李白的诗，但是没看明白。怎么请你的中文教授帮你？
＿＿＿＿＿＿＿＿＿＿＿＿＿＿＿＿＿

请教您 or 向您请教 is used to politely ask for information or instructions on something you don't understand. For example, to politely request a professor to explain the meaning of a classic Chinese poem, you may say 老师，李白的这首诗我读不懂，想向您请教一下 or 老师，我想向您请教一下这首诗的含义.

请教 is similar to 指点一下 in terms of the level of politeness, but it differs in the strategies for showing politeness. While the subject of 指点一下 is the other person (i.e., 请您指点一下), the subject of 请教您 is the speaker (i.e., 我想请教您 or 我想向您请教). In other words, using 指点一下, you honor the other person, whereas using 请教您 or 向您请教, you humble yourself. (That's a good thing!)

> **2/4**
>
> (下午,郑妮来到了秦老师办公室)
> 郑妮: 秦老师好。
> 秦老师:你好。来,坐吧。你想研究的话题是什么?
> 郑妮: 一个是关于中国人移民到国外的,一个是中国人对环境问题的看法。您看哪个更好?
> 秦老师:都是很有意思的话题。但是考虑到我们这次活动希望大家从中国人普遍关心的问题入手,所以,第二个话题可能更符合活动的目的。
> 郑妮: 好的,那我就做关于环境问题的研究。

3. 秦老师指出做研究时应该注意的地方,她说:"考虑到……"
(1) 你觉得组织一次文化活动要考虑哪些方面的问题?＿＿＿＿＿＿
(2) 有人提出放烟花庆祝独立日,你知道苏州市内规定不准放烟花。建议换一个活动的时候,你可以怎么说?＿＿＿＿＿＿

The phrase 考虑到 is normally followed by the rationale for making a decision. You can either state the complete reason or simply point out the type of reason that should be taken into consideration. For example, in response to someone's proposal of celebrating July 4th by setting off fireworks, you may say 考虑到苏州可能规定不准放烟花,我建议换一个活动 or you can say 考虑到苏州市的相关规定,我建议换一个活动.

4. 秦老师给郑妮的研究话题提建议,她说:"……希望大家从中国人普遍关心的问题入手。"
(1) 你认为学习外语,要先从什么入手?＿＿＿＿＿＿
(2) "做调查要先从做好采访计划开始",还可以怎么说?＿＿＿＿＿＿
(3) 当你接到一个很难的任务时,你不知道从哪儿可以开始,你可以说"我真不知道＿＿＿＿＿＿"。

从……入手 is used to indicate the first step of doing something. For example, you could say that to solve a problem you must start with an investigation: 解决问题要从调查研究入手. When you don't have a clue about where to start, you can say 我真不知道从哪儿入手 or, more formally, you can say 不知从何入手.

> **3/4**
>
> 秦老师:不过如果你只说"环境问题",话题太大,你能不能说得更具体一点。
> 郑妮: 其实我主要想了解中国人怎么看雾霾跟经济发展的关系。
> 秦老师:嗯,这样具体一些。你为什么想研究这个话题呢?
> 郑妮: 我觉得随着近些年中国经济的高速发展,环境污染越来越严重,生活环境好像成了经济发展的代价,我想知道中国人怎么看。

5. 郑妮告诉秦老师她的研究目的："我主要想了解中国人怎么看雾霾跟经济发展的关系。"

（1）这里"怎么看"是什么意思？ _____
（2）如果你想知道老师关于中国食品问题现状的看法，可以怎么问？ _____
（3）如果你想问老师中国的食品问题现状，可以怎么问？ _____

［someone］+ 怎么看 refers to someone's opinion on a certain issue. When used to ask about an opinion, it is often used in one of the following structures：a）［someone］+ 怎么看 +［issue］, and b）关于 +［issue］+［someone］+ 怎么看. For example, if you want to ask someone's opinion on the food safety issue, you can ask 您怎么看中国食品问题的现状？or 关于中国食品问题的现状您怎么看？If your question is about facts rather than someone's opinion, simply ask 中国食品问题现状是怎么样的？

6. 郑妮告诉秦老师她选择这个话题的原因，她说："我觉得随着近些年中国经济的高速发展……"

（1）郑妮觉得环境污染跟什么有关？为什么？ _____
（2）"由于电脑技术发展得很快，人们的工作和生活越来越依赖电脑"还可以怎么说？ _____
（3）你认为随着中国经济的高速发展，中美关系有什么变化？ _____

The pattern 随着……的高速发展 is similar to saying "with the rapid development of …". Common topics to use with this pattern are the economy, technology and computers. The result of the development always follows the statement. For example, to say that people's living standard has been improving as a result of the rapidly developing economy, you could say 随着经济的高速发展，人们的生活水平也不断提高.

7. 郑妮继续阐述经济发展和生活环境的关系："生活环境好像成了经济发展的代价。"

（1）郑妮为什么说生活环境成了经济发展的"代价"？ _____
（2）如果一个人想出名，他可能要付出什么代价？ _____
（3）年轻人常常喜欢感叹"这就是成长的代价"，你觉得"成长的代价"有哪些？ _____

The phrase ……的代价, literally meaning "the cost of something", usually refers to a negative consequence or the price that must be paid to achieve something good. In the dialogue, Zheng Ni is saying that the environment has been sacrificed (environmental pollution has worsened) as a consequence of the development of the economy. In another context, if a person betrays his friends for an opportunity to get famous, you may say 友情成了他出名的代价.

4/4

秦老师：你说的中国人是谁呢？
郑妮：　啊？就是我要去采访的那些普通中国人啊。
秦老师：你觉得他们的看法会是<u>一致</u>的吗？
郑妮：　可能不一定。噢，我明白了。您的意思是我应该把研究对象<u>按身份背景分类</u>，然后有针对性地对一些人群进行采访，对吗？
秦老师：对。这样你才能了解到不同身份背景的人看问题的视角有什么不同，他们的表达方式有什么特点。
郑妮：　好的。谢谢老师，现在我对这个研究活动的目的和方法都清楚多了。
……

8. 秦老师提示郑妮注意中国人之间的差异，她问："你觉得他们的看法会是一致的吗？"

（1）可以怎么用比较正式的语言说"大家全都同意小李的说法"？

_____

（2）如果一个人说的话与他的行为不一样，我们可以怎么形容这个人？

_____

一致 can mean unanimity or consistency, depending on the context. In the dialogue, 受访者的看法一致 denotes that the subjects' opinions are in agreement with each other. 一致 can also be followed by a verb in certain phrases as in 一致同意 and 一致认为. For example, when making a group decision, to indicate that people agree unanimously with someone's opinion, you can say 大家一致同意小李的看法. You can also use this phrase to denote consistency. For example, to describe a person whose behavior is consistent with his words, you may say 他是个言行一致的人. The phrase 不一致 can describe a situation in which two or more parties do not agree or are not consistent with each other. For example, when describing a person whose speech is not consistent with his behavior, we can say 他是个言行不一致的人 or 他这个人言行不一致.

9. 郑妮明白了怎么分析研究对象的看法，她说："您的意思是我应该把研究对象<u>按身份背景分类</u>……"

（1）除了按身份背景分类以外，研究对象还可以怎么分类？_____
（2）你觉得邮局的工作人员一般怎么把信件分类？_____
（3）你觉得图书馆的书一般按什么分类？_____

把 X 按 Y 分类 refers to the action of classifying or sorting item X according to certain criteria Y. 按 is the abbreviation for 按照, literally meaning "according to". For example, to describe the way post offices sort letters, you can say 邮局的工作人员一般把信件按邮

编分类. In another context, to introduce the way books are classified in libraries (according to the domain), you may say 图书馆的书一般按主题分类.

10. 郑妮继续说她的研究计划:"然后有针对性地对一些人群进行采访。"
(1) 怎样才能做到"有针对性"地对一些人群进行采访? _____
(2) 你听到一个朋友抱怨"我的老板最近总是针对我",你觉得他是什么意思?
_____

针对 literally means "to point the needle at". The phrase 有针对性地 + [action] refers to the manner of doing something with directed focus. For example, in the dialogue when Zheng Ni said 有针对性地对一些人群进行采访, she plans to organize her research participants according to social status and background in order to conduct interviews specifically directed at each group of participants.

In a different context, the phrase 针对 + [someone] can indicate the meaning of singling someone out and working against him or her. For example, to complain that a colleague recently behaves as if he is picking on you, you can say 我觉得丽丽最近总是针对我.

🎧 体演文本

Review the sections of the dialogue assigned by your teacher by listening to the audio and role-playing with another Chinese speaker. Be ready to perform the assigned portion of the dialogue from memory in class.

💬 举一反三

Answer the following questions and think about how the dialogue can be adapted for different situations.

1. 你觉得有哪些问题是你国家的人很关心的,但不一定是中国人真正关心的?
2. 秦老师反问郑妮:"中国人的看法会是一致的吗?"你觉得中国人的看法可能有哪些不一致?
3. 郑妮认为"生活环境成了经济发展的代价"。你能用你身边的两个例子证明或反驳这个观点吗?

🎧 熟能生巧

Listen to the audio and perform the following drills until you feel confident with the items practiced.

☞ **Drill 1 Recommending a better option based on certain consideration**

When asked to choose from two options, state the factor based on which you are making your choice, and then give your choice. The illustrations show the rationale based on which you should be able to make your choice.

例：

郑妮：这次做报告有两个话题，一个是关于移民的，一个是关于环境问题的。您看哪个更好？

李老师：都可以，但考虑到最好选中国人普遍关心的问题，关于环境的问题可能更好。

1. 成本 2. 方便 3.   4. 80%

☞ Drill 2 Improving upon a generalization

When someone points out a problem with your generalization, indicate that you understand where the problem is and suggest a way to improve your idea based on more careful categorization.

例：地域

李老师：关于经济发展影响环境这个问题，你能笼统地说南方人和北方人的看法都一样吗？

郑妮：我明白了，您的意思是这个问题应该按研究对象的地域分类。

1. 年龄
2. 职业
3. 收入
4. 性别

☞ Drill 3 Stating the negative result of a recent development

When asked why your research topic focuses on the relationship between economic development and another social aspect, explain that rapid economic development seems to have achieved at the price of the other aspect.

例：生活环境恶化

李老师：你为什么想研究经济发展和生活环境的关系呢？

郑妮：随着经济的高速发展，生活环境越来越恶化，生活环境好像成了经济发展的代价。

1. 人的身体健康差

2. 人际关系远

3. 社会风气差

4. 社会信用差

☞ Drill 4 Stating the next step

When the teacher gives a suggestion on how clear categorization will be helpful to your study, you recognize her help and state that you are going to design more targeted interview questions for the next step.

例：

李老师：把研究对象按身份背景分类，你就能知道不同身份背景的人表达方式有什么特点。

郑妮：谢谢老师，现在我对这个研究方向清楚多了。下一步我就针对不同身份背景的人群设计一些采访问题。

1.   2.   3.   4.

Narration

After her discussion with Miss Qin, Zheng Ni meets Zhao Yixin, who asks her if she has decided on a research topic. Assume Zheng Ni's role and explain how you have selected air pollution as your research topic and what you are going to do next.

赵奕歆：你的论文选题怎么样了？

言外有意

Read the cultural notes below and prepare questions for further discussion with Chinese people.

1. 有的放矢(yǒu dì fàng shǐ) Shoot the arrow at the target.

的(dì) means target here, and 矢 is an arrow. The literal meaning of this idiom is to shoot your arrow with a clear target, meaning to speak or act with a well-defined objective in mind. This idiom is used in both spoken and written discourses, especially in academic contexts. Your professor would very likely tell you that 做研究要有的放矢, meaning you should have a clear goal in mind when conducting research.

2. 与中国人讨论什么？

It is important for Chinese language learners to realize that what Americans like to talk about or know about China does not necessarily interest Chinese people themselves. Also keep in mind that there are many topics that Chinese people feel comfortable to discuss with other Chinese (especially people from the same region), but not with a foreigner. That is to say 与中国人讨论什么 is different from 中国人讨论什么.

One thing you will notice very soon while living in China is that Chinese people talk about food/cuisine much more often than you might expect. So if you meet someone for the first time in a relatively casual context, it is not a bad idea to talk about food, for example, asking about local specialties. If you know the person well and you really want to know their perspectives about certain issues, such as their opinion on environmental pollution, raise the question in a friendly way and avoid stating strong opinions. Keep in mind that certain sensitive issues such as Taiwan, environmental protection, homosexuality and the one-child policy might irritate certain groups of Chinese people. It is best to avoid these topics when you are trying to establish friendships or business relationships with Chinese people.

7.2 街头采访

循序渐进

🎧 投石问路

Listen to the five questions in the audio and answer them based on your own experience. Be ready to discuss these questions in class. You may write down some notes in the space provided below.

1.
2.
3.
4.
5.

🎧 边听边想

Listen to the audio and try to visualize the dialogue in your mind. Think about who the speakers are, the kind of social relationship they have, and what their intentions might be.

耳闻目睹

Listen to the audio again while following along in the printed text. As you listen, mark any place that you are unclear or have questions about.

循序渐进

人物：秦老师、郑妮、陈先生

（上课前，老师和同学们都在教室里）

秦老师：郑妮，听说你已经开始口头采访了，有什么有意思的发现吗？

郑　妮：我净碰钉子了！昨天下午我去公园采访了五个人，没有任何有价值的回答。

秦老师：怎么讲？（1/5）

郑　妮：我问的人都是一开始打招呼的时候还挺热情的，可是我一问他们"您对政府在治霾问题上的表现满意吗"，他们就不是找借口走掉，就是搪塞说"不好说"，还有一个人反问我"你说呢"。

秦老师：噢，你一个外国人问中国人对自己政府满意不满意，他们肯定会比较谨慎的。

郑　妮：那我应该怎么办啊？

秦老师：别着急，一会儿上课的时候我们会练习一些口头采访的技巧。（2/5）

（下午在万达国际电影城）

郑　妮：您好。

陈先生：你好。

郑　妮：您来看电影吗？

陈先生：是啊。你也是吧？

郑　妮：其实我是苏州大学的学生，我在做一个小调查，是为了完成中国文化课的一个作业。不知道您方不方便跟我说说您对雾霾问题的看法。

陈先生：方便，方便，反正离电影开始的时间还早。

郑　妮：太谢谢你了。一会儿如果有您不方便回答的问题，我们可以跳过。请问您贵姓？

陈先生：免贵姓陈。（3/5）

郑　妮：好的。陈先生，方便说一下您的年龄和职业吗？

陈先生：哦，58岁，退休了。

郑　妮：请问您是否觉得雾霾影响了您的生活呢？

陈先生：肯定。老觉得呼吸困难，本来平常还出来散散步、锻炼锻炼，现在一有雾霾就不敢出门了。

郑　妮：噢，是吗？那您觉得造成雾霾的最根本原因是什么呢？

陈先生：这个……应该是工业污染吧，跟路上跑的汽车数量增多也有关系。(4/5)
郑妮：　那您知不知道政府的一些治霾措施呢？
陈先生：限制车辆出行可能算一个吧。其实这个啊，我跟你说，没用。你看北京，限购限行了好几年，雾霾还不是照样厉害？
郑妮：　那么您觉得要怎样才能有效治霾呢？……(5/5)

知其所以然

The dialogue is broken down into sections below for explanation and analysis. Study the notes and answer the questions for the underlined text.

1/5

（上课前，老师和同学们都在教室里）
秦老师：郑妮，听说你已经开始口头采访了，有什么有意思的发现吗？
郑妮：　我净碰钉子了！昨天下午我去公园采访了五个人，没有任何有价值的回答。
秦老师：怎么讲？

---

1. 郑妮告诉秦老师她的口头采访不顺利，她说："我净碰钉子了。"
(1) 郑妮说她"碰钉子"，这说明她的采访做得顺利吗？_____
(2) 如果你星期六在家上了一天网，自己觉得很愧疚。晚上朋友问你做了什么，你可以怎么说？_____

净 indicates that someone has been doing the same thing repeatedly or running into the same situation, which the speaker finds undesirable. For example, in the dialogue Zheng Ni said that she kept getting rejected by others（碰钉子）. In a different context, after spending a whole day playing games online instead of being productive, you can tell your friend in a guilty tone 我今天什么都没干，净上网了.

The idiomatic phrase 碰钉子 literally means "to hit a nail". The nail refers to the big bronze nails on the doors of the 衙门, the government office in feudal China. In that context, "to hit the nail" was to be refused permission to enter.

2. 郑妮说她的采访"没有任何有价值的回答"，秦老师问她："怎么讲？"
(1) 这里的"怎么讲"是在问什么？
　　A. 郑妮采访时是怎么问的。　　B. 郑妮采访时问了什么。
　　C. 采访时发生了什么。　　　　D. 采访对象讲了什么。
(2) 这里的"怎么讲"还有别的问法吗？_____
(3) 你听过别人说"此话怎讲"吗？一般什么人会用这句话？_____

The phrase 怎么讲 here functions similarly to 怎么回事, asking for further clarification of the previous statement made by the interlocutor. In the dialogue, Miss Qin was in fact asking what happened during the interview. A similar expression is 此话怎讲, which also urges the interlocutor to explain something that has just been said. However, this expression is more commonly used in performance discourse, such as drama and crosstalk, rather than daily conversation.

郑妮： 我问的人都是一开始打招呼的时候还挺热情的,可是我一问他们"您对政府在治霾问题上的表现满意吗",他们就不是找借口走掉,就是搪塞说"不好说",还有一个人反问我"你说呢"。

秦老师： 噢,你一个外国人问中国人对自己政府满意不满意,他们肯定会比较谨慎的。

郑妮： 那我应该怎么办啊?

秦老师： 别着急,一会儿上课的时候我们会练习一些口头采访的技巧。

3. 郑妮说很多采访对象不愿意回答她的问题,她说:"他们……搪塞说'不好说'。"

(1) 这里的"搪塞"可以换成"拒绝"吗? 为什么? _____

(2) 一般会在什么情况下你可能"搪塞"别人? _____

(3) 如果有一位员工工作不太认真,他的经理提醒他认真工作的时候可以跟他说:"这工作很重要,别_____。"
   A. 搪塞   B. 敷衍

When doing research, if someone declines to answer your interview questions, you can say 那人拒绝了我. However, some people may agree to the interview, but give short and meaningless answers to certain questions because they either find them too sensitive or not important enough to answer seriously. In situations like these you can say 那人随便搪塞了我几句.

While 搪塞 is normally used to describe a noncommittal response to a person, 敷衍 can be used to describe half-hearted efforts in saying or doing something. For example, to remind an absent-minded employee to take his or her job seriously, you can say 上班时间专心工作,别敷衍.

4. 秦老师解释中国人为什么会有这种反应,她说:"……他们肯定会比较谨慎的。"

(1) 这里的"谨慎"可以换成什么词?
   A. 小心   B. 慎重   C. 严谨

（2）如果朋友开车来你家做客，晚上你送他出门时，你可以说什么？
_____

（3）你听说一个朋友准备炒股，想告诉他不要着急买，要做好研究，可以怎么说？
_____

Although 小心, 谨慎 and 严谨 can be used to describe paying close attention to people or things, they are used in different ways. 严谨 describes the manner of valuing precision and sticking to the rules strictly in order to deliver high-quality products. For example, to describe a stereotypical characteristic of German people, you can say 德国人做事很严谨. Both 谨慎 and 慎重 emphasize being cautious and careful to avoid making mistakes. However, 慎重 is mostly used to describe the thinking process rather than the actual conduct. Therefore, to advise someone to exercise caution in making a big financial decision such as investing in stocks, you can either say 一定要谨慎购买 or 做决定一定要慎重. In daily conversation, in order to avoid sounding too serious, use 小心 instead of 谨慎. For example, when guests are driving home from your dinner party, you can say goodbye and remind them to drive safely by saying 小心开车啊.

3/5

（下午在万达国际电影城）

郑妮：　您好。

陈先生：你好。

郑妮：　您来看电影吗？

陈先生：是啊。你也是吧？

郑妮：　其实我是苏州大学的学生，我在做一个小调查，是为了完成中国文化课的一个作业。不知道您方不方便跟我说说您对雾霾问题的看法。

陈先生：方便，方便，反正离电影开始的时间还早。

郑妮：　太谢谢你了。一会儿如果有您不方便回答的问题，我们可以跳过。请问您贵姓？

陈先生：免贵姓陈。

5. 在开始问问题之前郑妮告诉陈先生："一会儿如果有您不方便回答的问题，我们可以跳过。"

（1）郑妮为什么要在采访开始之前说这句话？_____

（2）这里的"跳"可以换成别的词吗？_____

（3）如果你觉得读写教材上有一部分内容很难，你想知道准备的时候能不能先不看那个部分，可以怎么问老师？_____

跳过 literally refers to the action of jumping over. It can also be used metaphorically to denote "skipping some routine procedures". For example, in the dialogue, Zheng Ni is reassuring Mr. Chen that he can skip any question that makes him uncomfortable. In another context, if you want to skip a section when preparing for a reading class because it's too difficult for you, you can ask the teacher 这一段我可以先跳过吗？The phrase 跳过 is rather fixed and 跳 cannot be replaced by other words.

4/5

郑妮：　好的。陈先生，方便说一下您的年龄和职业吗？

陈先生：哦，58岁，退休了。

郑妮：　请问您是否觉得雾霾影响了您的生活呢？

陈先生：肯定的。老觉得呼吸困难，本来平常还出来散散步、锻炼锻炼，现在一有雾霾就不敢出门了。

郑妮：　噢，是吗？那您觉得造成雾霾的最<u>根本</u>原因是什么呢？

陈先生：这个……应该是工业污染吧，跟路上跑的汽车数量增多也有关系。

---

6. 郑妮问陈先生对雾霾成因的看法："那您觉得造成雾霾的最根本原因是什么呢？"

（1）"根本"原来指的是什么呢？ _____

（2）这里的"根本"可以换成"根源"吗？ _____

（3）如果你听到人说"我根本不想骗他的"，这里的"根本"大概是什么意思？
_____

（4）你觉得中国经济快速发展的根本原因是什么？ _____

Both 根 and 本 refer to the root of plants originally. Combining them together, 根本 refers to or describes something fundamental. 根源 generally functions as a noun, referring to the fundamental origin of something. Therefore, in this context, 问题的根本原因 is interchangeable with 问题的根源. When used as an adverb, 根本 usually pairs with 不 or 没 to strengthen the negation. For example, to emphasize that you don't want to tell something to someone at all (no matter whether you actually did it or not), you can say 我根本不想告诉他的.

5/5

郑妮：　那您知不知道政府的一些治霾措施呢？

陈先生：限制车辆出行可能算一个吧。其实这个啊，我跟你说，没用。你看北京，<u>限购限行</u>了好几年，雾霾还不是照样厉害？

郑妮：　那么您觉得要怎样才能有效治霾呢？……

---

7. 郑妮问陈先生是否知道政府的一些做法："那你知不知道政府的一些治霾措

施呢？"

（1）这里的"措施"可以换成"方法"吗？为什么？＿＿＿＿＿＿＿＿＿＿＿＿＿

（2）发生火灾时有什么应对措施吗？＿＿＿＿＿＿＿＿＿＿＿＿＿＿

（3）你觉得自己老是记不住生词，想问问你的同学是怎么记的，可以怎么问？
＿＿＿＿＿＿＿＿＿＿＿＿＿

Although 方法 and 措施 both denote methods or measures, they differ in scope and formality. 方法 is a general term referring to all kinds of methods. For example, to inquire good ways of learning new vocabulary, you can ask 你有什么记生词的好方法吗？On the other hand, 措施 is often used in written discourses, referring to the formal measures taken to deal with issues which have substantial consequences. For example, when a natural disaster occurs, each person will have his or her own 方法 for surviving it, while the official measures taken by government agencies to deal with the situation can be called 应对措施.

（4）这里的"治"是什么意思？

　　A．治疗　　　　　　B．治理　　　　　　C．治愈

（5）你知不知道政府的一些治水措施？＿＿＿＿＿＿＿＿＿＿＿＿＿＿＿

（6）如果政府公布了一些针对污染的措施，用"治X"这个结构可以怎么说？
＿＿＿＿＿＿＿＿＿＿＿＿＿

You may have heard of 治病 before, in which 治 stands for 治疗 (to cure). In the structure 治 X, however, 治 stands for 治理 (to manage and put things back to order) and X usually refers to a significant issue. What you can put after 治 in this structure is a matter of convention. For example, 治霾 represents 治理雾霾, 治水 is 治理洪水, 治污 stands for 治理污染 and 治国 stands for 治理国家.

8. 陈先生觉得北京的治霾措施没什么用，他说："你看北京，限购限行了好几年，雾霾还不是照样厉害？"

（1）"限购限行"具体限制的是什么？＿＿＿＿＿＿＿＿＿＿＿＿＿＿

（2）如果你在路上看到一个写着"限高 10 米"的标牌挂在停车场的门口，大概是什么意思？＿＿＿＿＿＿＿＿＿＿＿＿＿

（3）如果你在学校里搞了一个活动，准备了一些 T 恤作为纪念品，你想告诉大家每人只能领一件，可以怎么说？＿＿＿＿＿＿＿＿＿＿＿＿＿＿＿＿

The structure 限 X refers to certain regularities that set a limit on something. The X here can be an action, such as 限购限行, which is a rule controlling the number of vehicles that can be bought and driven. In another context, when handing out free T-shirts at an event, to inform people that one person can only get one T-shirt, you can say 每人限领一件. Some properties can also fit in the place of X, such as 限高, which is setting a limit on the height of the vehicles coming through the gate.

体演文本

Review the sections of the dialogue assigned by your teacher by listening to the audio and role-playing with another Chinese speaker. Be ready to perform the assigned portion of the dialogue from memory in class.

举一反三

Answer the following questions and think about how the dialogue can be adapted for different situations.

1. 第二次出去采访的时候,郑妮用了什么策略使受访者同意接受采访?除了那些策略以外,她还可以怎么做?
2. 问完受访者基本信息之后的第一个采访问题很重要,你觉得什么样的问题适合做第一个问题?
3. 采访中国人的时候,有时候受访者回答可能很简短。你可以怎么让受访者多说几句?
4. 郑妮第二次去采访能够成功,跟她选择的地点和采访对象有没有关系?你觉得在什么样的地方的哪些人比较容易接受采访?

熟能生巧

Listen to the audio and perform the following drills until you feel confident with the items practiced.

☞ Drill 1 Emphasizing certain aspects of identity

When your friend states the difficulties he or she met conducting interviews, point out that it is a specific aspect of his or her identity that caused the problems. Each of the illustrations shows the aspect of identity that hindered the interview.

例:

郑妮:我问中国人"你对政府在治霾问题上的表现满意吗",他们好像不太高兴。
周丹锐:你一个美国人问中国人对自己政府的表现满不满意,他们肯定会不高兴的。

☞ **Drill 2　Asking for the fundamental cause**

Imagine that you are conducting an interview. Initiate the conversation by asking about the fundamental cause of an issue. Each of the cues shows the issue you want to ask about. Also try to catch the answers.

例：雾霾

郑妮：你觉得造成雾霾的最根本原因是什么呢？

陈先生：应该是工业污染和汽车数量的增多吧。

1. 高物价
2. 大城市高房价
3. 贫富差距
4. 城乡发展不平衡

☞ **Drill 3　Politely inquiring about basic personal information**

Image that you are conducting an interview. Initiate the conversation by politely asking your interviewees for personal background information and state that they may skip any questions they don't feel comfortable to answer.

例：年龄

郑妮：方便说一下您的年龄吗？如果不方便，我们也可以跳过。

陈先生：好的。我58。

1. 职业
2. 收入
3. 电话号码
4. 全名

☞ **Drill 4　Asking a follow-up question about an effective solution**

When the interviewee points out that the current solution to a problem is ineffective, follow-up by asking his or her opinion on how to solve this problem. Below are some expressions for "solving" followed by the types of problems they are commonly associated with：

- 治理雾霾/水土流失/交通拥堵
- 缩小贫富差距
- 解决地铁拥挤问题

例：

陈先生：限购限行了几年，雾霾照样厉害。

郑妮：那么你觉得要怎样才能有效治理雾霾呢？……

1.　　　　　2.　　　　　3.　　　　　4.

Narration

Zheng Ni did a second round of interview at the movie theatre after class. The next day, Miss Qin asked her how her interview went. Assume Zheng Ni's role and tell Miss Qin about your experience of interviewing people at the movie theatre.

1. Tell your experience with details about Mr. Chen's opinion on the negative effects of the fog and haze on his life.

2. Tell your experience with details about Mr. Chen's opinion on the causes of air pollution and the measures that the government has taken to control the pollution.

言外有意

Read the cultural notes below and prepare questions for further discussion with Chinese people.

1. 循序渐进（xún xù jiàn jìn）

This idiom is used to emphasize that the process of learning or working should progress gradually in a certain order. Another four-character idiom 急于求成 describes the opposite state: to be in a rush to achieve a goal. The two idioms are often used when giving advice on how to achieve a goal. For example, a teacher might say to a student who aims high but is impatient with readings and homework 做学问要循序渐进，不能急于求成.

2. 外国人问中国人对政府的看法

As mentioned previously in the notes, the topics Chinese people talk about among themselves can be very different from what they talk about with foreigners. Chinese people, just like people elsewhere, complain about their government for many different reasons. However, this does not mean Chinese people feel comfortable to talk about governmental decisions and issues openly with foreigners. A good strategy for foreign language learners who truly want to know Chinese people's opinions about their government is to discuss a recent news item and observe how Chinese people react towards it. However, instead of directly asking 你是如何看待这个问题的, the conversation would be more natural and meaningful if the foreigner can lead into the discussion by stating some relatively neutral opinions or posing non-threatening questions just like Zheng Ni did in our dialogue.

3. 采访的注意事项/技巧

A lot of Chinese people are willing to participate in foreigners' interviews, but they may not feel confident or comfortable to express their feelings and opinions in great depth. There are certain things you can say to increase the trust level, and make the conversation more bi-directional. For example, at the beginning of the interview, you could tell the people you are interviewing that they can skip any question they are not comfortable to answer or by assuring them that you have only educational purposes in mind. For example, you can say, 如果有的问题你觉得是比较敏感的话题, 我们可以跳过 or 我们的调查完全是出于学习的目的, 请你放心. During the interview, if you sense someone hesitating about saying something or not, you can tell him or her 我们也可以等一下再讨论这个话题 and then move on. Make sure you react to people's answers or comments positively so that they will continue talking. For example, you can say 你说的这点真有道理, 是我之前没有想到的. When you want to encourage someone to elaborate on a certain point, you can say 你说的这点给我很大的启发, 你能不能具体说一下? And, of course, don't forget to express your appreciation when the conversation ends.

7.3 口头报告
对答如流

🎧 投石问路

Listen to the five questions in the audio and answer them based on your own experience. Be ready to discuss these questions in class. You may write down some notes in the space provided below.

1.
2.
3.
4.
5.

🎧 边听边想

Listen to the audio and try to visualize the dialogue in your mind. Think about who the speakers are, the kind of social relationship they have, and what their intentions might be.

🎧 耳闻目睹

Listen to the audio again while following along in the printed text. As you listen, mark any place that you are unclear or have questions about.

对答如流

人物：郑妮、李女士、宋先生

（项目在活动中心开展文化沙龙活动，郑妮第一个做口头报告，有一些校外的人也来听）

郑妮： 各位老师、各位同学、各位苏州朋友，大家好！感谢大家来参加我们的文化沙龙活动。我今天想讨论的话题是"部分苏州市民对雾霾问题的看法"。我一共采访了15个人，包括5位大学生、5位在职人员和5位已经退休的人。我的研究问题主要有三个：一是他们是否觉得雾霾影响了他们的生活；二是他们认为造成雾霾的最根本原因是什么；三是他们知道哪些治理雾霾的措施以及他们对那些措施的评价。（1/5）

对于第一个问题，受访者普遍表示雾霾严重影响身体健康，大部分受访者也表示雾霾让他们心情不好，影响生活质量。有一位在职受访者提到雾霾天以来他跟太太吵架都多了。对于第二个问题，受访者提到最多的原因是工业污染、汽车尾气和施工修路。有一个很有意思的现象就是在职的受访者中没有人提及汽车尾气。对于第三个问题，所有受访者都提到限制私家车的措施，但是他们都表示这一措施对于治霾的效果并不明显，他们举了北京和上海的例子。有一位受访者说北京限购限行几年了但雾霾现象还是有增无减。（2/5）

总的来说，受访者普遍认为雾霾影响身体健康，影响心情，从而影响生活质量。在谈及造成雾霾的根本原因时，他们普遍认为工业污染是雾霾的罪魁祸首，其次是汽车尾气和施工。尽管这些原因都跟经济的高速发展有着直接或间接的联系，但是在谈论治霾措施时，没有人直接提到应该放慢经济发展的步伐。这让我很好奇，大家到底是喜欢经济发展多一些，还是讨厌雾霾多一些。今天借这个机会也想听听在场各位的想法。谢谢大家，欢迎你们的提问和建议。（3/5）

李女士： 郑妮同学，谢谢你的精彩发言。我就想问一下你自己怎么看中国的雾霾现象？

郑妮： 我觉得造成雾霾的原因是多方面的，所以要治理雾霾也应该多方面进行。汽车尾气可能不是造成雾霾的最主要原因。大家都说美国是"车轮上的国家"，私家车的使用率不比中国低，但是没有出现过像中国这样的雾霾现象。当然，这只是我个人的看法。（4/5）

宋先生：（激动地说）你说的很对，关键问题不在私家车。其实你的那些受访者都没有提到问题的症结。

郑妮：不好意思，我的中文词汇量还很有限，请问症结的意思是？

宋先生：就是造成雾霾的最根本原因。为什么工业污染严重？为什么到处采矿、修地铁？

郑妮：哦，我的采访确实没有深入到那个层面，谢谢您提出来。不知道您对这个问题怎么看？

宋先生：我看这个症结啊就在于政绩观……（5/5）

知其所以然

The dialogue is broken down into sections below for explanation and analysis. Study the notes and answer the questions for the underlined text.

1/5

（项目在活动中心开展文化沙龙活动，郑妮第一个做口头报告，有一些校外的人也来听）

郑妮：各位老师、各位同学、各位苏州朋友，大家好！感谢大家来参加我们的文化沙龙活动。我今天想讨论的话题是"部分苏州市民对雾霾问题的看法"。我一共采访了 15 个人，包括 5 位大学生，5 位在职人员和 5 位已经退休的人。我的研究问题主要有三个：一是他们是否觉得雾霾影响了他们的生活；二是他们认为造成雾霾的最根本原因是什么；三是他们知道哪些治理雾霾的措施以及他们对那些措施的评价。

---

1. Giving a research presentation

A research presentation generally contains the following steps：

(1) Introduce your topic：
- 今天我讨论的话题是……

(2) Introduce the subjects：
- 我一共采访了 W 个人，包括 X 位……，Y 位……和 Z 位……

(3) State your research questions：
- 我的研究问题主要有 X 个，一是……，二是……，三是……

(4) Report and elaborate on findings for each research question：
- 对于第一个问题，受访者普遍表示……
- 在谈到……的时候，受访者普遍认为……
- 有一位受访者提到……

(5) Conclude your research：
- 总的来说……

（6）End the presentation by welcoming comments and questions：
- 今天借这个机会我也想听听大家关于这个问题的想法。
- 谢谢各位，欢迎你们的提问和建议。

2. 郑妮介绍她的采访对象："……5位在职人员……"
（1）这里的"在职人员"指的是怎样的人？_____
（2）很多网站会统计自己的"在线人数"，这大概是什么意思？_____
（3）"生活在中国的留学生"，用简洁正式的书面语可以怎么说？_____

The structure 在 X refers to the state of being at a certain place or position, which usually functions as an adjective. X can be a concrete place, such as China. Since X is usually a one-character word, you can use 在华留学生 to refer to "overseas students in China" in written-style language. X can also be a more abstract concept. For example, 在职人员 holds a position in a workplace, and 在线人数 refers to the number of people who are simultaneously online.

3. 郑妮的第三个采访问题包括两个部分："三是他们知道哪些治理雾霾的措施以及他们对那些措施的评价。"
（1）这里的"以及"可以换成"和"吗？_____
（2）周丹锐：你最喜欢的运动是什么？
    孙浩：我最喜欢游泳_____打篮球。
    A. 和　　　　　　B. 及　　　　　　C. 以及
（3）北京、上海_____广州是中国的三大城市。（可多选）
    A. 和　　　　　　B. 及　　　　　　C. 以及

Although 和, 及 and 以及 can all be used to connect a list of two or more items, their usages slightly differ from each other, and none of them are equal to the use of "and" in English!

和, commonly used in both oral and written discourse, is used to connect short nominal and verbal words. For example, to tell a friend that you like to swim and play basketball, you can say 我最喜欢去游泳和打篮球.

及 and 以及 are normally used in written discourse. 及 is most commonly used to connect a list of two or more nominals. For example, to list the top three large cities in China in an article you can say 北京、上海及广州是中国的三大城市. In this context, 和 and 以及 may also be used in the place of 及. However, using 和, the discourse is more colloquial and less formal. Note that besides connecting nominal and verbal phrases, 以及 can also be used to connect clauses while neither 和 nor 及 can. Therefore, when Zheng Ni introduces her third interview question in the dialogue, 以及 is the only appropriate choice.

> **2/5**
> 郑妮：对于第一个问题，受访者普遍表示雾霾严重影响身体健康，大部分受访者也表示雾霾让他们心情不好，影响生活质量。有一位在职受访者提到雾霾天以来他跟太太吵架都多了。对于第二个问题，受访者提到最多的原因是工业污染、汽车尾气和施工修路。有一个很有意思的现象就是在职的受访者中没有人提及汽车尾气。对于第三个问题，所有受访者都提到限制私家车的措施，但是他们都表示这一措施对于治霾的效果并不明显，他们举了北京和上海的例子。有一位受访者说北京限购限行几年了但雾霾现象还是有增无减。

4. 郑妮介绍第一个问题的采访结果，她说："受访者普遍表示雾霾严重影响身体健康。"

（1）这里的"表示"可以换成"表达"吗？ _____

（2）"受访者表达了不满"和"受访者表现出了不满"有什么区别吗？
_____

（3）如果郑妮在跟好朋友介绍这个采访结果，她可能会怎么说这里的"受访者普遍表示"？ _____

（4）你认为环境污染问题中有哪些受害者？ _____

Zheng Ni uses rather formal language in her presentation. 受访者 and 表示 are both formal expressions. If she were speaking with her friend, she might just say 我采访的人都说……

表示 here functions similarly to 说, but it is a more formal way of quoting someone's statement. 表达 is usually followed by a noun or nominal phrase, such as one's thoughts or a certain kind of emotion. For example, to say that one expressed his opinion/anger, you can say 他表达了自己的看法/愤怒. However, 表现出 indicates that someone does not necessarily and explicitly convey his or her ideas. Instead, his or her facial expressions or gestures display the intention.

The structure 受 X 者 is rather formal, referring to the people who are X-ed. For example, 受访者 refers to people who are interviewed and 受害者 are people who are harmed, i.e., victims.

5. 郑妮提到了一个有意思的现象："在职的受访者中没有人提及汽车尾气。"

（1）这里的"提及"可以换成"提到"吗？为什么？ _____

（2）如果你的朋友给你介绍过一部电影，但是你忘记名字了，可以怎么问你的朋友？ _____

（3）你的博客里有一句话："谈到以前的事的时候奶奶哭了。"你的朋友建议你用

些更正式的词，可以怎么改？＿＿＿＿＿＿＿＿＿＿＿＿＿＿＿＿＿＿＿＿

One of the functions of 及 in classical Chinese is similar to 到 in modern Mandarin. Therefore，提及 can be viewed as a formal version of 提到. When asking a friend about a movie he once mentioned, you can say 你上次提到的电影叫什么？The phrase 提及, on the other hand, is normally used in written or more formal discourse. Another commonly used pair similar to 提及/提到 is 谈及/谈到. For example, to rephrase the sentence 谈到以前的事的时候奶奶哭了 with formal written-style language, you can say 谈及往事时，奶奶流下了眼泪。

6. 一位受访者评价北京治霾措施的效果："北京限购限行几年了但雾霾现象还是有增无减。"

（1）根据郑妮所说，那位受访者觉得北京的雾霾现象变严重了吗？＿＿＿＿＿＿＿＿

（2）有句歇后语叫"肉包子打狗——有去无回"，你能猜到是什么意思吗？
＿＿＿＿＿＿＿＿＿＿＿＿＿＿＿＿＿＿＿＿

（3）你觉得什么样的行为是"有勇无谋"？＿＿＿＿＿＿＿＿＿＿＿＿＿＿＿＿＿＿

（4）虽然中国房价很贵，但买房的人还是越来越多，你可以怎么描述这种情况？
＿＿＿＿＿＿＿＿＿＿＿＿＿＿＿

有 X 无 Y is a common structure in four-character Chinese idioms. These idioms often have a negative connotation, because the focus is on the second half of it, which is 无 Y. The first half, 有 X, generally only functions as setting a premise. It generally doesn't change the connotation of the whole idiom whether 有 X part denotes something positive or not. For example, the idiom 有勇无谋 is often used to describe a person who is courageous（勇敢的）but lacks strategy（无谋）or to criticize a person for taking ineffective actions without careful planning. For example, 我觉得小李那个人有勇无谋 and 他那样做是有勇无谋. Similarly, the idiom 有去无回 is often used to say that things or favors that are given out are by no means retrievable—like a meat bun thrown at a dog.

3/5

郑妮：总的来说，受访者普遍认为雾霾影响身体健康，影响心情，从而影响生活质量。在谈及造成雾霾的根本原因时，他们普遍认为工业污染是雾霾的罪魁祸首，其次是汽车尾气和施工。尽管这些原因都跟经济的高速发展有着直接或间接的联系，但是在谈论治霾措施时，没有人直接提到应该放慢经济发展的步伐。这让我很好奇，大家到底是喜欢经济发展多一些，还是讨厌雾霾多一些。今天借这个机会也想听听在场各位的想法。谢谢大家，欢迎你们的提问和建议。

---

7. 郑妮总结受访者对第一个问题的回答："受访者普遍认为雾霾影响身体健康，

影响心情,从而影响生活质量。"

(1) 这里的"从而"可以换成"而且"吗？为什么？_____

(2) 请选择适当的词完成句子："在苏州的生活很忙碌,很愉快,_____让我认识了很多新朋友。"

  A. 从而   B. 而且

The conjunction 从而 normally denotes a special type of causal relation with an emphasis on the progression of things. There are usually two stages of progression in a 从而 sentence：{[subject]→[result 1]}→从而→[result 2]. The result 2 following 从而 is the result of a second-stage progression and is only based on the premise of result 1, rather than directly on the subject itself. For example, in the sentence above, pollution directly impacts 身体健康 and 心情, and these, in turn, affect 生活质量. In another context, to state in an essay that the rapid development of agriculture provides sufficient food for people, which consequently improves life quality, you can say 农业的迅速发展为人们提供了充足的食物,从而改善了生活质量。

If there's no causal relationship between result 1 and result 2, the appropriate way to link a list of items is with 而且 rather than 从而. On the other hand, if the causal relation exists, using 而且 in place of 从而 won't be as accurate but is still acceptable.

8. 郑妮总结受访者对第二个问题的回答："他们普遍认为工业污染是雾霾的罪魁祸首。"

(1) "罪魁"和"祸首"意思一样吗？是什么意思？_____

(2) 你觉得什么是全球变暖现象的罪魁祸首？_____

(3) 你觉得中国的书籍可能会怎么介绍希特勒这个人？_____

Both 罪魁 and 祸首 can be interpreted as "head of a disaster" literally, so this four-character Chinese idiom denotes the leading cause of an undesirable situation or disaster. It can refer to a real person. For example, you may find 希特勒是二战的罪魁祸首之一 in a Chinese history book. It can also refer to abstract concepts, such as industrial pollution in the dialogue. In another context, to point out that deforestation is the cause of global warming, you can say 滥砍滥伐是全球变暖的罪魁祸首.

9. 关于第三个问题："没有人直接提到应该放慢经济发展的步伐。"

(1) "步伐"本意是什么？有什么更口语的说法吗？_____

(2) 如果你的一个受访者觉得中国的经济发展还不够快,你在做报告时可以怎么说？_____

(3) 如果你和几个同学在组织一项活动,你觉得有点来不及了,可以怎么跟大家说？_____

Originally 步伐 refers to the pace of someone, and it is a rather formal word. In spoken Chinese, one might simply say 步子. For example, to describe a fast walker you can say 他走路时步子很快. Here in the dialogue, 步伐 is used metaphorically, referring to the pace of economic development. For example, to state one's belief that China should speed up its economic development you can say 他觉得中国应该加快经济发展的步伐. However, 加快……的步伐 is usually used only in very formal discourse, denoting the progress of a large-scale undertaking, such as the economic development of a country. Therefore, it doesn't fit in the last question. Instead, you can say 我们得加快进度了.

4/5

李女士：郑妮同学，谢谢你的精彩发言。我就想问一下你自己怎么看中国的雾霾现象？

郑妮：我觉得造成雾霾的原因是多方面的，所以要治理雾霾也应该多方面进行。汽车尾气可能不是造成雾霾的最主要原因。大家都说美国是"车轮上的国家"，私家车的使用率不比中国低，但是没有出现过像中国这样的雾霾现象。当然，这只是我个人的看法。

10. 郑妮介绍她自己对中国雾霾的看法："造成雾霾的原因是多方面的。"
（1）你觉得郑妮直接回答了观众的问题吗？＿＿＿＿＿＿＿＿＿＿
（2）当你被问到"为什么中国学生的创造性没有美国学生强"时，你可以怎么开始你的回答？＿＿＿＿＿＿＿＿＿＿
（3）小组讨论的时候，你想提醒你的同学们要从各个不同的角度来看一个问题，你可以怎么说？（请用"多方面"）＿＿＿＿＿＿＿＿＿＿

When asked her "own opinion" about the severe smog in China, Zheng Ni started with "there are many reasons for the current problem". Emphasizing the complexity of the issue instead of directly answering the question is a strategic way for a foreign speaker to avoid offering a strong opinion in front of a Chinese. In addition to 造成……的原因是多方面的, another commonly used expression is 我们要从多方面来看这个问题（We should look at this issue from multiple-perspectives）.

5/5

宋先生：（激动地说）你说的很对，关键问题不在私家车。其实你的那些受访者都没有提到问题的症结。

郑妮：不好意思，我的中文词汇量还很有限，请问症结的意思是？

宋先生：就是造成雾霾的最根本原因。为什么工业污染严重？为什么到处采矿、修地铁？

> 郑妮：　哦,我的采访确实没有深入到那个层面,谢谢您提出来。不知道您对这个问题怎么看?
>
> 宋先生：我看这个症结啊就在于政绩观……

11. 观众宋先生认为那些受访者都没有提到问题的症结。
   （1）如果不用"症结",还可以用什么词替换?
      A. 根源　　　　　　　B. 特点　　　　　　　C. 性质
   （2）在你的报告中,当你要介绍造成雾霾现象的根本原因时,你可以用怎样的一句设问(rhetorical question)来开始你的报告?_____

症结 is a word from Chinese medicine, which literally means a hard lump（结）in the abdomen. Now, this word is used to indicate the crux of an issue. It can be replaced with 问题的根源（the root of a problem）. When used in a question, it is more common to ask 这个问题的症结在哪儿? instead of 这个问题的症结是什么?

12. 郑妮同意宋先生指出的问题,说:"我的采访确实还没深入到那个层面。"
   （1）很明显,郑妮这么说是因为她回答不上宋先生的问题,如果她就说"对不起,我的采访没有提到那个方面",你觉得有什么不同的效果吗?_____

When asked about something she is not able to deal with, Zheng Ni modestly admitted that her study did not delve into that depth. Unlike 没有提到那个方面 which seems to indicate that the question is somewhat unrelated, 没有深入到那个层面 is a self-criticism, indicating that the presenter takes responsibility for not being able to think profoundly. This is also an indirect compliment to the person who raised the thought-provoking question. The use of 确实 also strengthens the sense of modesty and self-criticism by showing agreement with the audience.

13. 宋先生告诉郑妮他对污染症结的看法:"我看这个症结啊就在于政绩观……"
   （1）政绩观是什么?
      A. 领导执政的成绩。　　　　　B. 领导对自己执政成绩的态度看法。
   （2）你认为领导应该有什么样的政绩观?_____
   （3）"对世界的总的看法和根本观点"是"世界观",那么"对人生的根本态度和看法"是_____。

XX观 refers to one's fundamental understanding and attitude towards a certain subject. For example, 政绩观 refers to how people perceive their political achievements. Similarly, 世界观 and 人生观 are the basic philosophical views on the world and life. Other commonly used items include 价值观,教育观,婚姻观,消费观。Do you know what they mean? Note that compound words like these are conventional expressions and can't be created as one wishes.

🎧 体演文本

Review the sections of the dialogue assigned by your teacher by listening to the audio and role-playing with another Chinese speaker. Be ready to perform the assigned portion of the dialogue from memory in class.

💬 举一反三

Answer the following questions and think about how the dialogue can be adapted for different situations.

1. 请在郑妮的报告中画出你觉得在你自己的报告中可以使用的表达（至少3个）。

2. 宋先生激动地说那些受访者"没有提到问题的症结"，你觉得他实际想说的意思是什么？

3. 郑妮在回答问题的时候，用了两个技巧帮助她巧妙地回避了尴尬。请你把它们找出来。

4. 除了郑妮在报告中使用的技巧，你还可以用什么方法回避一些不想回答的问题？

5. 对于有一些不适合在公开场合过多讨论的问题，即使你有想法也应该回避。在中国什么样的问题是不适合在公开场合过多讨论的？在美国呢？

🎧 熟能生巧

Listen to the audio and perform the following drills until you feel confident with the items practiced.

☞ **Drill 1 Introducing research subjects**

In this drill, describe the sub-categories of your research participants. The examples demonstrate some strategies you can use. In the first example, Zhou Danrui categorizes the 15 participants simply by their employment status: college students, employees and retired people.

例1：

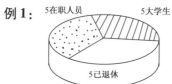

周丹锐：我一共采访了15个人，包括5位大学生、5位在职人员和5位已经退休的人。

In the second example, Zhou Danrui is able to describe his participants in more details: students who are still in school, white-collar employees of foreign companies, and self-employed people.

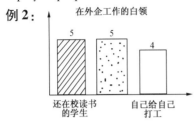

周丹锐：我一共采访了 14 个人，其中 5 位是还在校读书的学生，5 位是在外企工作的白领，还有 4 位自己给自己打工。

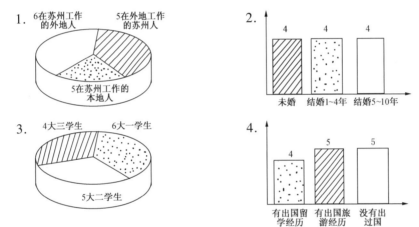

☞ Drill 2 Utilizing reported speech

The illustrations below provide the respondents' original words. Upon hearing them on the audio, practice reporting what each respondent has said. In the example, Zhou Danrui reports that one of his respondent mentioned that he argues more with his wife during smoggy and hazy days. You can report other people's speech with these commonly used verbs:

- 提到　　to mention
- 告诉　　to inform (someone)
- 说　　　to say
- 表示　　to express (one's opinion)

例：提到

受访者:"雾霾天以来我跟太太吵架都多了。"
周丹锐：有一位在职受访者提到雾霾天以来他跟太太吵架都多了。

1. 提到　　　　　　　　　　　　　　2. 告诉

3. 说　　　　　　　　　　　　　　　4. 表示

☞ Drill 3 Reporting findings on a specific question

In this drill, practice summarizing the various findings on a specific research question. Each of the illustrations provides the research question as well as two findings from the interview.

例：

周丹锐：在谈及造成雾霾的原因时,受访者普遍认为首先是工业污染,其次是汽车尾气和施工。

1.　　　　　　　　　　　　　　　　2.

3.    4.

☞ Drill 4 Making use of a public occasion

In this drill, take advantage of a certain occasion to make a public statement. In the example, Zhou Danrui uses the conclusion of his presentation as an opportunity to invite the audience to share their opinions about the research topic. Each of the illustrations shows the occasion as well as your personal agenda.

例：听听在场各位的想法，欢迎你们的提问与建议

周丹锐：今天借这个机会也想听听在场各位的想法，欢迎你们的提问与建议。

1. 感谢大家对我的帮助和支持   2. 敬王老师一杯，祝您生日快乐、工作顺利

3. 推荐一本书，叫《成语五百词》 4. 听听在场各位的看法，欢迎提问和建议

Drafting an oral presentation

Draft or revise the script of your own oral presentation. Make appropriate use of the strategies and expressions learned and drilled in this lesson.

言外有意

Read the cultural notes below and prepare questions for further discussion with Chinese people.

1. 对答如流 (duì dá rú liú) Able to reply quickly and fluently.

This idiom is mostly used in a complimentary way, often emphasizing that someone is well prepared. For example, after you have done a great job with your presentation, your professor may tell you that 你今天表现不错,对答如流. In response, you can say, 哪里哪里,应该谢谢您之前给我的建议.

2. 做报告的语言技巧

When giving a presentation in English, you want to avoid using words such as "perhaps" or "maybe" too often lest you sound too uncertain about your points. This rule also applies when you give presentations in Chinese. You do not want your ideas to sound too unrealistic or generalized. For example, in our dialogue, Zheng Ni's topic is 部分苏州市民对雾霾问题的看法. The word 部分 here skillfully shows that the speaker realizes she had interviewed a small group of people, therefore, avoiding the problem of over-generalizing her conclusion. When giving her presentation, Zheng Ni follows the sequence of introducing the research topic first, then subjects, questions and conclusions. This is an effective way to organize a presentation.

When being asked some difficult questions, Zheng Ni says 您的这个问题的确值得思考,不过,由于时间关系,我能不能活动结束后继续跟您讨论. This is an effective way to deal with a broad question or a question you did not expect. People will not ask you similar questions after that. In general, a successful presentation takes a lot of skill, practice and deep understanding of the topic being presented.

> 学而时习之

Before you actually do the field performances, rehearse doing them with a Chinese friend. The "Useful Expressions" box below provides you with some expressions you may use for these performances. For now, try saying them after the audio.

🎧 **Useful Expressions**

1. 您有没有空听听我的研究计划,给我提提建议?
2. 我的研究话题是/采访问题是……
3. 我想听听中国人对这个问题怎么看。
4. 我计划采访 X 个人。
5. 我觉得大部分受访者可能认为……
6. 你觉得我的研究计划怎么样? 可不可行?
7. 不知道你愿不愿意回答几个简单的问题?
8. 这个调查完全是出于学习目的,请您放心。
9. 你说的这点真有道理,是我之前没有想到的。
10. 你说的这点给我很大的启发,能不能具体说一下?
11. 方不方便留个联系方式,如果日后有什么问题我可以联系您? 不方便也没关系。
12. 感谢大家在百忙之中来听我的报告。
13. 我的报告是关于……

Make it a habit to carry a notebook with you and take notes on your interactions with Chinese people.

☞ **Performance 1 Discussing a research plan**

Talking to people about your research plan is always a good way to help you improve it. Get a Chinese instructor or a Chinese friend to walk through your research plan and collect feedback and suggestions.

　　____ Act 1: Start by asking if they have a minute to listen to your research plan.
　　____ Act 2: Introduce your research topic and the reason(s) why you are interested in studying it.
　　____ Act 3: State your research subjects and how you will categorize them.
　　____ Act 4: Describe how you will conduct the research (e.g., when, where, and how to approach potential subjects).

____ Act 5: Introduce your interview questions.
____ Act 6: State your hypothesis.
____ Act 7: Ask if your Chinese instructor (or friend) thinks your research plan is valid/practical and ask for suggestions.

☞ **Performance 2 Conducting a research interview**

Based on your own research design, approach a potential subject in the field. Initiate the conversation and get his or her consent to participate in your study.

____ Act 1: Start by either mentioning the obvious or making a compliment.
____ Act 2: Inform the person that you are an international student at Soochow University.
____ Act 3: Tell him or her that you are conducting a small research project as a course assignment.
____ Act 4: Ask if the person would like to participate in the study by answering a few questions.
____ Act 5: State that you can skip any question if he or she is not comfortable to answer.
____ Act 6: Assure the subject that the questions are only for educational purposes.
____ Act 7: Express gratitude and start by gathering the basic subject information (e.g., name, age, education background).
____ Act 8: Ask interview questions.
____ Act 9: Comment positively on the subject's answers and encourage further elaboration.
____ Act 10: Politely ask if the subject is willing to leave his or her contact information.
____ Act 11: Politely end the conversation by expressing your gratitude.

☞ **Performance 3 Rehearsing the report on your study with a Chinese friend**

____ Act 1: Start the presentation with greetings and self-introduction.
____ Act 2: Introduce the topic of your research.
____ Act 3: Introduce your research subjects (e.g., what's the total number and how many in each subject group).
____ Act 4: State the research questions.
____ Act 5: Report the findings on each research question.
____ Act 6: Elaborate on the findings by quoting subjects' comments.
____ Act 7: State the conclusions.
____ Act 8: End by welcoming comments and questions.

第八单元

话说苏州 Talking about Suzhou

8.1 漫谈苏州

月是故乡明

投石问路

Listen to the five questions in the audio and answer them based on your own experience. Be ready to discuss these questions in class. You may write down some notes in the space provided below.

1.
2.
3.
4.
5.

边听边想

Listen to the audio and try to visualize the dialogue in your mind. Think about who the speakers are, the kind of social relationship they have, and what their intentions might be.

耳闻目睹

Listen to the audio again while following along in the printed text. As you listen, mark any place that you are unclear or have questions about.

月是故乡明
人物：郑妮、周丹锐、孙浩、赵奕歆

（孙浩、赵奕歆两人在等周丹锐和郑妮下课，他们要一起去吃饭）

赵奕歆：这个项目结束以后，我打算去一趟北京。

孙浩：　你好像经常去北京嘛，是不是毕业了打算去那儿工作啊？

赵奕歆：我表姐全家都住在北京，所以有机会就会去看她。不过去的次数多了，越来越觉得自己还是习惯苏州这边的生活状态，虽然生活节奏也很快，但身边的人都不那么浮躁，从从容容地过日子。从小在这样的环境中长大，在北京挺不适应的。

孙浩：　哈，我看你是怕找不到正宗的江南美食吧。不过，我能明白你的意思，人对自己家乡的感情总是很特别的。（1/5）

（郑妮和周丹锐来了）

周丹锐：孙浩，奕歆，不好意思，我们今天下课晚了一会儿，你们等了很久吧。

赵奕歆：没事儿。

郑妮：　你们俩刚才聊什么呢？

赵奕歆：刚才在说我对苏州的感觉。对了，你们两个来了差不多两个月了吧，对苏州有什么看法？

郑妮：　我最喜欢美味的苏式糕点。而且感觉本地人对吃特别重视，就说学校附近的糕点店吧，每天早上都爆满。（2/5）

赵奕歆：吃一顿丰盛的早餐可是很多苏州人雷打不动的习惯，我外公今年快八十了，每天早上都会去买些不同花样的早点，回来和老邻居喝喝茶，聊聊天儿，日子过得特别滋润。（3/5）

周丹锐：苏州给我一种很亲切的感觉，这里高楼大厦很多，但老城区老街巷也还保留得很好。还经常能看到很多打扮很时尚的白领，下了班很悠闲地在老店排队买点心什么的。我很喜欢这种文化的平衡。

孙浩：　这就叫"包容并蓄"，既接受新生的现代文化，又保留着许多传统。苏州对外来文化的包容性也特别强，在苏州工作学习的外国人越来越多。

郑妮：　对，刚来的时候，我有点怕跟外面的本地人接触，因为他们说的话我有时候听不懂。后来发现他们都很友好不排外，我遇到困难的时候总有人很热情地帮助我。（4/5）

周丹锐：不过呢，我说了你们可别生气。我也碰到过不太友好、不守规矩的苏州人,比如在上公交车、上电梯的时候,又挤又抢。有些地方治安好像也不太好……

赵奕歆: 这些事儿不光是苏州有吧。再说,苏州这样一个文化大熔炉里,难免会有这些问题。

周丹锐: 可能我太喜欢苏州,总是希望它能完美。

孙浩: 哈哈,你越来越会说话了。(5/5)

知其所以然

The dialogue is broken down into sections below for explanation and analysis. Study the notes and answer the questions for the underlined text.

1/5

(孙浩、赵奕歆两人在等周丹锐和郑妮下课,他们要一起去吃饭)

赵奕歆: 这个项目结束以后,我打算去一趟北京。

孙浩: 你好像经常去北京嘛,是不是毕业了打算去那儿工作啊?

赵奕歆: 我表姐全家都住在北京,所以有机会就会去看她。不过去的次数多了,越来越觉得自己还是习惯苏州这边的生活状态,虽然生活节奏也很快,但身边的人都不那么浮躁,从从容容地过日子。从小在这样的环境中长大,在北京挺不适应的。

孙浩: 哈,我看你是怕找不到正宗的江南美食吧。不过,我能明白你的意思,人对自己家乡的感情总是很特别的。

---

1. 赵奕歆说到自己更习惯苏州的生活状态:"虽然生活节奏也很快,但身边的人都不那么浮躁。"

(1) 赵奕歆认为苏州人都不浮躁,你觉得她的意思是?

    A. 苏州人都很有礼貌。   B. 苏州人都很勤奋。

    C. 苏州人都很踏实。   D. 苏州人都很功利。

(2) 这些年,我们总是可以听到有人说"这是一个浮躁的时代",你同意这个观点吗?无论是同意还是不同意,请你举一个例子支持或者反对这个观点?_____

(3) 在你平时生活中,你有没有浮躁的时候?你有什么克服浮躁的方法?

When Zhao Yixin makes a comparison between people in Beijing and people in Suzhou, she says people in both cities live a fast-paced life, but people in Suzhou are not as restless, anxious or impatient as people in Beijing. These are all features associated with 浮躁的. You may often hear people make a statement such as 我们活在一个浮躁的时代. The pervasive effects of social media, the consumption of Internet-based information, or an interest in gossip can all be seen as symptoms of such an unfortunate age. The opposite of

浮躁的 are characteristics like 从容的（calm）,踏实的（steady）and 耐得住寂寞的（able to endure loneliness）, which are always considered positive. Therefore, 浮躁的 is something you should either overcome（克服）or completely get rid of（戒掉）. The Chinese idiom 戒骄戒躁 describes eradicating pride and impatience. 浮躁的 is close to 急躁的 in meaning, but 急躁的 is usually restricted to describing people's behaviors or mood; whereas, 浮躁的 describes an internal state.

2/5

（郑妮和周丹锐来了）

周丹锐：孙浩,奕歆,不好意思,我们今天下课晚了一会儿,你们等了很久吧。

赵奕歆：没事儿。

郑妮：　你们俩刚才聊什么呢?

赵奕歆：刚才在说我对苏州的感觉。对了,你们两个来了差不多两个月了吧,对苏州有什么看法?

郑妮：　我最喜欢美味的苏式糕点。而且感觉本地人对吃特别重视,<u>就说学校附近的糕点店吧</u>,每天早上都爆满。

---

2. 郑妮举例子说明苏州人重视吃,说:"就说学校附近的糕点店吧。"

(1) 如果郑妮是在一个正式口头报告里举这个例子,还可以怎么说?

_____

(2) 请选出所有符合的选项:

"最近同学们都很努力,就说_____吧,_____。"

　　A. 小文;每天都学习到半夜

　　B. 作业;每个人都完成得很好

　　C. 考试;还是有点太难

就说……吧 is commonly used to give examples in spoken Chinese. It is usually followed by a sentence or two, elaborating on the example. In the dialogue, Zheng Ni supports her argument that Suzhou locals really love food by taking the bakery near campus as an example, explaining that every morning the restaurant is filled with customers. A formal alternative would be 比方说…… or 比如说……. For example, to support the statement 最近同学们都很努力, you can either choose one student as an example, e.g., 就说周丹锐吧,每天都一早来教室学习, or choose a particular performance that reflected the hard work, e.g., 就说小考吧,每个人都答得很好.

3. 郑妮说学校附近的茶楼生意很好:"每天早上都爆满。"

(1) 你觉得郑妮说的那家茶楼怎么样? _____

(2) 如果你要跟中国朋友介绍纽约百老汇的音乐剧非常受欢迎,很难买到票,可

以怎么说？_____

You may often hear people complain about something being filled to capacity by saying 邮箱爆满，航班爆满，or 停车场爆满. However，爆满 doesn't necessarily indicate a negative tone. A sold-out Broadway show can be described as 场场爆满. Therefore，to describe the popularity of a Broadway show to a friend you can say 这部百老汇音乐剧非常受欢迎，场场爆满.

3/5

奕歆：吃一顿丰盛的早餐可是很多苏州人雷打不动的习惯，我外公今年快八十了，每天早上都会去买些不同花样的早点，回来和老邻居喝喝茶，聊聊天儿，日子过得特别<u>滋润</u>。

---

4. 赵奕歆告诉郑妮吃早餐对苏州人的重要性："吃一顿丰盛的早餐可是很多苏州人雷打不动的习惯。"

(1) 你有什么雷打不动的习惯吗？_____

(2) 你看到报纸上一条新闻写着"无论改革多少次，房价依旧雷打不动"，你觉得这是什么意思？_____

雷打不动 indicates that something won't be altered under any circumstances. Everyone probably has some 雷打不动的习惯. For example，for many young kids 每天睡前听一个故事是雷打不动的习惯. Some people may even have 雷打不动的规矩. For example，a Chinese learner who persists in an unshakable rule of memorizing a Chinese dialogue every day can say that 每天背对话是一个雷打不动的规矩. In both cases，the idiom 雷打不动 conveys a sense of strong determination and perseverance.

5. 赵奕歆说苏州人的生活特别舒服："日子过得特别滋润。"

(1) 你听到别人说"这小两口虽然挣得不多，可小日子过得很滋润"，你觉得可以用什么词替换"滋润"？请你想两个：a. _____ b. _____

(2) 除了说"生活滋润"以外，下面哪些东西也可以很滋润？（请圈出合适的选项，可多选）

    A. 皮肤   B. 收入   C. 空气   D. 话语

Literally meaning "nourishing（滋）and moist（润）"，滋润 is used to describe skin，air，soil and the environment that is well moistened，e. g.，四川人的皮肤很滋润. In recent years 滋润 has come to be used to describe a comfortable life. You can also use 你的日子过得很享受啊，or 你的日子过得很舒服啊 to communicate a similar idea. When commenting on a friend's glowing good looks，you can adopt a joking tone and say 你最近很滋润嘛，是找到女朋友了还是升职了？

4/5

周丹锐：苏州给我一种很亲切的感觉,这里高楼大厦很多,但老城区老街巷也还保留得很好。还经常能看到很多打扮很时尚的白领,下了班很悠闲地在老店排队买点心什么的。我很喜欢这种文化的平衡。

孙浩： 这就叫"<u>包容并蓄</u>",既接受新生的现代文化,又保留着许多传统。苏州对外来文化的包容性也特别强,在苏州工作学习的外国人越来越多。

郑妮： 对,刚来的时候,我有点怕跟外面的本地人接触,因为他们说的话我有时候听不懂。后来发现他们都很友好不排外,我遇到困难的时候总有人很热情地帮助我。

6. 孙浩总结周丹锐的看法说:"这就叫'包容并蓄'。"
(1) 你觉得一个"包容并蓄"的城市可能有什么特点？ _____
(2) 如果你听人说附近新开了一家餐厅,"风格包容并蓄",你觉得这家餐厅的菜肴可能是什么风格？

_____

Literally meaning "all-inclusive preservation", the idiom 包容并蓄 is often used to describe "a state where all coexist and accommodate each other". For example, when Zhou Danrui refers to an earlier observation that he often sees fashionable Suzhou white-collar workers buying food at traditional local food stands, Sun Hao uses the idiom 包容并蓄 to describe this harmonious coexistence of the traditional and the modern cultures. You may also hear people say 兼容并蓄 which conveys the same meaning.

5/5

周丹锐：不过呢,<u>我说了你们可别生气</u>。我也碰到过不太友好、不守规矩的苏州人,比如在上公交车、上电梯的时候,又挤又抢。有些地方治安好像也不太好……

赵奕歆：这些事儿不光是苏州有吧。<u>再说</u>,苏州这样一个文化大熔炉里,<u>难免</u>会有这些问题。

周丹锐：可能我太喜欢苏州,总是希望它能完美。

孙浩： 哈哈,你越来越会说话了。

7. 周丹锐委婉提到苏州的小缺点时,对赵奕歆和孙浩说:"我说了你们可别生气。"

(1) 周丹锐接下来说了什么？他为什么要先说"我说了你们可别生气"？

_____

(2) 当别人对你说"我说了你可别生气"的时候，你可以怎么回应？
_____

When Zhou Danrui implores his local friends not to get angry, he is actually signaling that he is going to tell them the downside of Suzhou after making several compliments. 可 here is an adverb preceding a verbal phrase describing the state of not intending to become angry, emphasizing or intensifying the phrase 别生气啊. This expression is usually used before making a negative comment. If someone said this to you and if you want to hear their true thoughts, you can encourage them to continue by saying 说吧, 没事儿, 我不会生气的.

8. 关于周丹锐提出的缺点，赵奕歆做出两点回应："这些事儿不光是苏州有吧。再说……"

(1) 这里如果不用"再说"，还可以用什么词？_____

(2) 孙浩：你怎么那么喜欢爬山啊？
　　周丹锐：我特别喜欢户外运动。_____山上的空气新鲜呀。
　　A. 而且　　　　B. 再说　　　　C. 两者皆可

(3) 孙浩：你平时喜欢做什么运动？
　　周丹锐：我特别喜欢户外运动。_____喜欢山上的新鲜空气。
　　A. 而且　　　　B. 再说　　　　C. 两者皆可

In spoken Chinese, 再说 is used to link two sentences that support the same argument, often in defense of an idea. Usually the sentence beginning with 再说 takes the argument further by presenting additional information to clarify the statement made in the preceding sentence. For example, in the dialogue 再说 links the two counterarguments Zhao Yixin made in response to what Zhou Danrui said about the downside of Suzhou. Generally speaking, 再说 could be replaced with 而且, as is the case in the dialogue.

9. 赵奕歆说这些缺点很难避免："苏州这样一个文化大熔炉里，难免会有这些问题。"

(1) 这里的"难免"有没有更口语的表达？_____

(2) 公司的新员工工作上犯了错，作为老员工你可以怎么安慰她？
_____

难免 carries the meaning of 不容易避免, implying that something is nearly unavoidable. It is used in both spoken and written discourse and has a relatively formal tone. A more casual way of saying this is 免不了. For example, if you want to comfort a new colleague who made a mistake at work, you can either say 刚开始工作难免会犯错，没关系 or 刚开始工作免不了会犯错嘛，没事的.

🎧 体演文本

Review the sections of the dialogue assigned by your teacher by listening to the audio and role playing with another Chinese speaker. Be ready to perform the assigned portion of the dialogue from memory in class.

💬 举一反三

Answer the following questions and think about how the dialogue can be adapted for different situations.

1. 你对苏州的看法跟周丹锐的一样吗？有什么不同？
2. 对话的最后丹锐说的话，你感觉是假话还是真话？为什么？
3. 如果你在一个苏州朋友家里做客，他的家人问你对苏州有什么感觉，你怎么说？如果是你的一个北京朋友打电话问你对苏州有什么感觉，你怎么说？

🎧 熟能生巧

Listen to the audio and perform the following drills until you feel confident with the items practiced.

☞ **Drill 1 Giving an example to support your opinion**

When asked about your opinion on a statement, agree and then provide an example with further elaboration.

例：糕点店/有很多人排队

赵奕歆：你觉得苏州人对吃重视吗？
郑妮：我觉得苏州人对吃特别重视，就说苏州的糕点店吧，总是有很多人排队。

1. 城市里/有新建的高楼　　　　2. 踢比赛/赢球

3. 他的房间/很干净

4. 糕点/很好吃

☞ **Drill 2 Stating your impression**

When asked what your impression of a certain place is, reply with how the place makes you feel.

例：亲切

赵奕歆：你觉得苏州怎么样？

周丹锐：苏州给我一种很亲切的感觉。

1. 现代化
2. 多元化
3. 浪漫
4. 自由

☞ **Drill 3 Accepting two opposing sides of something**

In this drill, upon hearing your friend debating between two opposing features of something, you state that the item under discussion possesses both.

例：

朋友：苏州是接受了新生的现代文化呢还是保留了许多传统呢？

郑妮：苏州既接受了新生的现代文化，又保留了许多传统。

1.　　　　　　2.　　　　　　3.　　　　　　4.

☞ **Drill 4 Mentioning demerits politely**

When your Chinese friend describes the positive aspects of his or her hometown or people, point out a negative aspect in a way that avoids sounding offensive.

例：

朋友：苏州人都很友好，我遇到困难的时候总有人很热情地帮助我。

周丹锐：不过呢，我说了你可别生气，我也碰到过不太友好的苏州人。

☞ Drill 5 Showing tolerance for flaws and faults

When your friend mentions a flaw, admit the existence of the problem while giving an explanation for why the problem may be unavoidable.

例：文化大熔炉

朋友：苏州的公交车上总是又挤又抢，很不守规矩。

郑妮：苏州是文化大熔炉，难免会有一些不太守规矩的人。

1. 1960 年建的
2. 业余比赛
3. 第一次用中文演讲
4. 梅雨季节

Narration

Zhou Danrui is visiting Sun Hao's family. At dinner, Sun Hao's mother asks what Zhou Danrui thinks of Suzhou. Assume Zhou Danrui's role and tell Sun Hao's mother how you like Suzhou.

孙浩妈妈：丹锐啊，你来苏州也快两个月了。对苏州有什么感觉？

言外有意

Read the cultural notes below and prepare questions for further discussion with Chinese people.

1. 露从今夜白，月是故乡明（lù cóng jīnyè bái, yuè shì gùxiāng míng）The season of white dew begins tonight, but the moon is brighter in my hometown.

This is a well-known line from one of the homesick poems by Du Fu（杜甫）, a famous Tang Dynasty poet. Moon or moonlight is often associated with thinking of or missing one's hometown in Chinese culture. This line is rarely quoted in daily spoken Chinese, but when people want to express homesick feelings in a relatively formal speech or a written context, they may use the second part of the line：月是故乡明(啊).

2. 中国人的家乡情结

As indicated above, homesickness is an important theme in Chinese literature, especially in ancient poems. Most Chinese people, no matter which part of China they are from, have a special feeling for their hometown. It is quite common to give special local products from one's hometown to friends. Interestingly, many Chinese people do not express their appreciation of their hometown in a direct way and may even appear to criticize it. For example, someone from Nanjing may say 南京有什么好呀!? Don't fall into the trap! Even in this circumstance you still need to reply by complimenting their hometown. Say something positive about the food, weather or famous attractions. By responding in this way, you will find yourself making new friends much sooner!

3. 中国人对每个地区的认识

There is a saying in China：不到北京不知道自己官小,不到上海不知道自己钱少,不到东北不知道自己的酒量好不好（There are many variations of this saying depending on the emphasis）. That is to say a lot of Chinese people tend to believe that many high ranking officials live in Beijing, people from Shanghai are rich and Manchurian people are good at drinking. Some of the stereotypes are actually valid, while others do not really apply since China is changing really fast. In our dialogue, Sun Hao used the word 包容并蓄 to describe Suzhou, to say it is a place with traditions and modernity, which is exactly what most of the Chinese people think of Suzhou. As a language and culture learner, knowing what Chinese people think about different cities can help you participate in conversations with your Chinese friends. For more information about "city stereotypes", you can read the book *Du Cheng Ji*(《读城记》) by a popular Chinese writer and scholar 易中天.

8.2 苏州攻略

痛并快乐着

🎧 投石问路

Listen to the five questions in the audio and answer them based on your own experience. Be ready to discuss these questions in class. You may write down some notes in the space provided below.

1.
2.
3.
4.
5.

🎧 边听边想

Listen to the audio and try to visualize the dialogue in your mind. Think about who the speakers are, the kind of social relationship they have, and what their intentions might be.

耳闻目睹

Listen to the audio again while following along in the printed text. As you listen, mark any place that you are unclear or have questions about.

痛并快乐着

人物：周丹锐

（周丹锐为苏大的留学生做了个视频，分享他在苏州的生活经历）

夏天在苏州学习，你就会体会到什么叫"痛并快乐着"。

之所以说痛，主要是因为苏州的天气。如果你们的项目也是六月中旬开始的话，那么你可能正好赶上苏州的梅雨天和桑拿天，又湿又热，让你只想在空调房里呆着。这样的天气大约要持续几个星期，可是既然是来学中文，你又不可能整天呆在屋子里吹空调，还得利用这宝贵的时间去外面跟各行各业的本地人交流。但是只要一出空调房，就会汗流浃背，那叫一个难受！不过比起我接下来要说的快乐，这点痛苦根本算不了什么。(1/5)

生活在苏州，学在苏大有四大快乐。第一大快乐就是住得方便。我们住在本部附近的姑苏饭店，环境优雅，安静又干净。出了宾馆，走几步路就有很多小饭馆，选择很多，价格也很公道。夏日的苏大到处都是一片绿意，吃完晚饭，在校园里散散步，闲适又舒服。(2/5)

第二大快乐就是学得充实。苏大的学习氛围非常浓厚，这座醒目的建筑就是图书馆，是看书自习的好去处。七月初学校放暑假之后，很多教室都会是空的，可以在那里学习或者和辅导老师见面。除此之外，社区服务、文化沙龙等丰富的课外活动，还可以让你收获新的经历、结识更多中国朋友。(3/5)

第三大快乐就是吃得过瘾。对爱吃的人来说，苏州真是美食天堂。从近处说，苏大的食堂在苏州的大学里是出了名的好。校园外的美食更是不用说。苏州人爱吃精致的糕点，苏式月饼、桂花糕、葱油桃酥……要是你也爱吃苏式点心，可一定不能错过几家苏州的老字号，比如黄天源和稻香村，通常都是天天爆满。除此之外，我还推荐平江路和凤凰街，一路逛下来各式各样的美食可以从早吃到晚。说着说着我口水都要流出来了，好了，不说吃的了，说说玩的。(4/5)

在苏州生活的第四大快乐就是玩得尽兴。不管你是喜欢大自然的美丽风景还是现代都市的人文气息，在苏州都能找到适合你的去处。灵岩山宜人的风景，能让你忘记一切不快乐的事情，全身心投入大自然的怀抱。大大小小的园林让我们感受到这座城市的历史底蕴和古典气息。晚上走在金鸡湖畔看着繁华的夜景，你又会觉得这是另外一个完全不同的、充满现代气息的城市。

既繁华，又安静，既现代，又古朴。朋友们，要想真正了解苏州这个城市，了解在这里学习和生活的快乐，还得你们自己来苏州亲身体演！再见了，拜拜！(5/5)

知其所以然

The dialogue is broken down into sections below for explanation and analysis. Study the notes and answer the questions for the underlined text.

1/5

（周丹锐为苏大的留学生做了个视频,分享他在苏州的生活经历）

夏天在苏州学习,你就会体会到什么叫"痛并快乐着"。

<u>之所以说痛,主要是因为苏州的天气</u>。如果你们的项目也是<u>六月中旬</u>开始的话,那么你可能正好赶上苏州的梅雨天和<u>桑拿天</u>,又湿又热,让你只想在空调房里呆着。这样的天气大约要持续几个星期,可是既然是来学中文,你又不可能整天呆在屋子里吹空调,还得利用这<u>宝贵</u>的时间去外面跟各行各业的本地人交流。但是只要一出空调房,就会汗流浃背,<u>那叫一个难受</u>! 不过比起我接下来要说的快乐,这点痛苦根本算不了什么。

---

1. 周丹锐解释为什么会"痛",他说:"之所以说痛,主要是因为苏州的天气。"
   （1）"之所以"可以换成"因此"吗? 为什么? ＿＿＿＿＿＿＿＿＿＿＿＿＿＿
   （2）在下面这句话中,哪一部分说的是原因? ＿＿＿＿＿＿＿＿＿＿＿＿＿
      "之所以说美国是'车轮上的国家',是因为这个国家有很多汽车。"
   （3）如果朋友问你为什么要花这么多时间学中文,你可以怎么回答?
   ＿＿＿＿＿＿＿＿＿＿＿＿＿＿＿＿＿＿

Although the phrase 之所以 contains 所以, it introduces a certain fact that needs further explanation, rather than indicating a result. Therefore, 之所以 is not interchangeable with 因此. In formal written discourse, Chinese people use 之所以 [situation]是因为[explanation] or 之所以[situation]就在于[explanation] to express a key explanation of a certain situation. For example, 之所以说美国是"车轮上的国家"是因为这个国家有很多汽车 or 苏州园林之所以有名,就在于它们很有江南特色. In a Chinese speech contest, one might state his or her motivation of learning Chinese by saying 之所以学中文,是因为我喜欢中国文化. However, in a casual conversation between friends, he may just say 我学中文是因为我喜欢中国文化.

2. 周丹锐说到苏州项目的时间:"如果你们的项目也是六月中旬开始的话……"
   （1）"六月中旬"大概指的是几号到几号? ＿＿＿＿＿＿＿＿＿＿＿＿＿＿
   （2）如果中国朋友问你感恩节一般是什么时候,你可以怎么用中国人容易理解的方式回答? ＿＿＿＿＿＿＿＿＿＿＿＿＿＿＿＿
   （3）如果说一个人"年过六旬",这人大概多少岁? ＿＿＿＿＿＿＿＿＿＿＿

When talking about an indefinite time in a certain month, Chinese people often use 上

旬, 中旬 and 下旬 to indicate the early, mid and late period. Since there are roughly 30 days in one month, each 旬 contains about 10 days. Therefore, to give people a rough idea of when Thanksgiving is, you can say 感恩节一般是十一月下旬. In other written contexts, 旬 can also denote 10 years and it's often used when talking about the age of someone relatively old. For example, 年过六旬 means someone is over 60.

3. 周丹锐继续介绍苏州夏天的天气:"……那么你可能正好赶上苏州的梅雨天和桑拿天。"
(1) "梅雨天"和"桑拿天"里的"天"指的是什么?＿＿＿＿＿＿＿＿＿＿＿＿
(2) 苏州的"梅雨天"一般从六月初开始,你知道那时苏州的天气是怎样的吗?
＿＿＿＿＿＿＿＿＿＿＿＿＿＿＿＿
(3) 你蒸过桑拿吗? 感觉怎么样?＿＿＿＿＿＿＿＿＿＿＿＿＿＿＿＿

天 here refers to 天气 (weather). For example, we have 晴天, 阴天 and 下雨天.
梅雨天 is a type of weather common in Southern China. It features humid weather and incessant rain. 桑拿 is the Chinese transliteration for "sauna". 桑拿天 is used to describe the muggy weather which reminds people of saunas.

4. 周丹锐说起桑拿天汗流浃背的感觉:"那叫一个难受!"
(1) 这里"那叫一个难受"的意思是＿＿＿＿＿＿＿＿＿＿＿＿＿＿＿＿＿＿＿
(2) 如果你刚参加了一个会议回来,你中国朋友问你那个会怎么样,你觉得特别没意思,你可以怎么用"那叫一个……"回答他?＿＿＿＿＿＿＿＿＿＿＿＿＿

那叫一个 + [adj./adv.] is a very colloquial way to intensify a description. It is more commonly used in northern dialects and is sometimes contracted to just 那 + [adj./adv.]. Other colloquial alternatives for this expression include 可难受了, 难受死了 or 特难受. To comment on a boring meeting, you may say 今天的会开得那叫一个没意思 or 今天的会那叫一个没意思.

那叫一个 may also be used with positive descriptions. For example, to describe a prize-winner's reaction upon receiving a big prize, a Chinese person may say 领奖的时候,小李那叫一个高兴,笑得半天都合不上嘴.

2/5

生活在苏州,学在苏大有四大快乐。第一大快乐就是住得方便。我们住在本部附近的姑苏饭店,环境优雅,安静又干净。出了宾馆,走几步路就有很多小饭馆,选择很多,价格也很公道。夏日的苏大到处都是一片绿意,吃完晚饭,在校园里散散步,闲适又舒服。

5. 周丹锐介绍在苏州生活的快乐之处:"学在苏大有四大快乐。"
   (1) "四大快乐"的"大"是什么意思? _____
   (2) 你听说过中国的"四大名著"吗?指的是什么? _____
   (3) 你听说过中国古代"四大发明"吗?指的是什么? _____
   (4) 如果你的中国朋友问你你的国家有哪些快餐店比较好,你可以怎么回答?
   _____

   The structure [number] + 大 + [something] can be used to identify the top [number] of [something]. For example, 四大快乐 refers to the four happiest things. 四大名著 in Question 2 refers to the four most famous novels in China and 四大发明 in Question 3 refers to the four most important inventions in ancient China. Usually titles like 四大名著 and 四大发明 are widely accepted as conventionally established cultural symbols. However, people can also use this structure to create their own lists like 四大快乐. Therefore, to talk about the famous fast-food restaurants in the United States, you can create your own list by saying 美国有三大快餐店 and proceed to introduce what they are.

6. 周丹锐说在苏大校园里散步:"闲适又舒服。"
   (1) "闲适"的"闲"和"适"分别代表什么词? _____
   (2) 你觉得怎样的生活算闲适? _____
   (3) 你什么时候有过闲适的感觉? _____

   闲适 can be understood as a combination of 悠闲 and 舒适, with the former one emphasizing the absence of pressure, and the latter one comfort. Therefore, you may use 闲适 to describe a day which you spent listening to music and tasting tea or canoeing on a peaceful lake surrounded by beautiful scenery:那天过得特别闲适 or 我喜欢这种闲适的生活.

   > **3/5**
   > 　　第二大快乐就是学得充实。苏大的学习氛围非常浓厚,这座醒目的建筑就是图书馆,是看书自习的好去处。七月初学校放暑假之后,很多教室都会是空的,可以在那里学习或者和辅导老师见面。除此之外,社区服务、文化沙龙等丰富的课外活动,还可以让你收获新的经历、结识更多中国朋友。

7. 周丹锐谈到在苏大学习的体验,他说:"苏大的学习氛围非常浓厚。"
   (1) 这里的"氛围"可以换成什么词? _____
   (2) 搞独立日庆祝活动时,你想让节日氛围更浓厚,可以怎么做?
   _____
   (3) 在给中国大学的申请材料中,你想告诉对方自己很喜欢中国文化,可以怎么说? _____

Generally speaking, 氛围 and 气氛 are interchangeable, both denoting the ambiance of a place. 氛围很浓厚 is a more formal way to say 氛围很好. 浓厚 can also be used to describe some other abstract concepts like 兴趣. For example, when writing an application essay to a Chinese university, if you want to express that you are very interested in Chinese culture, you can say 我对中国文化有浓厚的兴趣.

4/5

第三大快乐就是吃得过瘾。对爱吃的人来说,苏州真是美食天堂。从近处说,苏大的食堂在苏州的大学里是出了名的好。校园外的美食更是不用说。苏州人爱吃精致的糕点,苏式月饼、桂花糕、葱油桃酥……要是你也爱吃苏式点心,可一定不能错过几家苏州的老字号,比如黄天源和稻香村,通常都是天天爆满。除此之外,我还推荐平江路和凤凰街,一路逛下来各式各样的美食可以从早吃到晚。说着说着我口水都要流出来了,好了,不说吃的了,说说玩的。

8. 周丹锐说的第三大快乐是关于吃的:"第三大快乐就是吃得过瘾。"
 (1)"过瘾"的"瘾"是什么意思?＿＿＿＿＿＿＿＿＿＿＿＿＿＿＿
 (2)你对什么东西或者什么事情有瘾?＿＿＿＿＿＿＿＿＿＿＿＿＿＿
 (3)如果你去游乐园玩了一天,很开心,回来之后朋友问你玩得怎么样,你可以怎么回答?＿＿＿＿＿＿＿＿＿＿＿＿＿＿＿

瘾 here refers to addiction. 对……有瘾/上瘾 is a structure used to say that someone is addicted to something. For example, 我对苏州美食很上瘾. 过瘾 denotes the feeling of satisfaction after the present need has been met. For example, you can say 吃得过瘾 after eating a lot of delicious food. In another context, when your friend asks if you had a great time at a theme park, you can answer that 今天玩得很过瘾.

9. 周丹锐介绍说苏大的食堂非常有名:"苏大的食堂在苏州的大学里就是出了名的好。"
 (1)"出了名"可以换成什么词?＿＿＿＿＿＿＿＿＿＿＿＿＿＿＿
 (2)如果你的朋友问你在苏州吃得怎么样,你想告诉他中国人都知道苏州美食,可以怎么说?＿＿＿＿＿＿＿＿＿＿＿＿＿＿＿
 (3)如果你们公司的同事们都认为小李特别啰唆,在跟朋友说起小李时,你可以怎么说?＿＿＿＿＿＿＿＿＿＿＿＿＿＿＿

The structure 出了名的 X or 有名的 X are used to introduce a well-known feature of something. 是 is often used together with this structure to show the emphasis. For example, if a friend asks how you like the food in Suzhou and you want to say that Suzhou food is well-known for its good taste, you can say 苏州美食是出了名的好吃.

The structure may also be used to introduce a negative feature that is well-known. For example, you can also describe a talkative person known to everyone at work by saying 小李在公司里是出了名的啰唆.

10. 周丹锐解释他为什么不继续说吃的了,"说着说着我口水都要流出来了……"
(1) 用了"说着说着",周丹锐听起来好像_____
　　A. 刚刚意识到自己一直在说吃的。
　　B. 注意到自己一边说一边流口水。
(2) 如果你的室友晚上回来发现你躺在沙发上睡着了,但是电视没关,你可以怎么解释这个情况?_____

Zhou Danrui uses the sentence that begins with 说着说着 to transition to his next topic: 玩. The use of 说着说着 here leaves his audience an impression that he was so obsessed with talking about food that he did not realize his mouth almost got watery because of his description about food. [verb]着[verb]着 is used to describe a situation where a consequence of an action is unexpectedly reached before the person realizes the length and repetitiveness of the action. For example, to explain to your roommate why the TV was on while you were asleep, you can say 昨晚我看电视,看着看着就睡着了 or 昨晚我听新闻,听着听着就睡着了. To leave her boyfriend an impression that she did not intend to look at bags when shopping at a department store, a Chinese girl may say 不知道怎么搞的,走着走着就到卖包的地方了.

5/5

在苏州生活的第四大快乐就是玩得<u>尽兴</u>。不管你是喜欢大自然的美丽风景还是现代都市的人文气息,在苏州都能找到适合你的去处。灵岩山宜人的风景,能让你忘记一切不快乐的事情,<u>全身心投入</u>大自然的怀抱。大大小小的园林让我们感受到这座城市的历史底蕴和古典气息。晚上走在金鸡湖畔看着繁华的夜景,你又会觉得这是另外一个完全不同的、充满现代气息的城市。

既繁华,又安静,既现代,又古朴。朋友们,要想真正了解苏州这个城市,了解在这里学习和生活的快乐,还得你们自己来苏州<u>亲身体验</u>!再见了,拜拜!

---

11. 第四大快乐是关于玩的:"在苏州生活的第四大快乐就是玩得尽兴。"
(1) "尽兴"的"兴"是什么意思?
　　A. 兴趣　　　　　B. 兴致　　　　　C. 兴奋
(2) 这里的"尽兴"可以换成"过瘾"吗?_____
(3) 如果你在毕业晚会上发言,发言结束的时候,你可以对大家说"祝大家玩得过瘾"吗?_____

尽兴 can be literally understood as 用完兴致, which is "to use to the full extent of one's interest". Therefore, 尽兴 is quite similar to 过瘾, denoting the state of enjoying oneself to the full, and they are often interchangeable. However, 过瘾 denotes behavior that is a little bit over the limit and thus tends to be used in spoken discourse and less formal contexts. Thus 尽兴 is the more appropriate term for formal settings, such as in a speech at the program-closing ceremony.

12. 周丹锐说到灵岩山的风景能让人忘记不快乐的事情:"全身心投入大自然的怀抱。"
　　(1) 这里的"投入"能不能换成"进入"? _____
　　(2) "全身心"可以换成"完全"吗? _____
　　(3) 如果今天你的作业很多,朋友问你晚上有什么计划时,你可以说"我要全身心投入到学习中去"吗? _____

投入 X 的怀抱 is a rather fixed expression which has a strong literary flavor, meaning to lose yourself in the embrace of X. Here, X can be an environment (e.g., 大自然, 灵岩山, 祖国) or an idea (e.g., 现实主义). Therefore, 投入 cannot be replaced with 进入, which does not carry a literary sense.

A less literary use of 投入 can be found in the structure 投入到 + [an undertaking/cause] + 中去. For example, to formally describe a person who is participating wholeheartedly in environmental causes, a Chinese person may say 现在他已经全身心投入到环保事业中去了.

全身心 refers to both body and soul and communicates the idea of doing something whole-heartedly. It can be replaced by 完全, but 全身心 is more vivid and echoes better with 投入. Therefore, to tell a friend that you are determined to focus on studying tonight with a sense of humor, you may say 我今晚要全身心投入到学习中去. Normally, you would just say 我今晚要好好学习.

13. 周丹锐告诉大家真正了解苏州的方法:"还得你们自己来苏州亲身体演!"
　　(1) 这里"亲身"可以去掉吗? _____
　　(2) 如果你的朋友不相信你说的关于周丹锐的事,你可以怎么强调你的信息是可靠的? _____

亲 X, as in 亲身、亲耳、亲眼、亲口、亲手、亲自, is used to emphasize that you do something yourself in person. For example, to emphasize that the excitement about studying in Suzhou is true, you may say 我亲身体验过的, indicating that you have studied there yourself. To emphasize what you are saying about Zhou Danrui is from first-hand resource, you can say 是我亲耳听到的! or 是我亲眼看见的! or 是周丹锐亲口告诉我的! To emphasize that a dish is special and encourage your friends to taste it, you can say 快尝尝,这是我亲手做的. To emphasize the importance of an event, you may say 总统亲自去参

加了那个活动.

(3)这里的"体演"可以用什么词代替？ _____

(4)为什么丹锐在这里用"体演"而不用"体验"？他这么做有什么好处？有什么风险？ _____

亲身体验 is probably the word most commonly used in contexts where one sees things for oneself and gains first-hand experience. 体演 on the other hand, as in 体演苏州, is a term from the Performed Culture Approach（体演文化教学法）, which emphasizes that language learners should go beyond the role of an observer, and learn to do things (perform) in culturally appropriate ways. Zhou Danrui chooses to use 体演 here because the target audience of this video are his classmates and other foreign students at Soochow University, who have also used《体演苏州》as their language learning material and knows the meaning of this term. By using this term Zhou Danrui references a concept that is central to the program and familiar to the audience. It's a very nice way to summarize and end the video. However, if the audience were people with no prior knowledge of the 体演 concept, they may think Zhou Danrui made a mistake with the tone of the word. Always think about the audience when choosing your words!

🎧 体演文本

Review the sections of the dialogue assigned by your teacher by listening to the audio and role-playing with another Chinese speaker. Be ready to perform the assigned portion of the dialogue from memory in class.

💬 举一反三

Answer the following questions and think about how the dialogue can be adapted for different situations.

1. 周丹锐说到今年夏天的四大快乐。你有没有类似的四大快乐？它们是什么？

2. 如果你代表同学们给明年项目的同学做一个关于苏大和苏州的介绍,必须要介绍的内容有哪些?

🎧 熟能生巧

Listen to the audio and perform the following drills until you feel confident with the items practiced.

☞ **Drill 1 Elaborating on a previous conclusion**

In this drill, respond to an audience's question in the Q&A session in a public presentation by explaining the main reason for your conclusion.

例：苏州好玩的地方有很多

听众：你刚才说"在苏州玩得尽兴"，这是为什么呢？

周丹锐：之所以说在苏州玩得尽兴，主要是因为苏州好玩的地方有很多。

1. 宾馆附近什么都有
2. 来自全国各地的人
3. 有丰富的课外活动
4. 有丰富多样的美食

☞ Drill 2 Expressing your feeling strongly

When asked by a newcomer to China about certain aspects of your experience in China, express strong feelings in a somewhat exaggerated tone. The illustrations below show the situations you have strong positive or negative feelings about.

例：

新同学：桑拿天的感觉怎么样？难受吗？

周丹锐：那叫一个难受！

1. 2.  3.  4.

☞ Drill 3 Emphasizing that one aspect is nothing compared to another

When someone points out the high price you have paid for something, explain that compared with the benefit to be gained, the cost is nothing.

例：快乐

新同学：原来夏天在苏大学习那么痛苦啊？！

周丹锐：比起带来的快乐，这点痛苦根本算不了什么。

1. 收获
2. 便利
3. 快乐
4. 乐趣

☞ Drill 4 Emphasizing a well-known feature

When asked about something by a Chinese friend, state what it is well-known for.

Each of the cues indicates the feature for which the thing is well-known.

例：精彩

赵奕歆：百老汇的音乐剧怎么样？

周丹锐：百老汇的音乐剧在美国是出了名的精彩。

1. 糟糕

2. 强

3. 漂亮

4. 热闹

☞ **Drill 5 Making a recommendation**

When a new international student who just came to Soochow University asks you to recommend something, reply by emphasizing that a certain experience cannot be missed.

例：苏州的老字号

新同学：我很喜欢吃苏州的点心，有什么推荐的吗？

周丹锐：要是你爱吃苏州的点心，可一定不能错过苏州的老字号。

1. 平江路

2. 松鼠鳜鱼

3. 灵岩山

4. 猫的天空之城

言外有意

Read the cultural notes below and prepare questions for further discussion with Chinese people.

1. 痛并快乐着 Painful yet happy.

痛并快乐着 is originally the name of a Chinese pop song album by Qi Qin（齐秦）, released in 1995. However, many people who do not know that album know this expression since it is widely used in different media. The expression is now being used in written discourse to describe some difficult but worthwhile experiences.

2. "总—分—总"结构

Zhou Danrui's introduction to his experiences in Suzhou not only shows his knowledge about the city, but also presents one typical structure Chinese people like to use to organize a speech or essay: Introduction—Elucidation—Conclusion, called 总—分—总 in Chinese. Zhou Danrui began the speech with one introductory sentence 夏天在苏州学习，你就能体会到什么叫痛并快乐着. Then he began to illustrate the "painful" part of his time in Suzhou which was the hot, humid weather. It would be inappropriate in this context if Zhou Danrui had talked about more 痛 than 快乐. He began the 快乐 section with the sentence

生活在苏州,学在苏大有四大快乐, and then talked about the four positive aspects one by one. One advantage of adopting this structure is that it gives the audience a clear idea about the main ideas included in the speech. Try to use this structure in your presentations or compositions!

8.3 暂别苏州

依依不舍

🎧 投石问路

Listen to the five questions in the audio and answer them based on your own experience. Be ready to discuss these questions in class. You may write down some notes in the space provided below.

1.
2.
3.
4.
5.

🎧 边听边想

Listen to the audio and try to visualize the dialogue in your mind. Think about who the speakers are, the kind of social relationship they have, and what their intentions might be.

耳闻目睹

Listen to the audio again while following along in the printed text. As you listen, mark any place that you are unclear or have questions about.

依依不舍

人物：周丹锐

（地点：在项目的结业宴会上，周丹锐代表全体学生发言）

尊敬的各位老师，亲爱的同学们：

大家好！

我叫周丹锐，丹青的丹，精锐的锐。很荣幸代表我们项目的全体美国同学在这里发言。这个夏天我们在苏州的经历是充实而难忘的。能有这么充实又难忘的学习经历，我们要感谢很多人。首先要感谢在座的各位苏大的领导在项目期间对我们的支持与帮助，为我们创造了那么多难得的语言实践和文化经历。然后我们要感谢苏大的王老师、赵老师、张老师和周老师，是你们整个夏天的辛勤付出，让我们每天都能感受到自己在一点一点进步。我们还要特别感谢我们的秦老师，大家都深深感受到了项目各项活动和要求的用心良苦，而且从中学到了很多。"学而时习之"的学习理念会让我们受益终身。(1/4)

三人行，必有我师。能有这么丰富的收获，当然也要感谢苏大的同学们，你们不仅是我们的中文老师，更是我们在苏州生活的向导和知心朋友。我们很多同学都是第一次来苏州，刚到苏大的时候，很多东西对我们来说都很陌生。还记得第一次去苏大食堂吃饭的时候，要不是孙浩和奕歆跟我们一起，我跟郑妮都不知道该怎么买饭。在你们的陪伴与帮助下，我们很快地适应了这里的生活，并且爱上了苏州。短短的两个月之内，我们不仅提高了中文水平，而且结识了知心朋友，还了解了苏州这座美丽的城市。(2/4)

借此机会，我们也要感谢那些在项目背后辛勤付出的人，感谢俄亥俄州立大学为我们选择了苏州一个这么适合生活的城市，选择了苏州大学一个这么适合学习的校园，还为我们设计了这么充实的暑期经历。(3/4)

两个月一转眼就过去了，项目马上就要结束了。但是，项目的结束并不意味着我们中文学习的终止，更不意味着我们大家友谊的终点。虽然以后我们会在世界的不同角落朝着各自的理想去奋斗，但是"海内存知己，天涯若比邻"，我相信我们彼此都会永远记得这个夏天一起在苏州朝夕相处过的老师们、同学们和朋友们。

谢谢大家！(4/4)

知其所以然

The dialogue is broken down into sections below for explanation and analysis. Study

the notes and answer the questions for the underlined text.

1/4

（地点：在项目的结业宴会上，周丹锐代表全体学生发言）

尊敬的各位老师，亲爱的同学们：

大家好！

我叫周丹锐，丹青的丹，精锐的锐。<u>很荣幸</u>代表我们项目的全体美国同学在这里发言。这个夏天我们在苏州的经历是充实而难忘的。能有这么充实又难忘的学习经历，我们要感谢很多人。首先要感谢在座的各位苏大的领导在项目期间对我们的支持与帮助，为我们创造了那么多难得的语言实践和文化经历。然后我们要感谢苏大的王老师、赵老师、张老师和周老师，是你们整个夏天的辛勤付出，让我们每天都能感受到自己在一点一点进步。我们还要特别感谢我们的秦老师，大家都深深感受到了项目各项活动和要求的<u>用心良苦</u>，<u>而且</u>从中学到了很多。"学而时习之"的学习理念会让我们<u>受益终身</u>。

1. 周丹锐开始他的发言："很荣幸代表我们项目的全体美国同学在这里发言。"

（1）这里的"荣幸"可以换成"荣誉"吗？为什么？_____

（2）如果你和几个同学一起去一所小学做义工，结束的时候，校长十分感谢，你可以怎么很客气地回应校长的感谢？_____

（3）你听到身边的人打电话时说了"这是我的荣幸"，你觉得电话那头的人可能说了什么？_____

The structure 很荣幸 + [action] is conventionally used in formal contexts to politely express one's appreciation for the opportunity to do something, especially something done for the benefit of others. Here, Zhou Danrui is politely saying that the opportunity to give a speech on behalf of all the American participants is both an honor（荣）and a fortunate opportunity（幸）. In another context, when thanked by the principal at a primary school for volunteer work, a Chinese person may say 别客气,我很荣幸能为你们学校做点事.

荣幸 may also be used as a noun. For example, in formal settings a common response to expressions of gratitude is 这是我的荣幸. Therefore, if you hear a Chinese person say 这是我的荣幸, he is probably responding to an expression of appreciation, such as 谢谢你参加我们的会议.

Note that 荣幸 and 荣誉 are different in that the latter is associated with reputation, rather than good fortune. For example, people consider earning a doctoral degree as a 荣誉, so some universities award 荣誉博士学位 to honor distinguished individuals who have not officially earned a PhD. Other collocations of 荣誉 include 获得荣誉（gain good reputation）and 最高荣誉（the highest honor）. For example, 努力工作是不是为了获得荣誉? 诺贝尔奖(Nobel Prize)是科学界的最高荣誉之一.

2. 周丹锐表达大家对秦老师的感谢:"大家都深深感受到了项目各项活动和要求的用心良苦。"

(1) "用心良苦"指的是怎样的"用心"? _____

(2) 下面哪一种情况可以算老师的"用心良苦"?

　　A. 我生病了,老师带我去医院看病。

　　B. 我有点不舒服,老师让我在房间休息,不用上课了。

　　C. 老师为了让我们学好中文,精心设计了课程。

(3) 你觉得你父母为你做过的什么是"用心良苦"的? _____

深深感受到了[something]背后的用心良苦 expresses one's deep appreciation of someone's efforts that are behind some kind of difficult task or process. Here, Zhou Danrui is assuming that it is Miss Qin who has carefully arranged the program activities and created the requirements to maximize their gains in the program. 用心良苦, or 良苦用心, is a fixed expression. 用心 can be understood as diligence, and the whole phrase denotes careful thought and diligent effort. It specifically refers to those efforts that are not immediately obvious, such as a teacher's effort in designing a substantial curriculum or parents' efforts in engaging their children with regular outdoor activities.

3. 周丹锐高度评价项目的学习理念:"'学而时习之'的学习理念会让我们受益终身。"

(1) 你知道"学而时习之"出自哪本中国古书吗? 它的下半句是什么? _____

(2) 这里的"时"和"习"分别是什么意思? _____

(3) 你觉得自己在学习中文时做到"学而时习之"了吗? 是否有收获呢? _____

(4) 你能用更简单的汉语说出"受益"吗? _____

(5) "终身"是什么意思?

　　A. 全身　　　　　　B. 一生

(6) 如果你觉得你的一位大学老师对你影响很大,你从他那儿学到了很多东西,可以怎么简洁地说出来? _____

学而时习之 is a famous saying from The Analects of Confucius (《论语》). The whole saying is 学而时习之,不亦说乎, which can be understood as 学习,并且在合适的时机使用学到的知识,不也很快乐吗? It suggests that the pleasure of learning comes from timely application of what is learned.

[something] + 让 + [someone] 受益终身 is used to indirectly express one's appreciation. Here, by saying that the principle of 学而时习之 will benefit them throughout life, Zhou Danrui is indicating that Miss Qin has successfully taught them good learning strategies. For example, to tell people that you have benefited a lot from a professor's teaching, you may say 那位教授的课让我受益终身 or 那位老师的教导让我受益终身. To paraphrase 受益终身 or 终身受益 in more spoken-style language, you may say 对一生都有好的影响.

> **2/4**
> 三人行,必有我师。能有这么丰富的收获,当然也要感谢苏大的同学们,你们不仅是我们的中文老师,更是我们在苏州生活的<u>向导</u>和知心朋友。我们很多同学都是第一次来苏州,刚到苏大的时候,很多东西对我们来说都很陌生。<u>还记得</u>第一次去苏大食堂吃饭的时候,<u>要不是</u>孙浩和奕歆跟我们一起,我跟郑妮都不知道该怎么买饭。在你们的陪伴与帮助下,我们很快地适应了这里的生活,并且爱上了苏州。<u>短短的两个月之内</u>,我们不仅提高了中文水平,而且结识了知心朋友,还了解了苏州这座美丽的城市。

4. 周丹锐高度评价苏大的同学们,说他们不仅是中文老师,更是"在苏州生活的向导和知心朋友"。

(1) 这里的"向导"可以换成"导游"吗?为什么?＿＿＿＿＿＿

(2) 周丹锐给朋友介绍孙浩时说"这是孙浩,我在苏州生活的向导"合适吗?
＿＿＿＿＿＿

(3) 你觉得有没有什么人是你的"精神向导"?＿＿＿＿＿＿

向导 denotes more than "a tour guide". It can refer to someone who helps you get familiar with a certain place, as mentioned in Zhou Danrui's speech. 向导 is more often used in written or formal contexts. It rarely occurs in face-to-face conversation with friends. For example, when introducing Sun Hao to a friend, Zhou Danrui would say 这是孙浩,在苏州的时候他帮了我很多 instead of 这是孙浩,是我在苏州生活的向导. However, in an email or letter, Zhou Danrui may write 孙浩是我在苏州生活的向导. Similarly, in a Thankyou card for Sun Hao, Zhou Danrui may write 感谢你做我在苏州生活的向导.

向导 can also denote an intellectual or spiritual guide. Basically, anyone, either real or fictitious, who has an impact on your ideology, worldview, or spiritual life can be called 精神的向导.

5. 周丹锐深情地列举语伴对他们的帮助:"还记得……的时候,要不是……我跟郑妮都不知道……"

(1) 在这个例子里,孙浩和赵奕歆给了周丹锐他们什么帮助?＿＿＿＿＿＿

(2) 周丹锐对他们的帮助有什么感觉?＿＿＿＿＿＿

Like 记得……, which you have come across in 8.1, 还记得…… also begins a narration of past experience. However, 还记得 has a stronger nostalgic sense.

要不是[condition] + [negative result] is used to emphasize the significance of the condition for preventing the negative result from occurring. Here, Zhou Danrui is saying that he and Zheng Ni were fortunate to have Sun Hao and Zhao Yixin with them when they first ate at the campus cafeteria. For example, to narrate an experience in which you had a narrow escape from feeling embarrassed, you may say 我吃完饭才发现没带钱包,要不是结账的时候正好有个同学来吃饭,我真不知道怎么办好.

6. 周丹锐说他们的进步很快,收获很大:"短短的两个月之内,我们不仅……而且……,还……"

(1) 如果去掉"短短的",感觉会有什么不同? _____

(2) 如果是"两年"或者"二十年",也可以说"短短的"吗? _____

Here, Zhou Danrui uses 短短的 to emphasize their rapid progress and great achievement during a limited period of time. He is actually emphasizing the efficiency of the language partners' help. 短短的 does not have to be used with a short time in any real sense. Depending on how time-consuming it is to achieve something, you may say 短短的两天之内,我们已经成了好朋友 or 短短的三十年的发展,中国实现了从农业国到工业强国的历史性跨越.

3/4

借此机会,我们也要感谢那些在项目背后辛勤付出的人,感谢俄亥俄州立大学为我们选择了<u>苏州一个这么适合生活的城市</u>,选择了<u>苏州大学一个这么适合学习的校园</u>,还为我们设计了这么充实的暑期经历。

---

7. 周丹锐富有诗意地赞美苏州和苏州大学:"……苏州一个这么适合生活的城市……苏州大学一个这么适合学习的校园。"

(1) 周丹锐觉得苏州怎么样?他觉得苏州大学怎么样? _____

(2) 他可以怎么用富有诗意的语言赞美秦老师? _____

The expressions 苏州一个这么适合生活的城市 and 苏州大学一个这么适合学习的校园 convey a poetic sense. The structure 一个这么……的…… serves an extended apposition for 苏州 and 苏州大学. For example, to similarly compliment Miss Qin, Zhou Danrui could say 我们很荣幸遇到了秦老师一位这么经验丰富的老师.

4/4

两个月一转眼就过去了,项目马上就要结束了。但是,项目的结束并不意味着我们中文学习的终止,更不意味着我们大家友谊的终点。虽然以后我们会在世界的不同角落朝着各自的理想去奋斗,但是"海内存知己,天涯若比邻",我相信我们彼此都会永远记得这个夏天一起在苏州朝夕相处过的老师们、同学们和朋友们。

谢谢大家!

8. 周丹锐感叹时间过得快:"两个月一转眼就过去了。"
(1)"一转眼"表示时间过得快还是慢？＿＿＿＿＿＿＿＿＿＿＿＿＿＿
(2)如果你刚结束了一年愉快的实习,在欢送晚会上你要发言表达感谢与祝福,你的发言可以怎么开头？＿＿＿＿＿＿＿＿＿＿＿＿＿＿
(3)如果你看了一部三小时的电影,电影非常好看,那么朋友问你电影怎么样时你可以怎么说？＿＿＿＿＿＿＿＿＿＿＿＿＿＿

一转眼 can be used in various contexts to indicate the rapid passing of time. It can be used as a ritual opening for a speech in formal situations like graduation ceremonies. For example, at the closing ceremony of an intern program, you can say 一年一转眼就过去了,实习期马上就要结束了. It can also be used in daily conversation with friends to emphasize how fast time flies. For example, to tell a friend about an enjoyable long movie, a Chinese person may say 那部电影非常好看,三个小时一转眼就过去了.

9. 周丹锐表示项目结束后,同学们会继续学中文,大家还会是好朋友:"项目的结束并不意味着我们中文学习的终止,更不意味着大家友谊的终点。"
(1)如果把"意味着"换成"代表",周丹锐这句话给人的感觉会有什么不同？
＿＿＿＿＿＿＿＿＿＿＿＿＿＿＿＿＿＿＿＿
(2)有人觉得周丹锐的发言里带有一种留恋的意味,你同意吗？为什么？
＿＿＿＿＿＿＿＿＿＿＿＿＿＿＿＿＿＿＿＿
(3)如果你的同学在上课时吃早饭,老师对他说"不要影响其他同学上课",他不明白老师的话,你怎么给他解释？＿＿＿＿＿＿＿＿＿＿＿＿＿＿

意味 is a relatively formal word, and it can function as either a noun or a verb. As a noun, it is similar to 意思, but it specifically indicates an implied meaning. For example, what Zhou Danrui says in the dialogue implies his reluctance to depart with friends in the program, we may say 周丹锐的发言里带有一种留恋的意味. As a verb, it often occurs in the structure "A + 意味着 + B" to say A means or signifies B. In Zhou Danrui's speech, 意味着 may be replaced with 代表, but that would remove the literary flavor of Zhou Danrui's language. 意味着 is rarely used in casual spoken contexts. In such contexts, a Chinese person may use 意思是 instead. For example, 老师对你说"不要影响其他同学上课"意思是叫你不要在课上吃东西.

10. 周丹锐说项目结束后,大家会去不同的地方:"以后我们会在世界的不同角落朝着各自的理想去奋斗。"
(1)这里的"角落"可以换成"地方"吗？为什么？＿＿＿＿＿＿＿＿＿＿＿＿
(2)这里的"角落"指的是很小的国家吗？＿＿＿＿＿＿＿＿＿＿＿＿＿＿
(3)如果你拜访朋友的家,觉得他的家里到处都布置得很好,可以怎么称赞他？

Literally, 角落 means "corner", but here it does not necessarily denote very remote places in the world. 世界的不同角落 is a metaphorical way to say various places in the world, and it emphasizes how scattered everyone may be around the world. It makes sense if 角落 is replaced by 地方, but 世界各地 is more commonly used than 世界的不同地方. 角落 is also applicable to denote a smaller place, such as the "corners" of one's house. For (3), you can say 你家里的每个角落都布置得特别精致.

11. "海内存知己,天涯若比邻"

This quote is usually used in a formal speech to emphasize the importance and specialness of true friendship. The nice thing about citing an idiomatic expression like 海内存知己,天涯若比邻 is that it automatically activates in people all the feeling associated with the origin of that expression, in this case, the poem《送杜少府之任蜀州》("For Du Fu, who is leaving for Chengdu for an official post") by 王勃 of the Tang Dynasty. 海内存知己,天涯若比邻 is the third line in the poem and it emphasizes that true friendship will keep people close no matter how far apart they may be. In the following line, 无为在歧路,儿女共沾巾(wúwéi zài qílù, érnǚ gòng zhānjīn), the poet says "Therefore, we should not wipe our eyes like heart-broken children at the fork of the road (i.e., when parting)". In the particular context of closing ceremony, this sense is also relevant, so it is likely activated by Zhou Danrui's reference to the poem. Therefore, with this quotation, Zhou Danrui is encouraging everyone to be optimistic about the parting.

In other contexts, if your presentation is about friendship across cultures, you can nicely begin your talk by quoting this line. Or, when writing a sincere and polite email to your Chinese friend who is far away, you can refer to the idiom to express your appreciation of the friendship by saying things such as 海内存知己,天涯若比邻,希望距离不会冲淡我们的友谊.

12. 周丹锐说项目中的老师们、同学们和朋友们的关系很亲密:"一起在苏州朝夕相处过的老师们、同学们和朋友们。"

(1) 这里的"朝"和"夕"分别是什么意思?＿＿＿＿＿＿＿＿＿＿＿＿＿＿＿

(2) "朝夕相处"是指24小时都在一起吗?＿＿＿＿＿＿＿＿＿＿＿＿＿＿＿

(3) 如果你觉得有个人让你不太舒服,跟他说话也很容易生气,朋友问你这个人怎么样时你可以怎么回答?＿＿＿＿＿＿＿＿＿＿＿＿＿＿＿

In 朝夕相处, 朝 and 夕 respectively refer to "morning" and "night". The whole phrase generally denotes that a certain group of people spend a lot of time together every day, but not necessarily the whole 24 hours.

相处 can be understood as "get along with each other" and it is also commonly used in daily conversation. For example, to describe a person who is hard to get along with, a Chinese speaker may say 这个人很难相处 or 这个人很不好相处 or 跟这个人相处很累。To describe a person who is easy to get along with, he may say 这个人很好相处 or 这个人很容易相处 or 跟他相处很容易。

体演文本

Review the sections of the dialogue assigned by your teacher by listening to the audio and role-playing with another Chinese speaker. Be ready to perform the assigned portion of the dialogue from memory in class.

举一反三

Answer the following questions and think about how the dialogue can be adapted for different situations.

1. 周丹锐在对不同的人表达感谢的时候采用了怎样的顺序？你觉得那样的顺序好不好？为什么？

2. 在感谢苏大同学的时候，周丹锐举了去食堂吃饭的例子。根据之前学过的对话，你觉得他还可以举什么例子？如果是你，你会举什么例子？

3. 本单元三篇课文中，周丹锐都谈到在苏州的学习和生活，你觉得他谈论的重点跟观众期待是否符合？

熟能生巧

Listen to the audio and perform the following drills until you feel confident with the items practiced.

☞ Drill 1 Initiating an expression of gratitude

At the closing ceremony, you would like to express your gratitude to many people for making a particular experience or accomplishment possible. Each of the illustrations shows the particular experience or accomplishment.

例：充实又难忘的学习经历

周丹锐：能有这么充实又难忘的学习经历，我们要感谢很多人。

1. 丰富的文化经历

2. 明显的进步

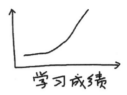

3. 难得的社会实践活动

4. 愉快的游学经历

☞ Drill 2 Formally expressing gratitude

At the closing ceremony, you are thanking different parties for their contribution to the program. The illustrations show the different parties and the cues above them indicate how each party has helped and how you benefited from the help.

例：大力支持→难得的社会实践经历

周丹锐：苏大的领导们，是你们的大力支持，让我们收获了这么难得的社会实践经历。

1. 辛勤付出→充实的暑期生活

2. 耐心帮助→愉快的学习经历

3. 悉心教导→明显的进步

4. 热情参与→丰富的文化经历

☞ Drill 3 Expressing appreciation indirectly

At the closing ceremony, you are recounting the moments when you felt especially grateful for someone's assistance. Complete each story using the information available from the cue. Each cue indicates where you were, what happened and what you were going to do if the help had not been available. Here is an example:

例：孙浩和周丹锐在食堂买饭/周丹锐考虑怎么买饭

周丹锐：还记得第一次去苏大食堂吃饭的时候，要不是孙浩跟我一起，我都不知道该怎么买饭。

1. 赵奕歆借给郑妮钱/郑妮考虑怎么回学校

    郑妮：还记得那天在金鸡湖的时候我的钱包丢了，要不是……我都……

2. 孙浩拿了出租车的发票/周丹锐考虑怎么找回护照

    周丹锐：还记得那次我把护照落出租车上了，要不是……我都……

3. 苏大青志协出面联系敬老院/周丹锐考虑去哪里做义工

    周丹锐：还记得那次我们联系志愿服务，要不是……我都……

4. 孙浩和周丹锐一起/周丹锐考虑怎么跟老板沟通

    周丹锐：还记得那次去书店联系文化沙龙活动，要不是……我都……

☞ Drill 4 Acknowledging the end of an enjoyable period

You are giving a formal speech towards the end of an enjoyable experience. After expressing gratitude, make a transition to express your sense of how quickly the time has passed and your awareness that the experience is about to come to an end. Each of the illustrations below indicates the experience you've been enjoying and its duration.

周丹锐：两个月一转眼就过去了，项目马上就要结束了。

☞ Drill 5 Looking beyond the endpoint

At the end of the speech you give at the closing ceremony of a program or an event, express your good wishes that the participants' commitments and friendships will last despite the end of the program or event. Each of the illustrations indicates the program or the event in which you have been engaged. The cue above each illustration indicates the duration of the program or event.

例：一个夏天

周丹锐：项目的结束并不意味着我们大家友谊的终点。我相信我们彼此都会永远记得这个夏天一起朝夕相处过的老师们、同学们和朋友们。谢谢大家！

老师、同学们：（掌声）

1. 四年

2. 六个月

3. 一年

4. 一个星期

言外有意

Read the cultural notes below and prepare questions for further discussion with Chinese people.

1. 依依不舍（yīyī bù shě） A sense of reluctance to part from somebody or some place.

This idiom is often used in both spoken and written contexts. However, it is not common to use this idiom to express one's own feelings, but rather to describe someone else. For example, you could say 我的小狗每天看到我出门,都一副依依不舍的样子 or 他对苏州产生了感情,走的时候特别依依不舍.

2. 学生代表发言

If you are representing your classmates while giving a speech at a graduation ceremony for a study abroad program in China, here are the things you might need to know: First, introduce yourself and express your gratitude for having the opportunity to represent your classmates, just as Zhou Danrui did in his speech. Second, and most importantly, be sure you thank everyone in the right sequence. Begin with the local institution, including its leaders and teachers. Third, express appreciation for your program, including the program director and resident director, your language partners and your classmates. Fourth, express your feelings about the local city, giving examples of places you enjoyed, such as your favorite place to study or to hang out with your friends. Last but not least, express your desire to return to the city and the local institution. Giving a fluent and sincere speech takes a lot of practice. It is not a bad idea for you to write down the script first and rehearse with your language partner or teacher.

学而时习之

Before you actually do the field performances, rehearse doing them with a Chinese friend. The "Useful Expressions" box below provides you with some expressions you may use for these performances. For now, try saying them after the audio.

> **Useful Expressions**
>
> 1. 你是苏州本地人吧?
> 2. 你说过你老家是山东的吧?
> 3. 为什么到苏州来读大学呢?
> 4. 当时为什么决定留在苏州工作的呢?
> 5. 习惯苏州这儿的生活状态吗?
> 6. 在自己的家乡读书/工作应该很舒服吧。
> 7. 其实我也是……
> 8. 俗话说"月是故乡明",人对自己的家乡的感情总是很特别的。
> 9. 苏州给我一种很……的感觉。
> 10. 就说……吧……
> 11. 你们也常去校门口那家糕点店吧?你最喜欢哪种点心?
> 12. 其实我刚来苏州的时候,看到有些人上公交车或者买票不排队,觉得挺不习惯的。
> 13. 是不是我太大惊小怪了?
> 14. 不过这些事儿不光是苏州有,大城市难免会有这些问题。
> 15. XX,我敬你一杯。项目马上要结束了,借这个机会我想感谢你对我的帮助。
> 16. 还记得我刚来苏州的时候……
> 17. 俗话说"海内存知己,天涯若比邻"……
> 18. 祝我们友谊长存!
> 19. 来,干杯!

Make it a habit to carry a notebook with you and take notes on your interactions with people you meet in Suzhou.

☞ Performance 1 Discussing personal feelings towards your hometown

Converse with a Chinese acquaintance to exchange your personal feelings towards your hometowns.

____ Act 1: Ask if the person is local. Or if you already know where his or her hometown is, ask the person to confirm it.

_____ Act 2: Make a comment on a positive/famous feature of the place.

_____ Act 3: Ask about the reasons the person stays at/ left his or her hometown to go to school or work.

_____ Act 4: Ask how the person likes living in/away from his or her hometown.

_____ Act 5: Relate to the person by sharing your personal experience living in/away from your hometown.

_____ Act 6: End by concluding that we have special feelings about our hometowns.

_____ Act 7: Support your statement by quoting famous sayings or lines from poems if applicable.

☞ Performance 2 Exchanging experiences in Suzhou

Talk to a Chinese friend about your experience living in Suzhou, including both things you enjoyed and things that gave you a hard time. Invite your friend to share his or her experience from a resident's perspective.

_____ Act 1: Start by stating your general impressions about the city of Suzhou.

_____ Act 2: List one or two aspects of life in Suzhou that you enjoyed most.

_____ Act 3: Give examples of your personal experiences to support your statement(s).

_____ Act 4: Ask if your Chinese friend also likes the things you mentioned.

_____ Act 5: Elicit his or her personal experience.

_____ Act 6: Ask for recommendations and propose to do it together in the future.

_____ Act 7: Mention one thing that you were puzzled about in a negative way. Bring up a personal experience when applicable.

_____ Act 8: Elicit his or her opinion by asking for help to see the issue from a Chinese perspective.

_____ Act 9: Make a sincere comment that shows your understanding for the flaws and faults.

_____ Act 10: End on a positive tone (e. g., by stating that your passion for Suzhou makes you a perfectionist).

☞ Performance 3 Saying farewell

Not everyone has the opportunity to be the student representative to say farewell at the commencement. But toasting is always a good chance to express your feelings publicly. Prepare a farewell toast to the Chinese friends/instructors who have always been there for you.

_____ Act 1: Propose a toast to the person(s) and briefly state the reason(s).

_____ Act 2: Recall some of the most memorable experiences you shared.

_____ Act 3: State your feelings (e.g., gratitude, luck, or reluctance to part).

_____ Act 4: Wish them very best of luck for the future.

_____ Act 5: Quote famous farewell sayings or lines from poems.

_____ Act 6: Promise to stay in touch and meet again in the future.

_____ Act 7: End the toast and invite everyone to raise their glasses.

附 录

附 录 1

Questions in "投石问路"

Unit 1

1.1 初次见面
1. 你的中文名字是什么意思？你怎么向中国人介绍你的中文名字？
2. 你是本科生还是研究生？读什么专业？有没有辅修？
3. 你在自己国家使用的是哪家公司的手机业务？你知道中国最大的电信公司是哪一家吗？
4. 在你的国家办手机卡麻烦不麻烦？需要做些什么？
5. 在你的国家有哪些可以节约手机话费的办法？

1.2 吃饭了
1. 你自己大学的食堂怎么样？
2. 如果你的朋友去你的大学看你，你会请他们去哪儿吃饭？为什么？
3. 你自己国家的大学生是不是都有一张学生卡？学生卡可以用来做什么？
4. 学生卡充值麻烦吗？在哪儿可以充值？
5. 你的爸爸或者妈妈菜做得怎么样？你会不会邀请你的朋友去你家吃饭？

1.3 买东西
1. 在自己国家你最爱吃的零食是什么？你觉得在中国能买到吗？在哪儿可能可以买到？
2. 在你的国家，你需要买鞋子的时候会去哪里？
3. 你买鞋子的时候总是买新款还是会买打折的老款式？
4. 在你自己国家买衣服或者鞋子，一般有些什么样的优惠活动？

5. 你觉得自己买东西的眼光怎么样？你是一个很会买东西的人吗？

Unit 2

2.1 去哪儿

1. 你有没有在中国参加过一些文化沙龙活动？在你自己国家呢？
2. 如果参加过，你参加的那个文化沙龙活动是在哪儿举行的？如果没参加过，你觉得在哪儿举行文化沙龙活动比较好？
3. 你在自己国家经常坐公交车吗？坐公交车的时候，你一般怎么买票？
4. 你在中国坐过公交车吗？在中国坐公交车和在你自己的国家有什么不同？
5. 在你遇到困难的时候，是否有过陌生人热心帮助过你？

2.2 与老师交流

1. 你在学习外语的时候，有没有背对话的习惯？你喜欢背对话吗？
2. 如果你是老师，你觉得学生什么样的行为会影响你上课？
3. 在自己国家学习的时候，你在什么情况下会在课堂上吃东西？
4. 你有没有过因为冒犯了老师而向老师道歉的经历？
5. 对你来说，中国文化中最难学的"规矩"是什么？

2.3 组织活动

1. 你自己国家的书店除了卖书之外，还有什么其他功能吗？
2. 你自己国家的书店里常常举行文化活动吗？
3. 在你自己国家庆祝国庆节的时候，一般有哪些庆祝活动？
4. 如果你要让中国朋友也体验一下你自己国家的国庆节，你会要他们参加什么活动？
5. 你在中国参加过中国节日的庆祝活动吗？你印象最深的是哪一次？

Unit 3

3.1 朋友小聚

1. 你自己的国家有什么特色小吃吗？
2. 你最爱吃什么样的菜？喜欢吃海鲜吗？
3. 你吃饭的时候喜欢喝什么饮料？
4. 在你自己国家，去餐馆里吃饭的时候有没有发票？在中国呢？
5. 你和中国朋友出去吃饭常常是谁请客呢？

3.2 家庭做客

1. 在你自己的国家，去朋友家做客的时候你会带什么东西吗？

2. 你去中国人家里做过客吗？是谁的家？
3. 你觉得去中国朋友家做客,要不要带什么礼物？带什么样的礼物比较好呢？
4. 在你的国家,在家吃的东西和在饭馆里吃的东西差不多吗？还是差很多？
5. 客人来你家做客,走的时候,你会送他们出门吗？

3.3　出席宴会
1. 你在自己国家参加过比较正式的宴会吗？是什么样的宴会？
2. 在你自己国家参加宴会要注意些什么？穿什么样的衣服？
3. 宴会的主人会坐在哪儿？你怎么知道自己应该坐在哪桌哪个位子呢？
4. 你第一次喝酒是什么时候？是和谁一起喝的？
5. 在你自己国家敬酒的时候要说些什么话？

Unit 4

4.1　团队游
1. 你参加过旅行团吗？如果参加过,你觉得跟旅行团旅游怎么样？
2. 旅行的时候如果你只有一个星期,你是喜欢在一个地方待久一点,还是多去几个地方,在每个地方待一两天呢？
3. 你在中国的时候有没有中国人要和你拍照片？
4. 你有没有要求过中国人和你拍照？是什么样的中国人？他们乐意吗？
5. 你去过苏州的哪些景点？印象怎么样？

4.2　自助游
1. 你喜欢自助游还是跟团？为什么？
2. 你想过去西藏旅行吗？西藏在中国的哪边？西藏为什么那么有名？
3. 你在中国坐过火车吗？最快的火车叫什么？
4. 如果你不想去火车站排队买票,有没有什么别的办法买火车票？
5. 火车上的硬卧、软卧、硬座、软座,你都体验过吗？感觉怎么样？

4.3　灵岩山
1. 你喜欢爬山吗？你爬过哪些山？
2. 你的家乡有山吗？是很高的山吗？
3. 苏州周围有哪些有名的山？你去过吗？如果还没有去过,有没有打算去呢？
4. 中国的山上常常能看到什么？
5. 你喜欢听导游说景点的故事吗？他们常常说一些什么样的故事？

Unit 5

5.1　钱包丢了

1. 你有没有过丢钱包的经历？后来找到了吗？是怎么找到的？
2. 你自己国家的出租车和中国的出租车有什么不同？坐出租车的经历也很不同吗？
3. 你坐出租车有没有拿发票的习惯？在什么样的情况下需要用到发票？
4. 你觉得苏州的出租车服务怎么样？有没有什么印象深刻的经历？
5. 要是你在出租车上丢了东西，你觉得能找回来吗？怎么找？

5.2　咨询前台

1. 你住的宾馆网络稳定吗？如果网络断了，你怎么办？
2. 你和宾馆前台的人员沟通过吗？他们解决了你的问题吗？
3. 你在苏州大学住的宾馆的服务怎么样？有哪些好的地方？哪些服务不到位的地方？
4. 要是在网上买东西，他们是通过什么方法送货的？最快的方法是什么？
5. 你想给在北京的朋友寄个小礼物，你会用什么样的办法寄？

5.3　空调病

1. 在你自己国家学中文的时候，如果你没办法去上中文课，你会事先告诉你的老师吗？
2. 在你的国家看医生需要带些什么？
3. 你在中国看过医生吗？是什么病呢？
4. 夏天的时候你喜欢把空调的温度调到多少？对于这个温度你身边的人都适应吗？
5. 你有没有吃过中药？你相信中药吗？

Unit 6

6.1　到社区去

1. 你在自己国家参加过社区活动吗？你们的社区活动一般有些什么内容？
2. 你在中国和年纪比较大的人交谈过吗？你们交谈了些什么？
3. 和年纪大的人交流的时候有什么困难吗？怎么办呢？
4. 你在中国有没有人想要你辅导他们的英文？你是怎么处理的？
5. 如果去参加社区活动，要你表演节目，你会表演什么？

6.2 志愿服务
1. 在你自己国家如果想做义工,可以通过什么样的方法联系?
2. 你做过什么样的志愿者活动?你觉得在中国也有这些活动吗?
3. 你在中国如果想去做义工,你要通过什么办法呢?
4. 敬老院是个什么地方?你自己的国家也有类似的地方吗?
5. 你觉得老人去敬老院是个好主意吗?

6.3 参加会议
1. 你在自己国家参加过比较正式的会议吗?是什么样的会议?
2. 参加正式的会议需要穿什么样的衣服?
3. 在会议的过程中又要注意些什么呢?
4. 你觉得中国人对食品问题关心吗?
5. 你听说过"转基因食品"吗?你们国家对"转基因食品"的态度是什么样的?中国关于"转基因食品"有什么新闻吗?

Unit 7

7.1 确立话题
1. 你在大学期间有没有做过调查研究的经历?是在哪门课上做的?
2. 你调查研究的课题是什么?
3. 你的调查研究用了什么方法?
4. 你觉得确立一个调查研究课题的时候,最大的困难是什么?
5. 你有没有用中文做调查研究的经历,这和你在美国大学做研究的经历有什么不同?

7.2 街头采访
1. 你有没有被采访的经历?如果有,那是一个关于什么的采访?如果没有,请想象一下你现在有一个被采访的机会,你最希望它是关于什么的?
2. 你有没有采访他人的经历?如果有,那是一个关于什么的采访?如果没有,请你说说如果有机会的话,你最希望采访谁?关于什么话题?
3. 你觉得在街头采访最大的困难是什么?
4. 当你和中国人交流的时候,有没有遇到过这样的情况——你虽然能听懂他说的每一个字,却发现他要表达的意思完全不是你所想的?
5. 当你问别人问题的时候,有没有被拒绝的经历?你觉得一般被拒绝的原因是什么?

7.3　口头报告

1. 如果你的中国朋友要用英语做一个口头报告,你能给他3条最重要的建议吗?
2. 当你的研究中有大量数据的时候,你觉得怎么才能在口头报告中把它们解释清楚?
3. 做口头报告紧张的时候,你有什么好办法缓解一下?
4. 如果观众在口头报告时提了一个特别难的问题,你怎么解决?
5. 我们已经知道了郑妮的报告和中国现在的"雾霾"有关,请你预测一个观众可能会问的问题。

Unit 8

8.1　漫谈苏州

1. 你在中国的哪些城市住过?你对那些地方有什么样的印象?
2. 中国哪些城市是比较现代的?哪些地方比较传统?苏州呢?
3. 你对苏州人的生活习惯有什么样的印象?
4. 你感觉苏州人对外来人口的态度怎么样?
5. 你在中国有没有遇到过什么让你不太开心的情况?

8.2　苏州攻略

1. 你用中文做过报告吗?听你报告的观众是谁?
2. 苏州夏天的天气怎么样?和你自己国家的哪儿比较像?
3. 苏大校园的环境怎么样?和你自己的大学比起来呢?
4. 苏州有哪些有名的点心?你吃过哪些?
5. 你在苏州有没有一个特别喜欢去的地方?为什么喜欢去那儿呢?

8.3　暂别苏州

1. 你有没有代表你的同学做过发言?如果有,发言的内容是什么?
2. 在苏州学习的这段时间里,有哪些人帮助过你?你想如何感谢他们呢?
3. 来苏州以前,你有过中国语伴吗?你们关系怎么样?
4. 你和在苏州认识的朋友之间有没有哪件事情让你印象比较深刻?
5. 从苏州回国之后你还打算继续学中文吗?在哪儿学呢?

附录 2

Sample Narrations

1.1 初次见面

1. 郑妮：哎，丹锐，你的新辅导老师叫什么来着，看上去人挺好的啊？
周丹锐：

嗯，对。	1) Respond to the interlocutor;
他叫孙浩，孙悟空的"孙"，浩浩荡荡的"浩"，是学中文专业的，今年也大三。	2) Provide basic information about your new friend (e.g., name, major, etc.);
我觉得他特别热情。	3) State your general impression of him or her;
刚才吃完饭，听说我们不知道在哪儿买手机卡，就要带我们去。我知道他下午有事，所以不想麻烦他，可是他坚持要陪我们去买。我再三坚持说自己能解决，他才放心去忙他自己的事情。	4) Give concrete examples of his words or behaviors to support your comment;
他人真是不错。	5) End the narration by expressing your personal feeling or making a comment.

1.2 吃饭了

张老师：郑妮，苏大食堂的饭菜挺不错的。你们去那儿吃过了吗？
郑妮：

对，昨天中午我和丹锐还有我们的中文语伴一起去过了，食堂的饭菜特别丰富。	1) Respond to the interlocutor;
我以前从来没有在中国大学的食堂打过饭，一开始我很紧张，因为有很多菜我都不知道怎么说。	2) State your ignorance of certain knowledge or wrong assumption due to lack of prior experience;
后来我发现有的菜我的语伴也说不上名字。	3) State the new information learned from the experience;

续表

她告诉我只要指着菜说要这个要那个就行了,我觉得很方便。	4) Elaborate on your experience if necessary;
老师,您经常去食堂吃吗?	5) End the narration by inviting the other person to comment.

2. 略

1.3 买东西

(略)

2.1 去哪儿

王老师:周丹锐,这个周末过得怎么样?

周丹锐:

这周末我去书店逛了逛,不过去的路上出了点小插曲。	1) Begin with a general comment on the story;
我上了公交车才发现身上没带零钱。我以为司机可以找钱,没想到他说找不了。	2) State the difficulty you encountered, elaborate on it if necessary;
多亏另一个乘客帮我刷了卡,要不然我就太尴尬了。	3) State the solution to your problem;
我觉得我挺幸运的,在苏州总能碰到这样热心的人。	4) End the narration with your personal feeling and comments.

2.2 与老师交流

秦老师:周丹锐,今天上课的时候怎么回事啊?

周丹锐:

秦老师,今天真是对不起。	1) Respond with an apology;
我早上背对话,没来得及吃早饭。上课的时候我挺饿的,就一边听课一边吃面包。张老师问我"你还没吃早饭吗",我以为她就是问一下,所以回答说"噢,刚才没来得及吃完",还接着吃。后来她说上课的时候最好不要吃东西,我才知道她不高兴了,所以马上就没吃了。下课以后我跟张老师道歉了。	2) Describe the incident and emphasize that you did not intend to offend the teacher;

其实您以前也告诉过我们不要在课堂上吃东西,以后我一定注意。	3) End the narration by repeating the apology and making a promise.

2.3 组织活动

秦老师:郑妮,关于独立日的庆祝活动你们有想法了吗?
郑妮:

昨天去书店的路上我和周丹锐他们一起商量了一下。	1) Describe the general background information;
一开始我提出组织同学们一起去金鸡湖边放烟花庆祝一下,但是周丹锐觉得我们应该组织一些不一样的活动。	2) State the original proposal (followed by a counter argument);
后来孙浩建议我们和校志愿队合作搞一次志愿服务活动。	3) Bring up the alternate suggestion;
大家觉得这个想法不错。所以孙浩打算去请示苏大的老师和领导。	4) State the final decision;
我们也想听听您的建议。	5) End the narration by inviting the other person's comment.

3.1 朋友小聚

郑妮:你刚才说"学了一招儿"是什么意思?
周丹锐:

哦,我发现在餐馆吃饭也可以砍价。	1) Briefly describe the new strategy;
今天我跟孙浩在"江南人家"吃饭,我们点了三菜一汤再加上饮料,本来一共是117块。结账的时候我跟服务员要发票,她说发票用完了,问我下次补上行不行。孙浩就顺口说了句"要不你就少收我们点儿",没想到服务员还真同意了,少收了我们两块钱。	2) Tell the story of how you have learned the strategy;
下次餐馆要是说没有发票,我们也可以试试这招儿。	3) End with a personal comment.

3.2　家庭做客

1. 周丹锐：孙浩邀请我明天去他家吃饭，你说我有没有什么要注意的？
   郑妮：

其实也没什么,去的时候最好带点小礼物,然后就是要做好吃很多东西的准备。	1）State the need to prepare for a certain kind of situation；
我去奕歆家的时候,她妈妈做了一大桌子菜,又好看又好吃。而且他们会一直叫你多吃一点。	2）Use personal experience to exemplify the situation being described；
要是你实在吃不下了,就要坚持说你真的吃好了。	3）Give advice about how to deal with the situation；
那天在奕歆家,我就说了好多次我真的吃好了,她爸爸妈妈才没有再让我多吃了。	4）Describe the kind of response that can be expected；
他们是真心怕我没吃饱,可我撑得第二天都没怎么吃饭,哈哈。	5）End with a personal reflection or comment on the experience.

2. 周丹锐：孙浩邀请我明天去他家做客，有什么要注意的吗？
   郑妮：

其实也没什么,就是要走的时候会有点尴尬。他们总是会留你多呆一会儿,让你觉得坚持要走的话会让他们扫兴。	1）State the need to prepare for a certain kind of situation；
我去奕歆家的时候,他们一直特别热情,我提出要走的时候觉得特别不好意思。不过奕歆的爸爸妈妈知道我第二天有课,就没有多留我,但是欢迎我常去她们家。	2）Use personal experience to exemplify the situation being described；
所以要是你想走了,可以说"今天时间不早了,我就不打扰了。你们也早点休息吧"。	3）Give advice about how to deal with the situation；
他们会很客气地欢迎你再去他们家,还会提出送你。如果你不想麻烦他们,一定要坚持说不要送。	4）Describe the kind of response that can be expected；
总之,我觉得拒绝中国人的热情挺难的。	5）End with a personal reflection or comment on the experience.

3.3 出席宴会

Mari：丹锐，我们合作单位的老板要请我跟他们公司的人吃饭，好像是个特别正式的宴席。饭桌上我有什么要注意的吗？

周丹锐：

中国宴席上的规矩可不少。	1）Remark that a lot of rules apply；
既然你是主要的客人，那么到时候你的客户应该会让你坐在他的右边。你一定要先跟他们客气一下，比如请年长的同事坐那个位置。如果他们坚持让你坐他右边你才坐。	2）Describe the process of getting seated and advise Mari on how to behave modestly；
到时候可能要喝酒，在敬酒或被敬酒之前，即使你渴了也千万不要自己喝酒。宴会开始的时候，主人，也就是你的客户，应该会敬大家，也可能会单独敬你。等他敬了酒之后，你再敬他，然后敬其他客人。敬其他客人的时候要按职位或者按年龄从高到低，所以他给你介绍其他客人的时候要记住他们的职位。	3）Remind Mari of the procedures and appropriate behaviors during proposing toasts；
对了，服务员上菜的时候都会先转到你面前，到时候你最好请主人先吃，如果他坚持让你先吃，你才先吃。	4）Describe how the dishes will be served and explain expected polite behavior；
这种场合就是说些该说的话，沟通一下感情，习惯了就好。	5）End with your personal feeling or comment.

4.1 团队游

王林：郑妮，你们这次旅行怎么样啊？

郑妮：

还好吧。	1）Give a reserved response；
我们只有两天半时间，但是去了上海好几个地方：外滩、城隍庙和浦东的国际金融中心。	2）Describe the busy itinerary；

续表

虽然这几个地方都在上海市区,但是这样赶来赶去、走马观花还是特别累。	3) State your opinion about the trip;
我知道我们来一趟不容易,老师想让我们尽量多去几个地方。	4) Acknowledge the good intention of the trip organizer;
但我还是希望去的地方少一点,在一个地方待得久一点。	5) Reinforce your opinion.

4.2 自助游

1. 郑妮:为什么啊?不是说好去西藏的吗?

   周丹锐:

我也想去西藏的,可是孙浩告诉我外国人去西藏都必须参加旅行团。	1) Indicate your understanding of Zheng Ni's disappointment;
你不是也不喜欢跟团旅游吗?所以我想我们还是退而求其次,去成都吧。	2) Indicate that you have considered Zheng Ni's travel preference;
成都也不错,也有很多可以看到西藏文化的地方,而且成都还是著名的休闲美食之都。去成都,我们可以自助游,不用被导游催着不停地走马观花,应该可以玩得很轻松。	3) Elaborate on the advantages of visiting Chengdu instead of Tibet;
你觉得呢?	4) End the narration by inviting Zheng Ni's comment.

2. 赵奕歆:你们不是要坐火车去成都的吗?怎么改飞机了?

   周丹锐:

我是很想坐硬卧去的,又便宜又舒服。	1) Explain that you would like to stick to your original plan;
可是现在已经没有15号去成都的硬卧了,只有硬座和软卧。	2) Describe the situation that made you change your mind and the two options of train tickets;
我本来想退而求其次,坐硬座去,正好可以体验一下坐硬座的感觉,而且秦老师也说过"没坐过硬座,就不算真正到过中国"。	3) State your initial alternative and rationale for it;

续表

可是郑妮觉得坐30多个小时硬座太受罪了。	4) Explain why you have to give up your initial alternative;
软卧呢,又太贵了,买软卧的钱都可以买飞机票了。	5) Explain the disadvantage of your second alternative;
所以我们就决定就坐飞机去。这样也不错,还可以多出一天时间去成都周边玩玩。	6) State your final decision and its advantage.

4.3 灵岩山

秦老师:怎么样,爬山累不累?

周丹锐:

累是有点累,不过挺值的。	1) Respond positively while acknowledging the difficulty;
一路上看了很多各种形状的岩石,大饱了眼福。还从导游那儿了解了不少关于灵岩山的历史。	2) Summarize the positive aspects of the experience;
据导游说这座山之所以叫灵岩山就是因为山上有各种奇形怪状的岩石。今天我还学会了一句诗文"山不在高,有仙则名"。用这句话来形容灵岩山很合适,因为灵岩山虽然不算太高,但风景很好。	3) Demonstrate your gain from the experience;
秦老师,您以前来过灵岩山吗?	4) End the narration by inviting the other person's comment.

5.1 钱包丢了

赵奕歆:丹锐,我听说你的钱包丢了?怎么回事儿啊,找回来了吗?

周丹锐:

还没有。	1) Respond to the question;
今天下午我和孙浩为了周五的文化活动去买吃的。	2) State the reason why you went out today which led to losing the wallet;
回来的时候可能钱包从裤子口袋滑出来了,就给落在了出租车上了。	3) Hypothesize a possible scenario resulting in leaving the wallet on the taxi;

续表

还好我们下车的时候跟司机要了发票,上面有那辆出租车的车牌号。	4）Remark that fortunately you asked for the taxi receipt;
我打电话给出租车公司,把车牌号和具体的上下车时间、地点告诉对方,服务中心说联系到司机以后就马上联系我。	5）Describe what you did to try to get your wallet back (e. g. contact the taxi company) and the result;
哎,还不知道能不能找回来呢。下次坐车可得当心了。	6）End with a comment or statement of your personal feeling.

5.2　咨询前台

周丹锐：今天房间里一直连不上网,我都约好了跟我朋友视频的。我得去问问到底怎么回事儿！

郑妮：

刚才我给前台打电话问了。	1）Respond to your interlocutor;
前台说是今天服务器出了一点故障,工作人员正在抢修。估计四点之前就能恢复正常了。	2）Report what you learned from the front desk about the WiFi malfunction;
现在整个楼都连不上网,要是你着急上网的话,可以去图书馆试试。	3）Mention an alternative solution to his need to use the Internet;
你也别着急,前台现在也没办法。	4）Suggest that Zhou Danrui shouldn't be upset as there's nothing the front desk can do either;
只能等等看了。	5）End with a comment or statement of your personal feeling.

5.3　空调病

孙浩：听说你昨天生病了,现在好点了吗？

郑妮：

现在已经好多了。	1）Respond to your interlocutor;
昨天晚上就开始拉肚子,还吐了。今天早上起来还是感觉头晕肚子疼,浑身没有力气,还有点发烧。	2）Describe your symptoms in a chronological order (e. g. last night ... this morning ...);

续表

我早上跟秦老师请了假,奕歆带我去了医院。	3) State how you dealt with the illness (e.g. ask for sick leave, go to the hospital, etc.);
医生说我这是空调病,给我开了点消炎药和藿香正气胶囊。	4) Report the doctor's diagnosis and prescription;
除了不要贪凉、晚上空调不要开得太低以外,医生还让我平时多喝水,少吃油腻辛辣的东西。	5) Mention the additional advice from the doctor;
没什么事儿,休息休息就好了。	6) End with a comment or statement of your personal feeling.

6.1 到社区去

1. 孙浩:郑妮,你们昨天下午的文化活动去哪儿参观了？有意思吗？
   郑妮:

昨天我们去了一个叫龙桥社区的本地社区参加活动。	1) Start with the general background of the event;
到了社区活动室以后,一开始先听社区的王主任给我们简单介绍了社区的情况。	2) State the first, second … and last activity in order of occurrence;
之后分别跟一些社区居民代表互相认识认识、聊聊天。	
最后是表演节目。	
跟我一对一聊天的阿姨特别直接,刚见面没说几句话就问我愿不愿意周末去她家帮她儿子辅导英文。我委婉地说周末项目有很多活动,最后留了自己的电子邮箱给她。	3) Elaborate on your own experience during one or more of the activities;
这个阿姨这么直接,我真有点儿不习惯呢。	4) End with a comment or statement of your personal feeling.

2. 赵奕歆：丹锐，你们昨天下午去哪儿搞活动了？
周丹锐：

昨天我们去了一个叫龙桥社区的本地社区参加活动。	1）Start with the general background of the event；
到了社区活动室以后，一开始先听社区的王主任给我们简单介绍了社区的情况。	2）State the first, second ... and last activity in order of occurrence；
之后分别跟一些社区居民代表互相认识认识、聊聊天。	
最后是表演节目。	
昨天和一个很有意思的孙大爷聊了会儿天。他年轻的时候也喜欢搞乐器，所以看见我在调吉他，就过来跟我说话。他虽然70多岁了，身板还很硬朗，我们聊着聊着就变熟了。	3）Elaborate on your own experience during one or more of the activities；
这次我发现我挺喜欢跟中国的大爷大妈聊天的，他们让我想到了我自己的爷爷奶奶。	4）End with a comment or statement of your personal feeling.

6.2 志愿服务

秦老师：我听孙浩说你们几个同学想去敬老院做义工，联系得怎么样了？
周丹锐：

正好想跟您商量这件事儿呢。	1）Respond to the interlocutor；
本来我们想又不是所有同学都参加的活动，不需要通过苏大的青志协提前帮我们联系。	2）State your initial hypothesis that led to the failed attempt；
我们自己打电话过去了以后，对方听说我们是美国来的留学生，还说很佩服我们献爱心的热情。	3）State the response from the other side that causes the misunderstanding；
我一开始以为这就是同意了的意思。	4）Explain your initial understanding；
结果那边很客气地说现在暂时没有公开招募志愿者的计划。	5）Provide the final result（what was really meant by the other side）；

续表

| 看来不以学校的名义联系,对方真的不会轻易接受。 | 6) Conclude with a reflection on the reason behind the unsuccessful negotiation; |
| 您觉得是不是应该请青志协的会长帮我们沟通一下? | 7) Ask for your interlocutor's opinion/Request help from your interlocutor. |

6.3 参加会议

秦老师:郑妮,你觉得今天的文化活动怎么样,有收获吗?

郑妮:

今天的收获特别大。	1) Respond to the interlocutor;
我听了一个关于转基因食品的报告,跟我的专业很有关系,我也对这个话题特别感兴趣。	2) Explain what made this conference a valuable experience for you;
休息的时候,我还主动跟一位在会上发言的张经理聊了聊。	3) Elaborate on your experiences reaching out to a professional at the conference;
特别巧的是,她还去俄亥俄州立大学参加过学术研讨会!	4) Mention a surprising common ground you discovered between you and the person, which led to the exchange of contact information;
所以我就跟张经理交换了联系方式,以后有问题可以多向她请教。我还邀请她有机会再来哥伦布,我给她当向导!	5) State that you intend to establish further connection;
这可是我第一次在中国比较正式的专业场合向别人毛遂自荐呢!	6) End with a comment or statement of your personal feeling.

7.1 确立话题

赵奕歆:你的论文选题怎么样了?

郑妮:

| 我今天请秦老师指点了一下我的选题。 | 1) State that you sought help from Miss Qin; |
| 原本我有两个题目,一个是关于中国人移民到国外的,一个是中国人对环境问题的看法。最后我选了第二个,因为秦老师说这个话题更符合活动的目的。 | 2) Describe the two topics you had, which one you chose and the reason; |

续表

中国的环境污染越来越严重,我想了解中国人是怎么看雾霾和经济发展的关系的。	3) Explain your research interest in the topic you chose;
秦老师建议我把受访者按身份背景分类,然后有针对性地进行采访。	4) Tell your friend about Miss Qin's suggestion to you;
这样我可以关注不同身份背景的人看问题的视角有什么不同,表达方式有什么特点。	5) Elaborate on the intended outcome from following the suggestion;
所以下一步我打算针对不同的研究对象设计一些采访问题。	6) State what you plan to do next.

7.2 街头采访

1. 秦老师：昨天的口头采访还顺利吗？

郑妮：

嗯,昨天课上练过口头采访的技巧以后,下午进行得挺顺利的。	1) Respond to the interlocutor;
我在万达影城的大厅采访了一位已经退休了的陈先生。	2) Introduce the background information of your interview (e.g. where, when, who was your interviewee);
我问了他几个问题,包括雾霾是否影响他的生活,造成雾霾的根本原因是什么,还有政府的治理措施。	3) List some of your interview questions;
在问他是否觉得雾霾影响他的生活的时候,他说到现在会觉得呼吸困难。以前还能出门散散步什么的,现在一有雾霾都不敢出门了。	4) Elaborate on one (or more) interchange(s) between you and the interviewee;
那个陈先生很愿意跟我谈话,他的观点也挺有代表性的。	5) End the narration with a comment on the experience.

2. 秦老师：昨天的口头采访还顺利吗？

郑妮：

嗯，昨天课上练过口头采访的技巧以后，下午进行得挺顺利的。	1) Respond to the interlocutor;
我在万达影城的大厅采访了一位已经退休了的陈先生。	2) Introduce the background information of your interview (e.g. where, when, who was your interviewee);
我问了他几个问题，包括雾霾是否影响他的生活，造成雾霾的根本原因是什么，还有政府的治理措施。	3) List some of your interview questions;
在问到造成雾霾的根本原因的时候，他表示工业污染和汽车尾气都对雾霾有很大影响。而关于政府的治理措施，陈先生提到了限制车辆出行，但他也说到这一措施效果并不明显。	4) Elaborate on one (or more) interchange(s) between you and the interviewee;
他的这个观点很有意思，我也想看看其他中国人是不是也有类似的看法。	5) End the narration with a comment on the experience.

8.1 漫谈苏州

孙浩妈妈：丹锐啊，你来苏州也快两个月了。对苏州有什么感觉？

周丹锐：

阿姨，我非常喜欢苏州这边的生活状态，给我一种很亲切的感觉。	1) Respond to the interlocutor and bring up the first characteristic of Suzhou that you like;
生活节奏虽然很快，但是身边的人都不浮躁，从从容容地过日子。	2) Elaborate more on the first point you made;
而且我觉得苏州的文化包容并蓄，既接受新生的现代文化，又保留着许多传统。	3) State a second characteristic of Suzhou that you like and elaborate on;
不过我说了您别生气，苏州也有一些不太完美的地方。比如上公交车、上电梯的时候有些人不排队什么的。	4) Politely mention a negative observation you made about Suzhou;
但我觉得在苏州这样一个文化大熔炉里，这也是难免的吧。	5) Continue to say that you think these drawbacks are understandable;
可能我是太喜欢苏州了，总是希望它能完美。	6) Summarize and end on a positive tone.

《体演苏州》英文版在美国同步出版，以下为英文版《体演苏州》的相关出版信息：

© 2016 National East Asian Languages Resource Center, all rights reserved

Library of Congress Cataloging-in-Publication Data

Names: Jian, Xiaobin, author. | Wang, Jianfen, 1981 – author. | Jia, Junqing, 1985 – author. | Feng, Chenghua, 1971 – author.
Title: Perform Suzhou : a course in intermediate to advanced spoken Mandarin / Jian Xiaobin, Wang Jianfen, Jia Junqing, Feng Chenghua.
Other titles: Course in intermediate to advanced spoken Mandarin
Description: 1st edition. | Columbus, Ohio : National East Asian Languages Resource Center/The Ohio State University, [2016] | Series: Perform China series; Volume one
Identifiers: LCCN 2016016505 | ISBN 9780874153835 (alk. paper)
Subjects: LCSH: Chinese language—Textbooks for foreign speakers—English. | Suzhou Shi (Jiangsu Sheng, China)—Description and travel.
Classification: LCC PL1129. E5 J533 2016 | DDC 495.1/82421—dc23
LC record available at https://lccn.loc.gov/2016016505

ISBN: 9780874153835

This volume prepared and published by
  National East Asian Languages Resource Center
Distributed by
  Foreign Language Publications
  The Ohio State University
  198 Hagerty Hall
  1775 S. College Road Columbus, OH 43210 – 1309
  614 – 292 – 3838
  http://Flpubs.osu.edu; http://nealrc.osu.edu

Funded partially by The Title VI Grant of the U.S. Department of Education

Producers: Galal Walker, Chenghua FENG
Managing Editors: Minru LI
Distributions Manager: Lauren Barrett
Cover design: Hanning CHEN

图书在版编目(CIP)数据

体演苏州 /(美)简小滨等著. —苏州:苏州大学出版社,2016.5

(体演中国)

中高级中文听说教程

ISBN 978-7-5672-1728-7

Ⅰ.①体… Ⅱ.①简… Ⅲ.①汉语—口语—对外汉语教学—教材 Ⅳ.①H195.4

中国版本图书馆 CIP 数据核字(2016)第 114573 号

书　　名:	体演苏州
体演中国系列主编:	(美)简小滨
体演苏州系列主编:	(美)简小滨　逄成华
策　　划:	(美)吴伟克(Galal Walker)　逄成华
著　　者:	(美)简小滨　(美)王建芬　(美)贾君卿　逄成华
责任编辑:	董　炎
封面设计:	陈寒凝　刘　俊
出版发行:	苏州大学出版社(Soochow University Press)
社　　址:	苏州市十梓街1号　邮编:215006
印　　刷:	苏州恒久印务有限公司
厂　　址:	苏州市友新路28号东侧　邮编:215128
邮购热线:	0512-67480030
销售热线:	0512-65225020
开　　本:	787 mm×1 092 mm　1/16　印张:20.25　字数:499千
版　　次:	2016年5月第1版
印　　次:	2016年5月第1次印刷
书　　号:	ISBN 978-7-5672-1728-7
定　　价:	40.00元

凡购本社图书发现印装错误,请与本社联系调换。服务热线:0512-65225020